# 360 DEGREES OF GRIEF

## REFLECTIONS OF HOPE

*May 2014*
*To the Sugar Grove Library,*

Volume I.

*Debbie Richards,*
*Contributing Author*

# A *Selah Press* Anthology

Managing Editor, Kayla Fioravanti

# 360 Degrees of Grief, Reflections of Hope, Volume 1

**Authors:** T.G. Barnes, Duane Bigoni, Heather Blair, Jacquelyn Bodeutsch, Joyce Bone, Beverly Brainard, Tom Burgess, Sharon Steffke Caldwell, Elin Criswell, K.A. Croasmun, Clay Crosse, Renee Crosse, Kimberly Crumby, Paul Dengler, Kolinda King Duer, Wendi Fincher, Kayla Fioravanti, Zachary Fisher, Bruce Fong, Gary Forsythe, Lona Renee Fraser, Cherie Funderburg, Charles Garrett, Maria Gelnett, Steve Green, Valerie Geer, Chuck Hagele, Drenda Howatt, Mary Humphrey, Emily Joy, Cathy Koch, Kyle Koch, Shila Laing, Bethany Learn, Shirley Logan, Dana Lyne, Rebecca Marmolejo, Lynn McLeod, Ric Minch, Ginger Moore, Ellen Peacock, Cheri Perry, Deborah Petersen, Karyn Pugh, Lane Reed, Linda Reinhardt, Mandalyn Rey, Debbie Richards, Loral Robben, Lisa Rodgers, Prevo Rodgers, Jr., Rex Paul Schnelle, Sara Shay, Tammy Lovell Stone, Debra Sturdevant, Michelle Titus, Melodie Tunney, Rachel Turner, Dorothy Wagner, Wayne Watson, Marc Whitmore, Lisa LaCross Wethey, Carol Wilson, Jessica Mills Winstead

**Managing Editor:** Kayla Fioravanti

**Editors:** Carol Wilson, Lynn McLeod, Debbie Richards, Mary Humphrey, Robin Schmidt, Shila Laing, Kim Jones, Darcy Hickey, Ginger Moore, E.F. McAdams, Carol Hattaway-Richey, Rose Cunfer, and Caiden Fioravanti.

**Cover Design:** Dawn Fitch
**Cover Photo:** Kayla Fioravanti
**Interior Photography:** Lisa Rodgers

ISBN-13: 978-0615987613 (Selah Press)
ISBN-10: 0615987613

Copyright © 2014 Selah Press, LLC
Printed in the United States of America
Published by Selah Press, LLC

# 360 DEGREES
## BOOKS

**Find out how to become a 360 Degrees contributing author at**
**360DegreesBooks.com**

# DEDICATION

To my mother.
The great void she left in my life inspired this anthology.

And to all of the people who inspired the stories within these pages.

# TABLE OF CONTENTS

# Chapter 1

# WHAT GRIEF TAUGHT ME

By Managing Editor, Kayla Fioravanti

My first awkward experience with grief was in grade school as I tried to tame my quivering bottom lip at my neighbor's funeral. Over the span of my lifetime grief has become more than an acquaintance. I've stood by loved ones in their valleys and they've stood by in mine. I've had the honor of being present at both the first and at the last breath of life.

I've been the strong one stroking the belly of a loved one filled with cancer so advanced I could feel it under his thin skin. I assured him it was okay to die that day. I sat beside him when his last breath escaped his body, relieved his pain was over and mine had begun.

I've been the weak one sitting in my husband's office weeping openly when the news came that my mother needed life-threatening surgery. I've been the adult, who felt like the little child trying to be brave, as my mother was wheeled down the hallway to uncertain outcome. My shoulders heaved as my legs barely held me up in the hospital hallway. I've held my mother's hand when all there was left to do was let her die at her appointed time.

I've been the weeping one while witnessing the pain of a mother who lost her son all too early and suddenly. He wasn't mine, but I ached completely for her loss. I've prayed with a mother I barely knew, as she signed the papers to turn off life support for the daughter I did know. I've kissed the warm hand of a brain dead friend. I've said goodbye knowing her warmth came from the machines and that coldness would invade her body once the machines were disconnected.

I've experienced the joy of celebration and hope and then suddenly collapsed in despair. I've wept into the tiny holes of the phone to my mother when loss was so common and constant, even my kitten died. I've walked away from a future that would have destroyed me. I've said goodbye when my heart wanted to stay and I've run away when warning bells rang. I've regretted my absence when I learned of an old friend's tragedy too late. I've been compelled to respond when news of another's grief relentlessly chased me.

I've been guilty of causing heartbreak I can't undo. And I've forgiven those who've never asked. I've looked back and surrendered my sins to Christ. I've walked forward knowing I've already been forgiven. I've lived through the complete spectrum of life—from ecstatic joy to the darkest grief—and have learned some lessons along the journey.

> ➤ The walk through grief is paved with precious milestones. You cannot sneak past grief in the night, run through it or sit still in one spot. Grief is a passage

not a place to wallow in, skip past or tunnel under. If you don't go through the grief, it will fester and consume you in another way or at a later time. You must walk, not run, through at grief's own pace.

➤ It is good to read your way through grief. Read the experiences of others. There is benefit in knowing you aren't alone in your thoughts and struggles. When numbness caused by shock vanishes you will need to know others survived the day after, the week after, the month after, the year after, the lifetime after their loved one died.

➤ It is good to cry. Even if you aren't a *crier*, allow yourself to cry, weep and sob. Even though crying can leave you exhausted and spent, it still washes away a stronghold of hurt. Crying does not miraculously close a wound. It facilitates the cleansing of a festering sore.

➤ Love your way through grief. The instincts of hurt can cause us to withdraw within ourselves, but loving others is a salve of healing. Bottled up love causes the vacancy left in our lives to feel enormous. Actively loving others multiplies the joy in our lives. Even a glimpse of joy can be enough to carry you through the next hour.

➤ Forgive those who don't know how to be there for you in your deepest hurt. People will say stupid things, they will pull away and some will tell you to come to them when you need them. None of it feels good, but give them grace. Your grief journey is new to them too. Listen to their intentions, not what the clouded perception of emotions makes you hear.

➤ Learn to live with a hole in your life without falling into it. You can't join the dead while you are grieving. You have the right to grieve, but not at the expense of losing the very essence of life. It is okay to laugh again, live again and adopt new people into your life. Accept the fact life will never be the same, but you will find a new normal even with an ever-present hole in the middle of your life. Decorate it, rejoice in it, and glorify the very hole you would wish to fill.

➤ Have realistic hope about grief. You'll never stop missing your loved one and the vacancy is forever deep, but it will get better. Even though the grief will never ever end, you must continuously move forward into your new life.

➤ Don't starve, nor gorge your way through grief. You will need sufficient sustenance to walk grief's exhausting and long journey. On the other hand gluttony will make the burden heavier and wear you out too. Don't try to numb the pain of grief with anything--drugs, alcohol, busyness, and any other numbing technique. Feel it. Go through it so you can grieve in the here and now, not sometime in the far off future.

➢ Remember, to remember, to breathe--moment by moment. As sorrow engulfs you, it is easy to hold your breath, tighten your muscles and give into the tension caused by loss. Take life one breath at a time, one step at a time, and one jagged sob at a time.

➢ Grief is a price of love, but you must continue loving even at the risk of paying a price. Your loved one enriched you, made you who you are and you must honor their lives by living yours. Love others, love often, love openly, love fervently, love expectantly, and love completely into the lives of others.

➢ Write your way through grief. Even if you aren't a writer and have no aspirations of becoming an author, write your way through grief. Use a journal to purposefully write when memories flood you and you feel you may drown. Writing it out is a healing life preserver.

➢ Lean into God as you walk through your grief. There is no rescue or instant remedy that will offer relief from grief--only daily walking, talking, reading, writing and crying our way through grief on the lap of our Father. Grieving in the arms of the Lord is the most intimate exposure you will ever experience with Him. God is near to the brokenhearted. He will walk beside you on the messy path of grief.

The writers of *360 Degrees of Grief* have allowed the written words to assist them in their grief process. They've been blessed. Our prayer is that you will be encouraged by our reflections of grief in the aftermath of our crises as you walk through your own dark valleys.

## Section One
# CHILDREN OUTLIVING PARENTS
Photo by Lisa Rodgers

CIRCLE OF BREATH

THE NIGHT MY FATHER DIED
THE MOON SHONE ON THE SNOW.
I DROVE IN FROM THE WEST;
MOTHER WAS AT THE DOOR.
ALL THE LIGHT IN THE ROOM EXTENDED
LIKE A SHADOW. TRUANT FROM KNOWING,
I STOOD WHERE THE GREAT DARK FELL.

THERE WAS A TIME BEFORE, SOMETHING
WE USED TO TELL--HOW WE PARKED
THE CAR IN A STORM AND WALKED INTO
THE FIELD TO KNOW HOW IT WAS TO BE
CUT OFF, OUT IN THE DARK ALONE.
MY FATHER AND I STOOD TOGETHER
WHILE THE STORM WENT BY.

A WINDMILL WAS THERE IN THE FIELD
GIVING ITS LITTLE CRY, WHILE WE
STOOD CALM IN OURSELVES, KNOWING
WE COULD GO HOME.
BUT I STOOD ON THE SKULL OF THE WORLD
THE NIGHT HE DIED, AND KNEW THAT
I LEASED A PLACE TO LIVE
WITH MY WHITE BREATH.
TRUANT NO MORE, I STEPPED FORWARD
AND LEARNED HIS DEATH.


WILLIAM STAFFORD, "CIRCLE OF BREATH" FROM ASK ME:
100 ESSENTIAL POEMS (GRAYWOLF PRESS, 2014)

# Chapter 2

# UPON GOODBYE

By Kayla Fioravanti

In mid-January I picked my parents up from Sea-Tac airport after they cut their Hawaiian vacation short. We had no idea within days my mother would go from the emergency room to ICU then move to an oncology unit and finally home with hospice. In exactly three weeks she was gone.

After her diagnosis of Hodgkin's disease forty-four years earlier, my mom was given a life expectancy of three to ten years. She intentionally raised my brother and I to be strong and independent enough to live without her for she always knew her time was limited. Her goal was to raise us and she did. Her next goal was to know her grandchildren and she did that too. Finally her desire was to die at home with her family. Which she did.

Growing up in my mom's shadow I learned to express myself, try new things, and to be creative. She taught me to dance through life with love and laughter pouring out freely. I learned to be strong and brave. To accept a time would come when there would be nothing left but to accept death.

My mom taught me to see the beauty in everything and in people. She expressed her beauty on canvas. My expression is on paper with words. I wrote for the first time three weeks after picking mom up at the airport. I needed to be brave for mom those three weeks. One morning I walked down to the safety of the ocean, letting go of my brave face began writing these words in my journal:

*I've been here three weeks now caring for Mom. She's been unconscious since Saturday. Today is Wednesday and it's the first time I've made it to the beach. I decided today would be a good day to come to the beach as a signal to her I will be okay. I am giving her the space to let go. She would want to be free and not trapped in her stagnant body with her eyes closed.*

*There is hoarfrost covering the grass and rocks, even on the log where I sit. I remember mom telling me about the hoarfrost coating North Dakota the winter her mother died. Sitting on this island beach, my mind is filled with memories of watching her enjoy this place with her grandchildren. She loved the beach. She spent endless hours throwing rocks in the ocean and hunting for tiny crabs.*

*She's given me a thousand memories in the past three weeks to hang onto. She reminded me of how important it was to know people, even if it was for only a short period. She wanted to know everyone's name and to learn a piece of their story when she was with them. These last weeks, I've seen her laugh and cry, love and give, mourn and worry, and say goodbye.*

*Mom is most alive in her smiles. The smiles have been gone for many days. There's no conversation. Mourning has begun. At first, goodbye seemed like it was rushing at us. Now it feels unhurried, but still painful.*

*Today is a perfectly clear crisp Whidbey Island day. It's a perfect day to say goodbye.*

At 10:00 a.m. I had nothing left to write. I stared at the ocean for a few moments wishing I could bring the perfect beach scene to her bedside. After a few minutes the contentment I felt sitting there left. I felt compelled to return to the house. To symbolize each member of our family letting her go I took a moment to throw a rock for every one of us into the ocean.

I returned to Mom's bedside carrying the beach scene in my heart. Sitting beside her still body I recounted, "Mom, hoarfrost has settled over the island today—just like when your mother died. It's even on the beach."

With a catch in my voice I continued my monologue, "Mom, the mountains are so visible today. I felt like I could almost touch them. The ocean is reflecting a beautiful bright blue sky. You would enjoy the cool gentle breeze and the hypnotic sound of the ocean caressing the beach. Mom, can you smell the scent of the ocean? It's a perfect day to let go, Mom. We will be okay."

She remained still as she had for days. I walked away from her bedside for a few minutes. When I returned, her breathing had changed. She was surrounded by love as we gathered around her. Within moments at 10:25 a.m. she released her final breath.

A few hours later I wrote a poem for her memorial service.

**Upon Goodbye**
It is nearly impossible
to think of you in the past tense.
Your life is colorfully woven into the fabric of ours.
I know you are gone,
I saw you leave,
but in my memory you are vividly alive,
with your mischievous smile
teasing the corners of your mouth.
Saying "she was…"
doesn't fit comfortably on my tongue yet
because you left bold strokes upon my life.
I see you *alive* all around me
You live in the impression
you left upon your grandchildren.

Your life is etched in the laugh lines
worn deeply into my father from a lifetime
of joy shared with "the love of his life."
I see you in the bold brush strokes you left on canvas
and the lives you touched.
I can hear you in the language of my motherhood
and the dialect of my life.
I feel your strength that you wove deep
into the hearts of my brother and me
because you always knew that you would leave us too soon.
Death may have taken you,
but what you left behind
Will echo in our lives
for generations to come.

# Chapter 3

# MOM'S LAST DAYS

By Wayne Watson

My dear Mom passed away last night. One more of the greatest generation has slipped away. They weren't given such a title casually. It fits. She was a great lady.

Mom was eight-eight years old and dealt with lots of annoying physical ailments for years. Three and a half years ago she moved into the nursing home a quarter of a mile from my childhood home. She willingly left the house she'd lived in for fifty-plus years. Living alone in the house had become lonely and at night, from time to time, she would hear noises making her nervous. Every now and then she'd fall and would have to wait for someone to come and help her up. So the nursing home provided a safe place. A place where there was an abundance of friends and caregivers interacting with her every day.

She quickly became a favorite around the home. Before much time had passed she established a small library (she loved to read) encouraging everyone to check out books and enjoy the variety of materials. Mom diligently proofed all the reading material to make sure there were none of "those words" in the text.

A couple of Christmases ago we gave her a Kindle not knowing if she'd take to the new-fangled gadget or not. She loved it even though the little tiny buttons frustrated her. At the time there wasn't a wireless network in the nursing home so she'd roll her wheelchair to the end of the hall facing the First Baptist Church (*They* had wireless . . . and it was powerful!) to tap into their network. I had her on my Amazon account and about once a week I'd get an email from Amazon thanking *me* for *my* order.

She studied all week to teach Sunday school. She was always excited to see who would come to class even though more than a few would sleep through the lesson.

She played piano for some of the functions at the nursing home with fingers seriously bent from arthritis. I bet she still didn't make many mistakes. I suppose I got my music ability from my mother and possibly a sense of humor too. She was very sharp and funny until the very end.

She'd lost use of her hands and feet by the time she was admitted to the hospital. Her kidneys were failing. She was firm in her decision to not have dialysis. She was just too frail to make the trips to have the treatments and didn't want to live such a life. The doctors told us without dialysis, she wouldn't have a chance. So, we convinced her to try three treatments with the hopes her kidneys would kick-start. It was a long shot but she agreed.

She endured the dialysis the first two days. An hour into the third round she was exhausted. She told the doctors, "Stop. I can't do this." We made plans for hospice to take over two days later on a Sunday. The clock started. Lots of family began to gather.

At one point in the day mom asked me "Who's teaching my class today?" Even as I'm writing this the little things she said to me don't really translate well to the printed page. They might seem insignificant and pale to most people. But as I counted the days – I had no idea how many we had left – the brief dialogues were and will always be priceless to me. All week long her clouded mind gave way to moments of clarity. She would say to me, "Let me go. I want to go."

One day during the week before, she told me – and I don't know which mind this was, cloudy, clear or visionary – "I saw your daddy through the window." "How did he look?" I asked. "Oh, he's young and his hair is dark and wavy . . . he's so handsome," she said with a smile.

Another time, she pulled the oxygen mask down off her face enough to ask me, "How did I get this sick?" I told her the saga of the past week and her response was, "Well, if my kidneys aren't working, I'm not gonna make it." I raised my eyebrows a little and nodded. She asked, "How long do I have? Hours?"

I said, "You've got as long as you want, Mom." A few seconds passed, she pulled the mask down again and asked me, "Have you ever watched anybody die?"

"No," I said.

"I have," she replied. Another few seconds passed and she whispered, "It takes a while to die. I love you, honey."

From there, it took a little more than twenty-four hours.

She fought to breathe the last day with all the effort of a marathon runner at the finish line. Her face grew more and more red and the veins on her temples stood out. After her last breath, her face was as sweet and clear as a porcelain doll. Race over. Winner.

What a fascinating life is this life. The flesh was formed of the dust of the earth and the earth is all it knows. It fights with all it has to stay in the dirt. The spirit knows the future and knows its destiny. The One who formed us calls out to the spirit to break out.

One of our friends who visited the hospital shared a quote (origin unknown to me) something like this: *The spirit exits the body like a schoolboy on the last day of class . . . with great joy and abandon!*

That she did.

# Chapter 4

# DAD BELIEVED IN ME

By Debbie Richards

I once heard the sweetest words from my dad. He laughed and asked, "You know what you should have been? A vet. You would have been good at it. You love all animals . . . well you'd have to pretend when it comes to cats."

My heart swelled to know that he could see this much potential in me, for I had always secretly wanted to become a veterinarian, but never pursued it for a hundred different reasons. It seems that no matter my age, I continued to long for acceptance from my parents. Those words were a gift from dad. I am forever grateful.

Little did I know when we had this conversation that my dad was in the process of dying. Maybe I knew, but my right brain tendencies – the emotional, loving, caring part of me – allowed me to deny it. He had come to live with me and my husband. His health had been declining for months. Ever so gradually, like a parent not noticing their toddler has grown until someone else brings it to your attention, I didn't notice my dad's decline.

He told just about anyone who would listen that he had lived a long life and did not enjoy the limitations that old age delivered. He was ready to go, but at the same time, his strong character and discipline kept him from giving in easily. He did not like to think of himself as old. Even though it became more and more difficult, he was determined to be up and dressed at a decent hour each day. About a week before he died, he spoke of how hard it was to wake up that morning and how he could barely get himself out of bed. I told him, "If I were you, I'd just stay in bed all day long. Give yourself a break from your normal routine." But he would not allow himself that. With less and less strength, he still pushed through the days.

He resisted my pleading requests that he use a cane or walker. The idea of relying on a walker or, God forbid, a wheelchair infuriated him. No matter how many times I suggested it, he never agreed to even *try* to ride in the power grocery carts at the store, even when I tried to make it sound fun. I told him, "C'mon Dad, I'll go first!" His physical body became weaker each day, but he did not think of himself as old. He finally agreed to try to use the cane I'd bought him, but he could not grasp the idea of the cane's purpose. On the rare occasion he remembered to pick it up he simply would grasp it around the neck and carry it, usually with me holding one elbow and him holding the cane in his other hand. To an onlooker it may have looked comical. Neither of us was laughing about it though. Those were difficult times.

It's only now, looking back, that I see this as an amazingly positive character trait. At the time I simply thought he was being obstinate. He was in my care and I worried all the time; and I confess, it was a power struggle. The worry made me sick and didn't help either of us, but I continued to worry – in the end he won the power struggle and I thank God that he did.

One Tuesday night, I helped him walk to bed. Those were his last steps--not mighty steps, they were more like a weak shuffle. The following morning an ambulance took him to the hospital. I observed Dad yanking out the EKG leads each time the paramedic attached them. At first glance it seemed his arms were randomly moving about and accidentally knocking the leads out. Then I realized he was still winning the power struggle to be in total control. He knew exactly what he was doing. He did things his way. I'm proud of him for that. At eighty-six, he outlived all his relatives by a long shot. He lived with inner-strength and dignity until the end.

It meant the world to me to read the stories from old friends who generously shared their memories in sympathy cards. Laughter-filled canasta games and front porch chats were some of the shared memories that reminded me of the positive impact my dad had on others' lives. During his later years, he may not have heard what people said much of the time, but he always smiled and nodded. He laughed at the appropriate times, somehow.

Being his caregiver was a huge responsibility, but I'll never stop missing him. A friend of mine wrote the most honest words of sympathy I've ever heard. She said, "Sorry to hear about your dad, but I'm glad he is at peace and that your life can go back to normal again. It was a tough road for both of you."

Yes, it *was* a tough road. But I am deeply blessed and grateful. I'm honored to have been Dad's caregiver. I'm even glad that I lost the power struggle, which allowed him to live and die with dignity. I'm glad I was present, so that I could be on the receiving end of a heart-to-heart gift of the sweetest words with far deeper meaning than a casual observer could have. My dad believed in me. I should have been a vet.

Chapter 5

# THE LUCKIEST GIRL

By Debra Sturdevant

In her early years my mother longed to have a baby of her own. She loved children so very much. Since this could not happen, I became the luckiest girl in the world when she adopted me at only three days old. As the only child of a selfless woman, I never thought of myself as anything other than her very blessed daughter.

Mother was my rock, independent and strong, until Alzheimer's struck. The roles then reversed. It was violent from the sudden beginning turning my life upside down. Without hesitation I left the outside world, my job and social engagements, to cocoon myself for three brutal years in the world of my mother an Alzheimer's patient. I experienced every moment of the tortures of this devastating disease as if they were my own.

I sought frantically for answers, but found none. Moments, hours and days would pass with her in constant turmoil, confusion, and violence. A brief time of lucidity would tease me into thinking she might *be back*, only to be plummeted too quickly into the abyss of Alzheimer's ugly clutches. It was pure torture witnessing the agonizing process of losing my beloved mother. I often cried so intensely I couldn't see. I cried for her, not myself.

There was no respite care in our area, which left the responsibility of my mother with my family. The stress nearly ended my marriage and kept me almost always exhausted. When I tried to reason with Mother to no avail, I often lost patience and yelled back at her. The guilt from those memories still haunts me. I yelled at God in private moments pleading for answers. Why should a woman suffer such an injustice after dedicating her entire life to giving care to many old, sick and abandoned souls of both humans and animals.

I asked my pastor why someone so good-hearted had to suffer. I also explained how downright mad I was with God. He told me it was okay, God wants us to talk to Him and He would understand. He also said maybe I was the one supposed to learn from this experience. It was part of His plan.

Looking back, I found the strength I didn't know I possessed, for putting one foot in front of the other each day. The last days of her life were spent in the quiet night hours laying beside her talking, not knowing if she could hear me. I apologized for the quarrels and injustices a mother of a daughter sometimes endures. I told her my wish was to have her back again as she once was. Somewhere in those last hours I found the courage to let her go and found myself in the process.

I still have moments when my heart clenches or when tears flow. I cry for my own loss now. I still grope for answers with the faith I will see her again. I also take solace from a precious gift Mother gave me just weeks before she died. During a lucid moment when tucking her in for the night, she took my hand and said, "I love you, Debbie." Then she slipped away again forever. The memory carries me through the days of grief I will have until we see each other again. *Momma, I miss you so much. Thank you for making me the luckiest girl in the world.*

# Chapter 6

# MEMORIES OF A FATHER

By Marc Whitmore

As I turned to leave my mother's house after an all-too-short visit, she handed me a photograph.

"Have you seen this before?" she asked.

It was a high school photograph of my father. He was handsome, in a dark suit, staring somberly at the camera.

"Take it. I have others," she promised as she kissed me goodbye.

When my plane took off from southwestern Missouri to fly home to Los Angeles, I pulled out the photo. Pictured was my father in the prime of his life at seventeen years old. And then it struck me—that's exactly how old I was when my father was taken from me, nearly forty years ago.

I was in my fourth period speech class on a cold winter's day when I received a note to come to the principal's office. As I walked in the secretary looked up with an expression I now recognize as pity. She told me my mother had called and asked for me to come directly to the hospital. This was unusual, but not unexpected. My father had been in the hospital for a couple of weeks suffering from complications from diabetes. It never occurred to me this was to be the last afternoon of his life.

By the time I reached the hospital my father was already in a coma. Much of the family had gathered. At the time, it still didn't register with me there was even a possibility he wouldn't pull through this. In my teenage mind I optimistically believed he was going to make it and things would soon be back to normal.

The hours stretched into early evening. At about eight o'clock, as I sat in the family waiting room reading a magazine, the door opened with my mother, aunt, and grandmother coming in as they cried uncontrollably. They all wore a look of utter despair I will never forget. Finally, at that very moment I realized the thing I never imagined could happen, *had* just happened. My father had transformed in the twinkling of an eye from a flesh-and-blood father into a flood of memories. Those memories were all I would have left of him.

I spent the rest of the evening in a state of shock. The next morning when I awoke there was just pain left in my chest. Not the idea of pain, but *real* pain--like someone had ripped my heart out of my chest. The next few days were a blur and then finally . . . a funeral.

At seventeen years old there was nothing I ever wanted to do *less* than attend my father's memorial service. The idea of saying goodbye to the man I most admired, to the person who taught me just about everything I knew about life, who believed in me and thought I could accomplish anything . . . well, it was just about more than I could take. I wasn't sure I could endure the pain of seeing his face for the very last time and hearing the finality of his life with the closing of the casket lid. If there were any way I could have escaped this ordeal, I would have jumped at the chance. But in our family we were taught to always do the right and proper thing. So I went.

My father's service was packed. Many friends and family had jammed into the chapel. There were also a number of people I never expected to attend: businessmen and farmers, highway patrolmen and preachers, a college president and the wealthiest man in our part of the state, simple people and important people.

I remember most clearly one man at my father's funeral. He was an uneducated farmer who lived in a shack on top of a rocky God-forsaken piece of land. He drove a rusty old pickup truck and spoke with some sort of speech defect. He attended the service in overalls, work shoes, and an old suit jacket. On his head was a battered hat he wore whether he was going into town or working in the fields. When he passed by the casket to pay his final respects, he took off his old hat and took a handkerchief out of his pocket to dry his eyes. I remember how utterly embarrassed I was that this bumpkin was there and he was crying--a grown man! What would my friends think?

Looking back I realize how important the memories of my father are to the way I've chosen to live my life. Although he's been gone for forty years, I cherish the way he always made me feel important and special. My father thought I could do anything. Now I possess the confidence to go after big dreams largely because of his faith in me. I watched my father take care of people who had less than we did. If I have a generous spirit, it's because I watched him live generously. If I do the right thing today, it's because my father always demonstrated how important it was to do the right thing.

Death robs us. It steals birthdays and anniversaries. It steals opportunities for heartfelt chats. It takes away the chance to sit around the Sunday dinner table holding hands with the ones we love while we pray together. We lose the opportunity to experience the joy of sharing all the intimate moments we hoped to experience with our loved ones.

But God gave us a temporary replacement: the gift of memories. Like faith, a memory can't be seen or smelled or tasted. It can't be held in our hands. Memories have life and power that can impact the rest of our lives. They can teach us things and are a great substitute until the day we are reunited with those we love. Memories allow us to pass on the values that we hold dear. Now, I want to imbed a storehouse of memories into my children's minds that will have very real and tangible effects.

I still grieve the loss of my father. I still ache to talk to him one more time. And yet, memories of my father continue to teach me forty years later. I realize of all the things my father taught me, the old farmer represents the best of them all. That everyone matters. The rich and the poor. The important and the socially insignificant. I don't remember a single word those influential people said about my father that day. But I'll never forget the grief of one man as he stood in front of my father's casket. The eloquent words of the rich paled in comparison to the tears of one poor man.

# Chapter 7

# FOR LIFE, I HONOR HER

By T.G. Barnes

For several weeks afterwards I dialed her cell phone number to hear her voice again on the voicemail greeting, knowing she would not pick up. Each time I prayed her boyfriend would not answer. He had been using her phone after her death. It was really starting to hit me. The woman whose face I see in the mirror every day. The one who birthed me, yet was never my protector or nurturer, was gone. My mind replayed the last scene of our goodbye as my husband and I prepared for the drive back to Virginia from Tennessee.

I recalled the scowl on her face as I finalized paperwork to have her released from hospice. Miraculously, she had begun to recover and no longer fit the criteria to remain in hospice. The staff reminded me over and over it was rare for this to happen. I did not understand the scowl she gave me. *Did she think I was out to get her?* It was revealed to me the reason she ended up in ICU was due to years of drug use weakening her heart

Her prognosis was grim when my husband and I arrived. She was on a ventilator in the ICU. The doctors insisted it was the end. I walked into her hospital room with tubes and machines everywhere. The rhythm of the bleeps and burps of the machinery reminded me of the science fiction thriller, Frankenstein, with the intricate assembly of his near dead existence. *Can these machines create life or the appearance of life?* The doctor vaguely probed. I wasn't sure what he was getting at until finally the doctor asked, "Do you know why your mother is here?"

I stood at the end of her bed. She opened her eyes and smiled. She couldn't speak because of the tubes. She reached for my hand as I walked closer to her side. I embraced her. The doctor came in and explained they needed to know what her final wishes would be should she stop breathing. Did she want to be resuscitated, remain on a respirator or did she want to sign a DNR (do not resuscitate) order? Based on their assessment, she would probably remain on the machine to stay alive. "Can you speak with her, Mrs. Barnes, so we can know what she wishes? She won't give us an answer." At the moment her final wishes were not my concern.

Since I was a child I had prayed for God to change my mother's heart. I prayed He would save her from her sins and she would truly know the Lord. If this was the end I wanted to make sure I presented the opportunity to her. No holds barred, I said, "The doctors don't think you are coming out of here alive. I don't want you to die in your sin. I don't want you to leave here not knowing Jesus as your Savior." I prayed and asked her if she knew Him. She nodded. In a small whisper through the tubes she responded, "I know Him." One single tear rolled down her cheek. *Was this just deathbed religion?* The doubt crept in, but it wasn't for me to judge. The truth was between her and God.

My husband and I stayed overnight in a hotel. My sleep was restless. Thoughts and memories--some good and some bad--raced through my mind. Constant reoccurring dreams kept me up. I was taking care of the person who never cared for me. This brought new meaning to Exodus 20:12: "Honor your father and your mother, so that you may live long in the land." It doesn't say to honor them only if they cared for you, provided for you or gave you your heart's desires. My mother had done none of it for me. I had long ago released my bitterness. She had chosen to bring me into the world. She allowed me to be cared for by her sister who was able to do the job she couldn't or wasn't willing to do.

Her transfer from ICU to hospice was filled with unknowns. Because I was next of kin and her only child it was left up to me to answer the questions I had absolutely no clue how to answer. Our relationship had improved over her last five years. We talked every day. But our conversations were often about the news, family things, world issues or just catching up. Never had we discussed how we had become strangers. The family secrets I witnessed as a child through whispers remained mostly hidden. We only came close to revealing some secrets when I found out I had a half-sister who was six months older than me. We shared the same father and her mother was my mother's cousin. The conversation, however, was shut down quickly. It was closed for discussion even among family who could provide answers, but refused.

The chaplain and hospice did everything they could to guide me through the process. I was left to handle my mother's business including dealing with disability, social services and so much more. I spent the first night with her while my husband went back to the hotel. I prayed. I read through every packet hospice had given me about the stages of death including what to expect when your loved one is dying.

I wanted God to help me understand what I was to do. *If this was going to be her last days, what should be the focus?* The answer came, "No matter what, care for her as if she had cared for you all your life." Human nature would have made it easy for me to just say, "This person was never there for me. Why should I put my life on hold? Why should I leave my children in the care of someone else, travel to another state for someone who never sacrificed anything to be a mother?" The answer: Honor. Honor for the life that could have been aborted, honor for her being sober-minded enough to bring forth my life regardless of how she screwed up hers. At least she knew her child deserved a chance.

That night I read scripture to her. Sometime in the night I dozed off. I awoke to the sound of her losing oxygen. She had flipped on her side and was chewing her tube. She looked like a newborn baby staring at me as if she had no clue what was going on. The doctor suspected some brain damage. They really could not predict how long she had left to live.

That afternoon her landlord met my husband and me at her apartment. When we entered the apartment I was shocked at the wall in the living room. It was covered with pictures of me from the time I was a child until I got married and everything in between. Her landlord was a local minister whose church was in the neighborhood. He invited us back to his office. He talked about what he knew of my mother and how nice she was. He said he could tell we were not very close. I explained she did not raise me. His answer, "No matter what, honor her."

I started to feel the blood rise to my head. He knew absolutely nothing about what I had gone through as a child. *Who was he to tell me to honor her?* But I did. I had been mad all my life about all the unanswered questions. It looked as if I probably would not receive the answers. The next day's events seemed miraculous. My mother improved beyond the criteria to stay in hospice. We were faced with finding a facility for her. But she wanted to go home and have a nurse come to her. Arrangements were made and supplies for oxygen were to be delivered.

My husband and I had to get back home. I finalized paperwork to have her released from hospice. We contemplated having her live with us, but there was no guarantee she could make the travel. The chaplain came in to speak to me before I left. My mother glared at me. We said our goodbyes. I could not forget the glare. I kissed and embraced her, but she did not respond. My husband hugged and kissed her. She smiled and hugged him back. *What had I done?* I told her I loved her and would call. As I walked out the door I glanced back at her. She still was glaring at me. Her look is forever ingrained in my memory.

She went home and a nurse came in daily. She called to let me know she was sending something Western Union to cover our expenses for coming to see her. I told her it was not necessary. Truthfully I wasn't expecting her to follow through. All of my life she had never followed through. Her next call was to give me a confirmation number. There was something in the atmosphere. I sensed it would not be long before she died. She was different. She seemed happy and enthusiastic about life. Our conversations were different. She seemed like a brand new person. We talked and talked, just because.

One day I was going about my day, but I didn't feel *right*. I had playtime with my oldest and put the baby down for a nap. I did some housework, but felt everything was going in slow motion. Then the baby screamed and the phone rang. My mother's sister was on the other end, "Why aren't you answering your cell? Someone is trying to reach you about your mom!" My cell had not rung until then. I heard the sobbing sounds of mother's boyfriend. Through his sobs he said my mother had been rushed to the hospital. Her heart had stopped and she had been revived. But I knew she was gone. My baby had screamed the same way when my grandmother had passed away. I felt it in my heart she was already gone. I couldn't cry, I just sat there holding my baby and I hung up.

Reality became apparent as I made arrangements and wrote her obituary. I combed through her things trying to find anything I could. I called cousins for information because the truth was I did not know her. *What can I say about the woman who did not raise me?* She had lived running the streets and using drugs. She had a few rehab stints. *Memorials should be positive to honor someone's memory, right?*

Then my cell rang. It was her pastor giving his condolences. He began to tell how she had planned to come to service the Sunday of Mother's Day to give her testimony. *Testimony?* He said my mother had told him God had delivered her. The drug dealer had showed up at her home and she told him she didn't do drugs anymore. She began to witness on her porch to everyone who would listen. Her neighbors stood outside of her home listening to her story of how she died and came back because of God's mercy. I received several calls from people telling me the story. God had answered my prayer. She was prepared. Now I could write about a woman who had experienced obstacles in her life, but in the end found freedom in Christ.

I found her birth certificate. I did the math and learned my grandmother had been fourteen and my grandfather twenty-four when they had my mother. Back then, a few generations after slavery, it was not unusual for girls to be married at a young age. Perhaps her family pathology was the reason her life was filled with such chaos. She was a baby being raised by a baby.

I was sad for days. Some people could not understand why, since she did not raise me. *How could I grieve for someone who was never there?* All my unanswered questions were lying dead in a casket. My grief escalated from not truly knowing the circumstances surrounding my birth, but she was my mother. She chose to give me life and that was her love. For this, I honor her.

# Chapter 8

# FREEDOM FOUND IN FORGIVENESS

By Kayla Fioravanti

My mother consumed her sixty-nine years of life with vitality and love. She loved family, friends, and strangers. An outing often ended with my mother bringing home a stranger in need of a meal, companionship, or encouragement. Relationships were important to her.

My mother lived her life out loud. Sometimes she spoke too soon, said too much and occasionally caused friction in her relationships. She was normally quick to say she was sorry. On rare occasions she would stick to her guns about being right. On her deathbed she was determined to make all the things right which she felt she had gotten wrong. She spoke to each loved one individually at the hospital. Our conversations created peace, erased burdens, and lifted spirits.

When we arrived to my parents' home for hospice care she felt there was one more wrong to right. She and a neighbor friend had experienced a falling out. It was vital to my mother they speak. She sent me over to the neighbor's house to ask her to come over. When the neighbor didn't answer her door, my mother sent me back with a note asking her again.

This wrong she needed to make right was at the front of her mind until her tearful neighbor showed up at the door. Suddenly in the face of my mother's final moments, both were ready to lay down their argument, give and receive apologies, and pick up their friendship where they dropped it. They spoke privately. I never heard what was said. A few days later I saw the tear-streaked face of the neighbor at my mother's funeral. I could see she had been set free from their former feud. Unforgiveness had separated two friends and robbed them of precious time to enjoy each other. Forgiveness set them both free.

Life gives us countless opportunities to ask for forgiveness as well as to forgive others. The opportunity to right wrongs on our deathbed is not the ordained future for all of us. We all have the present. We have this moment to take inventory of our lives and right any wrongs.

We can say "I am sorry" even if there is no guarantee of forgiveness.

We can say "I forgive you" even if there is no hope of an apology.

We can celebrate life and experience the gift of freedom found through forgiveness.

# Chapter 9

# GONE BUT NOT FORGOTTEN

By Ellen Peacock

My dad was from a generation of men who did not show or discuss their feelings openly. He was our family's John Wayne. This was both strength and weakness. Maybe it is an inherited behavioral trait, because I can be the same way at times.

When my dad passed away after a lengthy battle with cancer I felt both sadness and anger. I'm sure other people knew the blasted disease was going to win, but I failed to see even when his death was inevitable. There are a million discussions I wish I'd had with him before he passed. I knew he loved me, but we never talked about how he felt, what his wishes were or anything like that.

My father had a military funeral and was buried in the local national cemetery. There wasn't a graveside service. I remember noticing when we were leaving the funeral new graves were being dug by a pond. It was beautiful there. My father loved to fish and I thought it would have been a great location for his remains.

I was not aware of my father's burial location. None-the-less I went to the cemetery on the chance I could find him. While walking by the pond looking at all the identical headstones, I said out loud, "Where are you?" Soon, it was as if I became a divining rod when suddenly I sensed a really strange feeling. I turned around and his tombstone was a stone's throw from the picture perfect pond. The epitaph said, "Gone but not forgotten."

Grief was a hard thing for me to deal with. I was a private griever and felt very alone. I carried a tremendous weight of anger because something I dearly loved was taken from me. I was mad at the doctors. I was mad at the researchers. I was mad there was such a thing as cancer. I was mad that both young and old get cancer. I was mad the world was full of cancer-causing elements and no one was safe.

The anger just seethed within me. Sadness settled in on top of it. It's an awful thing to watch a loved one's vitality waste away. I tried to put on a good face while feeling as though I walked around in concrete shoes with a millstone around my neck. Even so, anything reminding me of him—a song on the radio, seeing another elderly man, someone's words—would cause me to break down into a bumbling mess of tears. No one seemed to understand.

I realized being mad was futile. Nothing could bring my father back. There was no way I could possibly remove all of the cancer-causing elements from my life. The reality was I could not remove them from anyone else's either. Moderation is the key to almost everything and so I learned to accept things as they were and moderate my anger.

I often wondered: *When will this terrible feeling end? Will it ever end? How long am I going to feel like even the slightest effort is almost impossible?* The truth is it took me years. It was very hard to give myself permission to move on with life and not feel guilty for just living. What finally helped the most with the healing process was learning to accept things as they are and being thankful for what I have.

I am thankful for having him as a father, for his guidance and advice, for many things he taught me—those things I will never lose. My father will always be with me in my heart and mind. That is a comfort to me. Death cannot remove his essence from those places. He is gone, but not forgotten.

Chapter 10

# NO REGRETS

By Kolinda King Duer

As far back as I can remember my Mom's zest for life and steadfast faith inspired me. When life got tough she was always my biggest encourager and trustworthy friend. Over the years, we had the kind of relationship where we could talk about almost everything. I always knew she would give sage advice worth more than gold. She taught me about Jesus and more than a few times, she took me to Sunday school and vacation bible school. Her faith was real to her and something she valued more than anything in this world.

My family loved to sing Gospel songs. Mom would play the piano every morning. She would wake me up with those songs of faith beckoning me to "see what God has done for you today." She opened my eyes to nature, to the *diamonds* in the glistening snow, to the jaw-dropping beauty of sunrises and sunsets, and to stars on ebony summer nights. I learned to see the good all around me because of her childlike faith that never changed. Even though the years pressed on, her heart stayed young.

So in February of 2012, when we got the call her doctors had found a mass requiring exploratory surgery, my heart sank. When my family was called into the "little room off to the side," we knew things weren't good. The doctors found she had ovarian cancer, stage 3c. They wanted to do chemo right after having surgery to remove her ovaries and reproductive parts. However, they waited because of a complication with a pre-existing condition in her stomach. By June, her cancer progressed to stage four. She moved from the care of her doctors in Illinois to my home near Nashville, Tennessee to begin treatments at a nearby a cancer care center. For four months, she and Dad lived with my husband, our youngest daughter and me as we tried to find balance, in healing for Mom and peace in the midst of the storm. At the end of that time, the doctor called us in and said the chemo wasn't working. They had done all they could. They sent her home to Illinois wanting to set her up with hospice.

Now, you have to know Mom. The day after she got home and received the call from hospice she told them, "I'm a long way off from needing you!" So, from September of that year until December she started being more intentional about her self-care. We researched everything we could find on the Internet and in the latest cancer treatment books that gave even a ray of hope for healing. Mom ate, drank and took natural remedies like a champ. We prayed for a miracle and we got one. Before Christmas her hometown doctor ran more blood tests. Based upon those results her cancer was in remission.

Our family rejoiced in the miracle and breathed a sigh of relief thinking she had beaten the disease. We would have her around for many more years. Unfortunately, our joy was short lived. Just two months later she started feeling ill again. The doctors found cancer. This time it was a tumor. She began more chemo and by May she seemed to be doing better. Again, we thought, the storm had passed. For Mother's Day my husband, oldest daughter and I took her, Dad, her sister, her best friend and sister-in-law on a train trip in Northern Illinois. It was one of her bucket list items. That day, she was more alive than I had seen her in a long time. She was happy, greeting everyone in her path and just being "Mom." She was the person who never met a stranger.

Life always seems to either roll in as a storm or rise like a beautiful sunset. It was a little more than a month after the train ride we were preparing for our oldest daughter to be married on our farm. All focus and energy was on the big event. It was two weeks before the wedding and Dad called us, crying. The cancer doctor had used an experimental chemotherapy on her and it hadn't worked. He sent her home with hospice to take care of her. This time for real. We talked to Mom about whether or not to cancel the wedding. She told us emphatically to go ahead. She didn't want to take away from our daughter's joy. We kept pushing on through what felt like a tempest of hardship knowing Mom would have to be with us in spirit. We tried to balance our rollercoaster emotions as the wedding preparations kept our lives in a flurry of details.

Eight days before the wedding I made a special trip to see Mom. I remember walking into her room seeing her tiny frame on her bed and knowing there wasn't anything left we could do to help her on this side of Heaven. As always, she greeted me with a smile and lifted her frail arms toward me for a hug. I sat by her side with tears flowing wanting so much for the clock to rewind and to spend more time with her. But I couldn't. The only thing left was to just be with her. To hold her hand, sing to her and reminisce about the times when she once played her piano for me, leading me heavenward.

I stayed with her for the weekend. When it came time for me to leave, I told her I would be back to see her the Monday after the wedding, but if she needed to go home to be with Jesus I would understand. I said I would be okay if I didn't see her again this side of Heaven. She looked right at me, reached for my hand and said, "I have no regrets with you." My mind flooded with a lifetime of memories, of laughter, songs sung, special moments and a love that stood the test of time and would extend into eternity.

It was her last gift to me, one of completion and thankfulness for the beauty and meaning of our relationship with each other. I have carried this moment, this memory with me since she went to be with Jesus one week after our daughter's wedding. I won't see my Mom again this side of Heaven. I believe she is free now enjoying Heaven's grandeur and unspeakable beauty. And she is in the presence of the

One who made all those starry nights and snow laden mornings of long ago. I rest in knowing I will see her again. When I do, I plan on having many stories to share of how I tried to carry on the legacy of her last words and live my life with no regrets.

# Chapter 11

# WHEN DEATH IS PERSONAL & PIERCING

By Kayla Fioravanti

Death can make acquaintance with us on many levels. Some remotely connected deaths, such as distant relatives or celebrities, give your heart pause. On the opposite end of the spectrum there are the deaths that hit you full force in the heart. It can also impact at various levels in between.

My mom once snuck me into a classroom at the University of Texas Health Science Center in San Antonio. The large, sterile room was cold and infused with a queer aroma. Evenly spaced tables exhibited cadavers under fluorescent lights. My mom wanted me to see them because I was a science geek. It was strange walking through the classroom filled with cadavers waiting to be dissected by students.

At the time I was only remotely acquainted with death. I had lost friends, but not a family member yet. Our solemn walk amongst the cadavers introduced me to the detached clinical side of death. This was bearable. Then the day I experienced death full force arrived. No science geek trait within me could detach from my own mom's death.

I often think of the doctor telling us my mom's condition was terminal. We weren't surprised by the news. Her next words hit like a sucker punch broadsiding us when the doctor told us mom had seven to ten days left to live. Staggering back from the doctor as if distance would remove her words, we sucked in air and sobs escaped. She stood calm and collected watching quietly as we regained our equilibrium.

Sure enough within the timeframe the doctor predicted, my mom passed away at home with us holding her hands. It was nothing, nothing at all, like seeing cadavers in the classroom. It wasn't clinical and cold. My mom's death was personal and piercing. Her life had contained ours. The loss forced us to spill out into the world of uncertainty, no longer contained by her life.

Now a few years later, we have shored our lives up a bit. There are still leaks from holes that can never be filled by anyone else. One of these is the moments I'd give anything just to call and at the sound of my voice hear her say, "Well, hello Kayla" with singsong joy filling the airwaves.

On her deathbed, my mother told me you never quite stop missing your mom. Of course she knew because she never stopped missing her own mother. She knew too, I would never stop missing her. Her death will always be personal and piercing to me.

Chapter 12

# EVENSONG

By Beverly Brainard

*EVENSONG, even-SONG, EVEN-song.* I loved the feel of it on my tongue. Ever since reading P.D. James' who-dun-it, *Death in Holy Orders*, the word had stuck with me. I thought it referred to some sort of religious service, what kind exactly, eluded me. All I knew was each time I mouthed it, I felt reassured. I did not know why except the word conjured images of hand chiselled, blue-gray stone, dancing shadows across flying buttresses, and the murmur of Gregorian chants resonating heavenward. The word brought delight, even during a less than delightful year.

New Year's Day arrived with its promise of a new beginning. I desperately needed a fresh start. I reflected on all that had happened since January the year before, since the call Granny had taken a turn for the worse. It did not matter to either of us she was not my real grandmother. Granny was my steadfast support, despite divorcing a favorite grandson some twenty years earlier. Granny ignored her children when they said she should no longer associate with me. She loved me and I loved her. No one was going to tell Granny whom she could associate with.

Granny wanted to see me. I drove to the next town where she was staying with her daughter. Acutely aware Granny's life was ebbing away, we clung to each other. Soon Granny was bedridden. I went to see her in the hospital. The bed next to Granny glared an ominous sign of emptiness. Mouth agape, eyes clenched close, Granny lay comatose.

I lamented her loss. I knew Granny's essence had fled the antiseptic drenched room and prayed her pain would soon be gone as well. I caressed Granny's gnarled hand, heart flooded with sadness, until she had to flee. Granny died a short while later. The day of the funeral arrived with leaden sky and gusts of pelting rain forcing the graveside service inside among the crypts. The family closed ranks and I mourned alone.

Golden daffodils, scarlet tulips, sunset-colored azaleas, and longer days heralded the onset of spring. Easter arrived with its promise of new birth. I awoke as though from a strange land. Surprised by its suddenness, I celebrated God's gift with a self-indulgence of my own. Savoring the look and smell of the glistening, semisweet chocolate covered caramel, I bit into something hard, too hard.

Spitting the stickiness into my upturned palm, my tongue recoiled at the crevasse in my mouth and then the ragged molar. Points of light sparked before my eyes as I willed myself not to pass out. My gloom returned with the dentist's bill for an enamel-covered gold crown and a sense of my own encroaching mortality.

June brought another school year's march toward completion. One week until commencement and then I could focus on my administrative duties as vice president. The college president I so admired was retiring and I would assume his job along with my own until a new leader was chosen. I refused to dwell on the sense of foreboding I felt from the departure of my mentor and friend. State licensure renewal forms and an application for accreditation added to the weight of my duties.

A call came. My mother was not feeling well in the stifling California desert. *Could I come? Of course, why hadn't my parents told me Mother was ill?* They said they did not want to worry me. Upon arriving, I recoiled at how much my parents had aged since the summer before. Mother's short curly hair was completely white and her smooth skin shone translucent. She said she felt much better with me there. After a doctor's appointment two days later, Mother reported her red blood count was up. She was on the mend. I stayed a few more days and then returned home.

Three weeks later another call came. *Could I come back? Mother had a minor setback. It was nothing serious just a bad case of anemia.* I said I would leave at the end of the week. Arriving I noted my mother appeared paler still. After voicing concern, my parents told me not to worry. *Really it was nothing serious.* When Mother was napping, I pressed my father to tell me what was wrong. *It was nothing serious. Her blood count was down and she was feeling blue. She would perk up since I had returned.* He was sure of it.

A week later Mother seemed stronger. As I prepared to leave, I discovered they had not told my sister, Chriss, Mother was ill. *Did they want to call Chriss or should I? Could I?* Chriss was livid. *Why had she not been told? She would come at once.* I picked her up at the airport the next day. Chriss stayed a week. Mother seemed stronger. Maybe the worst was over. Chriss agreed to stay another week so I could return to work.

Mother's illness and everything that needed to be done before the fall semester made me feel nauseous. My response to the endless state and accrediting questions, student recruitment, and last minute preparations for the upcoming school year made me edgy from the guilt. I was amazed two weeks had passed when Chriss called. Mother was worse. I had to go. My sister had a problem with her kidneys and just gotten out of the hospital. *Was she all right? Yes, but not up for travel.* Father was doing his best, but one of us needed to be there. I had to sit down. Chriss was Mother's favorite. She was closest to Mother. I was afraid. I knew I had to go, what else could I do?

When I reached my parents' house, a middle-aged woman was washing my mother's hair in the kitchen sink. Father said she was from hospice. The only thing I knew about hospice was it was for the terminally ill. After the woman left, I confronted my parents. They insisted Mother only had pernicious anemia. I did not believe them.

I wanted to ask Mother's doctor myself but felt it would be a violation of my parents' trust. *Surely they would not lie to me.* Mother seemed so frail, like a pink-and-white porcelain doll. My gut told me my mother would never get well. I called Chriss. She was better. She would come the next day. I picked her up at the airport. After Mother fell asleep that evening, Chriss demanded the truth. Father stared with an expressionless face into the cold fireplace. With much throat clearing he confessed Mother had leukemia. My father, Chriss, and I huddled together with arms interwoven oblivious of the tears splashing to the floor.

Chriss spent her days stretched out beside my mother on the king-sized bed. She barely left Mother's side. I tried to keep busy, but grew more resentful with each passing day. I willed Mother to call for me or to display some act of maternal affection. Finally Chriss said I should go and sit with Mother. She smiled faintly as I balanced myself on the edge of the bed. I prayed my mother would speak to the pain in my soul, to reach across the chasm of forty silent years. Mother appeared to perk up speaking excitedly of people and places across the decades. I mourned my aloneness.

The next day Mother felt better. She slumped in her favorite chair after dabbing on a bit of red lipstick and robin-blue eye shadow. She said she decided to have a blood transfusion. That was all she needed. We could go home. She would be fine. We would see. I felt weak with relief since school started in three weeks.

Chriss insisted we take a Polaroid picture of all of us under the walnut tree. We said our farewells. When I arrived home I could not let go of the revelation I experienced in my soul as the plane flew over Crater Lake. The opposite of love was not hate, but indifference. Father called to say Mother seemed stronger. The transfusion must have worked. I felt euphoric. Maybe we still had a chance for intimacy.

Another call came three days later. Mother had died in her sleep. Two funeral services were planned. One at the church my parents attended in the desert and a graveside service at the coast where I had grown up. During the church service I barely looked at my mother lying in the casket. I would not remember her that way. When I tried to read the Psalm Mother had requested, the words floated off the page and I had to start over. I have no memory of the drive to the graveside service, only of Father sitting silently beside me.

Kind words of sympathy were spoken before the visitors left. I made no effort to rise from the linen-draped chair under the green-stripped graveside awning. I had not moved since the copper-colored casket was lowered into the waiting hole. I watched the ebony hearse depart with its black-frocked driver. The workers had not wanted me to stay and watch the grave being filled. I could not will myself to leave. Only after an immense mound of dirt had been hammered into place did I get up and let myself be driven back to the desert.

The next morning, Father insisted I go through Mother's things. He begged Chriss and I to take everything of hers home with us, especially the shoes. He had paid a lot of money for them. Chriss packed a few bags. I said I would never wear the clothes and the shoes were too big. My father refused to take no for an answer. He also insisted I take Mother's diamond wedding set. I told him I already had two of Mother's rings and the wedding set should go to my sister. Chriss wept as she held me tight.

The following afternoon, I began the thousand-mile drive back home with two bags of clothes and three pairs of shoes. Collapsing on the motel bed that evening, my exhausted mind refused to quit replaying the previous week's events. I tossed and turned. I flopped on my side. I clutched my knees to my chest in a fetal position. Convulsively I sobbed for my mother and myself. For what could have been and now would never be, until every tear was shed. Exhausted I slept.

Students and faculty returned for the fall semester. Licensure and accrediting applications were sent off. The dark days of fall mimicked the numbness shrouding me. As I went through the motions of eating breakfast the last Thursday of October, I hastily scanned the morning newspaper. My eyes focused on a small box in the bottom right hand corner, which contained a public invitation to an Evensong at the downtown Episcopalian church. A four o'clock celebration for the dead would be held the following Sunday afternoon. I mouthed the word to myself. *EVEN-song, even-SONG, EVENSONG*. Unexpected joy welled up inside me, and I was comforted.

# Chapter 13

# IF I COULD TURN BACK THE HANDS OF TIME

By Paul Dengler

I remember the last time.
Said you'd be returning real soon.
Never dreamed it would be the last time . . .
I'd see you.
Now I'm here, and I'm just staring . . .
At your name carved in the stone.
I listen over and over . . .
To your final message on my phone.
If I could turn back the hands of time,
I would have your hands again in mine.
If I could turn back the hands of time,
I wouldn't throw it away. I'd make it shine.
I know we had unfinished business.
Too late now to reconcile.
All the times we shared that made me cry . . .
They don't compare to all the times that made me smile
If I could turn back the hands of time,
I would have your hands again in mine.
If I could turn back the hands of time.
I wouldn't throw it away. I'd make it shine.

# Chapter 14

# THE VALLEY OF THE SHADOW

By Elin Criswell

"Blessed be the God and Father of our Lord Jesus Christ, the Father of mercies and God of all comfort, Who comforts us in all our tribulation, that we may be able to comfort those who are in any trouble, with the comfort with which we ourselves are comforted by God." 2 Corinthians 1:3-4 NKJV

"What do you think Heaven will be like?" she asked.

The question pierced through me. I immediately turned away to stare out the hospital window into the cold, rainy dark night. The question hurt so because I knew mom would be going there soon.

"I don't know exactly," I replied. "But I think there will be a lot of people all praising God."

"Yes," she agreed, "Lots and lots of singing."

It was a Friday in 1995 and it had been one of the worst days of my life. Hospital officials called to inform me we would have to make a decision on what to do next. They wanted to move mom into the rehabilitation unit, but under hospice care status. They expected her to die soon. No resuscitation orders. No heroic measures. They would give her medication to make her comfortable but nothing more. It was agonizing to face the details.

When I came to the hospital that night, I didn't know what to expect. In the previous few days there were times when she was coherent and other times when she was not. But thankfully on this night she was lucid. After explaining the events of the day, mom agreed to make the move to the rehabilitation unit. When it was time to go I hugged and kissed her. Then turned back to look at her as I went out the door.

She was looking at me and said, "I really thank God for you."

Tears welled in my eyes as I walked down the hall.

I had not always enjoyed a close relationship with my mom. In fact, it had only been since the birth of my first child six years earlier, when things between mom and I really began to improve. Mom was the daughter of Swedish immigrants to Texas. She had experienced a hard life and a lot of heartache. At only thirteen her mother died. She grew up during the Great Depression and married young. She was a hardened, opinionated and strict woman. She was harsh at times. She was my mom.

Saturday morning started off with another phone call from the hospital. Only this time, informing me we needed to come right away. Mom was dying. For the next few hours family and friends gathered to hold a vigil on the second floor of the hospital. It didn't take long. A little after eleven she was gone.

My precious momma was gone.

I've heard it said losing someone is easier when it is expected and when he or she is old. I couldn't disagree more. Such circumstances may make one more prepared, but I think a lot of a person's response is connected with how close you are to the person regardless of their age or health. My mom was eighty-one years old and she had fought cancer for two and a half years. The depth of despair I experienced along with the sense of loss, this created a void that is hard to put into words.

To me grief is like a serious wound. If a wound does not receive the proper medical attention it requires, it will get infected and things will go from bad to worse. It cannot be ignored but must be tended to.

Growing up I did not have the pleasure of knowing my grandparents; but my Great Aunt Maude was like a grandmother to me. Years before I came on the scene, she lost part of her ring finger in a lawn mower accident. Although she was immediately taken to the hospital, it was impossible to reattach her finger. She lived the rest of her days with a shortened finger. Often she experienced phantom pain from the part no longer there. Grief is like that. It demands attention to initiate a measure of healing. Just like my aunt's finger there will always be a void in our life. We will always miss the loved one lost.

The night after my mom's funeral I went to bed exhausted and numb from the sadness. My husband did his best to console me, but I was inconsolable. At two in the morning I awoke with my back in extreme spasms. I had been running on adrenaline for days dealing with details. Now all that was over and the full force of pain and stress hit me all at once. I went into the living room and sat on the couch for what seemed like hours. All I could think of was I would never see my Momma on this earth again.

In the weeks to follow I found it hard to be around others. I just didn't feel comfortable being in a group of people. In a sense it was like I just wanted to go it alone for a while; yet, the very thing helping the most were phone conversations with my friend. I found simply talking about how badly it hurt, just being able to talk, really enabled me to begin to deal with my grief.

I'll never forget when there was a knock on our door two days before my mom's funeral. It was the daughter of an elderly friend of mine. My friend passed away the previous year. When I opened the door she tenderly smiled saying, "I heard about your mom and I just wanted to stop by to give you this." Then she handed me a spiral ham. Hardly any words were spoken. They weren't needed. I knew she knew what I was going through. Her simple act of kindness was a great encouragement.

During this time we were all really concerned for my dad. My parents had been married for sixty-one years. *How would dad do now with mom gone?* We did our best to be there for him. To our surprise dad did fine. He missed mom, but he went on the best he could.

He loved his house in the country. Yet he wanted to go into town all the time. His favorite activity was going for coffee. Our local Walmart® had a snack bar where the locals would meet for coffee. They even had a coffee club where members stored their favorite coffee cup to use every time they came. The Arby's® on the highway near his home was another favorite hangout. He enjoyed watching the travelers come and go.

Dad lived alone for two and a half years; however, the day came when he fell and broke his leg. Everything changed. After surgery there were only two choices. Either he would go into a nursing home or someone would have to live with him. My husband and I became dad's primary caregivers.

Caring for my elderly Dad required a huge role reversal as now I was the one taking care of him. Being around him so much brought me face-to-face with some unresolved issues in my life that I didn't know I had. The major issue was concerning love.

I knew that Dad loved me; but his love had always been distant. As a child I felt like he kept me at arm's length. I wanted to spend time with him. He always seemed to be too tired. Granted, I was born late in my parents' lives. Dad was forty eight and mom was forty-seven years old when I was born. They were tired! He would make promises to me he ultimately didn't keep. He broke his promises to build me a playhouse in the backyard and to take me fishing. I just wanted him. I wanted his love. I needed my parents' love and affection. Instead, I felt rejected.

My parents did the best they could. I think there is this tendency to expect your parents to be perfect when there is no such thing as perfect parents. When I became a parent myself it was like a switch turned on. I realized my parents did love me and they had done their best.

My parents were Christians. We went to a good Bible teaching church. I was taught the truth from the Bible and understood we are all sinners in need of the Savior. At the tender age of six years old I prayed the sinner's prayer. Yet simply reciting the words of a prayer will not save a person unless it is mixed with real faith in Jesus. I held back from God. Deep down I really didn't believe God loved me. So when I prayed to accept Jesus, I didn't mean it. To me it was the thing to do, yet it was just words. I did not put my faith in Christ at that time. For the next three decades I went on to live my life as I thought a Christian should. I was the good girl. Very religious. Very deceived. Very lost.

While taking care of dad I began to question my salvation. For months I struggled with the very idea that I didn't know Jesus personally. How could I not be a Christian when I knew so much about God? One Saturday morning my husband said, "God is not your daddy." Hearing that was what it took for me to break. His words switched the light on for me. Dad was the first father figure in my life. My dad may have been distant and unavailable to me, but God is not distant. God does not hold me at arm's length. He loves me more than I will ever really comprehend. I finally surrendered and prayed. This time I told God not only did I know I was a sinner, not only did I accept Jesus' sacrifice for me on the cross to pay for my sins, but I also accepted the fact that God indeed really does love me.

During the first week of December in 2001, Dad came down with a cold that quickly put him in the hospital. He seemed to get better at first. Then his condition changed and he was transferred to intensive care. For most of his time in ICU he was unconscious. I remember visiting and praying over him while holding his hand. I would gaze at my daddy's hands. They were large and weatherworn from many hard-working years farming, doing construction work and house painting. Later in the week I received a call from Dad's doctor who informed me Dad had developed Acute Respiratory Distress Syndrome. The condition was usually fatal for both the very young and very old.

Each night before going to bed I would call the ICU nurse to check on Dad. After making my call on Friday night I went to sleep. I was awakened shortly before midnight. "Mrs. Criswell, I am so sorry. Your dad has taken a turn for the worst. You'll want to come right away." Before we could get there, Dad was gone.

The grief that I had after Dad's passing was different than it was with my mom. Now that I knew the Lord, God's grace sustained me from within. Still the pain was just as deep.

Each December when the weather gets cold and gloomy, I am apt to think of when my parents passed. Sometimes grief comes when I least expect it. Like the time I went to IKEA with my oldest daughter, Becky. We ended up in the kitchen section of the store where I picked up a Swedish cookbook. Suddenly I found myself thinking of mom and began to tear up. Becky stood by my side simply saying, "Some people might think it strange for a grown woman to start to cry in the middle of a store. But we don't. No. We don't." She said just the right thing. Through my tears, I just had to laugh and my mood lightened. She understood and that was what I needed.

Sooner or later, we all have to travel our own journey of grief. Eventually you will lose someone you love. It is comforting to know that God loves us and desires to walk with us through each step of life. He can and will help you make it through your own valley of the shadow.

# Chapter 15

# GLIMPSES OF JOY

By Kayla Fioravanti

I've suffered the loss of someone so deeply personal. She was the one person whose place in my life went down to the very roots of who I am. Loss and hard times are familiar to me. Still nothing could have prepared me for the loss of my mother.

Grief doggedly tugged me downward. Yet, I know my mother would never have wanted my own momentum in life to stand still from the loss of the time. She would have wanted me to move forward. I choose to honor her by following the example she set to always search for glimpses of joy, even in the heaviest of moments. She captured the bright side of every occasion finding laughter there. My choice to intentionally follow her has helped me regain equilibrium in life.

Like mom, I've discovered glimpses of joy flash all around me like fireflies in the southern night sky. The flashes are illuminating and wonderfully effective in distracting me from the heavyweight of grief even if only momentary.

I spent three weeks where the world was only as large as the space surrounding her hospital bed. Once she passed, rejoining my already-in-progress-life was like jumping on a spinning carousel ride. I bobbed and bounced while the lights of the ride flashed and music played. I've adjusted to riding the carousel knowing my mother isn't coming around the corner any moment. Her voice won't greet me on the other side of my phone again.

It was disconcerting jumping onto the spinning carousel in the midst of my grief. I felt fear and resistance at first. If I refused to adjust, the ride would have been an unrelenting nightmare. I learned if I chose to relax and embrace the opportunities for joy I could ride through my days with renewed perspective and energy.

I am taking the time to relish in the music of my children's laughter, the dependability of my husband, my history still alive in my father, the familiarity of my chaos, the certainness of my faith and the care of friends and family. Sure some days are darker than others. In those days my glimpses of joy shine more brilliantly, like fireflies emerging in the night sky.

# Section Two
# THE UNNATURAL EVENT OF PARENTS OUTLIVING CHILDREN

Photo by Lisa Rodgers

# Chapter 16

# BLESSED BY THE PROCESS

By Jacquelyn Bodeutsch

We found out we were pregnant with our third child on New Year's Eve. We knew this was going to change everything. A few weeks later, after the shock wore off, we became excited about this new life inside me. At our twenty week ultrasound the technician took a very long time reviewing the various parts of our baby's body. Having been through this twice before I knew something wasn't right. I asked, "Is that six fingers he has? Well I can handle six fingers; we can handle that." The tech just smiled and went about her business. I honestly had no concerns at this point.

Several days later the phone rang and it was my midwife. Before she could say anything, I knew something was wrong. I fell to the floor weeping. My heart broke in two. Our son had a rare genetic disorder. His chances of survival after birth were close to zero. Such a deep sorrow overwhelmed me. I was grieving and hurting so badly. I tried to enjoy my baby, but at the same time I was afraid to get attached. I decided to not even name him or dream a life for him.

Weeks later the darkness lifted. We embraced our unborn son with open arms and loved him as much as possible. It wouldn't be easy to bury our son. We were going to choose joy, love, and hope through it all. I kept praying for a miracle. Ultimately I said to God "Whatever you want to use to shape us and grow us then that's what I want--even if it means watching my baby die." I wrote and journaled a lot through the next few months and trusted God to get us through it.

The hour came for him to be born. It was the most excruciating pain. I believe my body was afraid to let him come into this world only to be taken away.

It was the most beautiful thing once he was born. They placed him on my chest. I thought he looked totally healthy and did not suspect otherwise. I held him close and smooched him (not enough). Until I saw my husband's tears, I had no idea my son was going to sleep and would not wake up. I was in shock and did not know what to do. We held him for two hours even though he had passed within an hour of his birth. Realizing it was just his body and his soul had gone away made it easier to release him to the nurses and say goodbye. As they took his body from our room we sat and cried together. We noticed the sunset outside our fourteenth story window and knew God was holding us. He would continue to hold us as we went on with our lives.

Our nearly four-year-old daughter looked at me confused when we came home. She asked, "Mommy where is the baby?" I turned my head away bursting into tears as I fell to the ground. *How could I carry on normal activities and not cry? How could I explain this to my sweet little children and not be sobbing all day long?* And somehow it felt like it had never even happened. We gave birth thirty miles from our town. It seemed like a dream entering back into our home. *Did I really just send away my child? Did he really die in my arms?* Then I would look down and see my belly speaking it all too be true.

We immediately had to make plans for his burial and funeral. We chose a funeral home we wouldn't pass by too often thinking it would be helpful with our grief. Unfortunately, we are disappointed now we did not choose the funeral home closest. We would love to be able to walk over to him and say hello at any time. Each time I drive by the funeral home within two blocks from where we live I nearly cry because of the opportunity we lost to have him much closer to us. Judgment is always clouded at the beginning of grief.

Within weeks of the loss I began experiencing intense anxiety, nightmares, insomnia and panic attacks. I thought maybe I was losing my mind. I certainly wasn't blaming it on my loss. I was not aware at how much his death had affected me. It was causing a bit of chaos in my mind. I began clinging closely to these two little lives I was still taking care of. I was holding so much tighter for fear of losing them both as well. I became obsessed with germs and would go into a panic if anything were out of my control. I would plan my husband's funeral whenever he was traveling or gone for the evening. I wouldn't allow my children to go or do things that might put them in danger. I hardly left the house for many months. My reactions may have made sense, but it certainly wasn't healthy. I eventually had to put my life on hold. I just couldn't function anymore.

I began seeing a counselor who allowed me to be completely honest with no judgments. It was the most amazing thing I could have done at the time. I was able to see how everything in my life had led me to this place. It all made sense. Our connection and my comfort surprised me because I expected it to take several different counselors to find the best fit. He helped me see it was all right to cry every single day. It is good to talk with God openly with questions and confusion. Asking questions is not wrong. I learned when we stop asking questions and become silent it is the most dangerous. Healing from a trauma takes time and time doesn't always heal.

I had to learn to be honest with myself. To process as much as possible with others who were able to validate me. Validation was a huge part of my healing. I never chose to go to a support group, but how I wish I would have. I am planning to start attending next month. I recently met with a woman in town who experienced something so similar to me. It was such a blessing to talk with her. Even four years later I still need this validation.

I believe action is much more important to healing than time. In the beginning little steps are all it takes. Bigger leaps came as I let go of the fear and the weight the world placed on me. Or maybe what I had put on myself. I decided to shave my head and *wow* was it ever freeing! Throwing off the expectations of others and saying to the world *this is who I am and it is good! I am OK! It is OK to feel how I feel! It is OK to be true to myself,* whatever it may look like. I also tattooed the words *hope* on my right wrist and *mercy* on my left wrist. I do not regret it one bit. Every single day I am reminded of the mercy God has shown me through the years and the hope I have in Him. He held my hand the past four years and will continue to carry me each day. Stepping out of the comfort zone of safety and into the realm of adventure is something I found so liberating.

I don't know if I will ever be finished healing, but I do not care. Through this process old wounds are being treated and closed. Things I wouldn't have had the courage to address were no longer avoidable anymore. If it were not for this life-changing event I would not be who I have become. A person who is stronger than I ever imagined. I cannot be angry with what has happened to me when it has brought about so much fruit in my life. I have been truly blessed by the process.

# Chapter 17

# A BEND IN THE ROAD

Collected Stories by Jessica Mills Winstead

I still have a recurring nightmare of a tragic July 4th day . . .

> *"Jessica has anyone called you? There's been an accident . . . they've been doing CPR for twenty minutes . . ."* *I arrive at the hospital emergency room doors and looked in the ambulance. I wonder if Noah had been in there. I can see myself walking through the emergency room doors. I wonder if I am the mother of two living children. I still don't know what's happened. A nurse gets a doctor and they try to talk to me. I won't listen. Then I'm in a scene where I try to get in touch with my parents and best friend, but I just couldn't speak the words. Many people hover around me. I see my daughter's dad carrying Haleigh Raye into the waiting room. Our eyes lock. I know I have to tell Haleigh Raye her brother Noah is gone and not coming home.*

And then . . . usually I wake up. I try not to let myself wake up too much. I have a fear of not going back to sleep and more memories will return of the day my world came to a crashing halt.

It was a day when I left my house to go to the gym with plans to have lunch before joining friends for a July 4th celebration. The celebration never happened.

Instead I received a phone call, "Noah's been in an accident at the lake."

I lost Noah Dean my ten-year-old son. I remember little of my life in the months to follow. I can't imagine ever wanting to celebrate during the July 4th holiday again.

When the nightmares awaken me I usually grab a heating pad, my newest staple since losing Noah. It's warm and helps me not to feel so alone. It takes me back to July 2nd, my last night with Noah when he climbed into bed with me. He was warm and I was not alone.

After Noah's death, people suggested it might be therapeutic to journal my thoughts and feelings. I smiled politely, but secretly wondered, *"My thoughts? I don't even know what my thoughts are. They are so scattered and don't make sense to me. How could I ever get them down on paper?"* But then there's this social media tool we all know as Facebook®. It became an outlet for me. Through Facebook® I connected to a community of people whose comments encouraged me through my darkest hours lightening my burden. Most importantly I felt strengthened by their promises of prayer.

I am still amazed at the outpouring of love and support shown. As we were making arrangements for the funeral I can somehow recall thinking, "*Noah was only ten. Did he know enough people to even come? Would he just be someone passing through this earth no one would know or remember?*" Humbly I now smile because Noah made more of an impact in his ten years than many people do in a lifetime. I have made it my mission for people not only to know about Noah and his spunky personality, but also to tell them where Noah is now. I have come to somewhat of an understanding and acceptance Noah doesn't need me now in heaven. I need him more than he could ever need me.

I can mourn, I can grieve and I can cry for him. I still have to live. I have to live for my daughter, I have to live for myself and, most importantly, I have to live for God. I have no idea why I'm on this journey. It goes without saying it is not one I voluntarily signed up for. But I am on it. I have a choice to either turn away being bitter or accept and embrace this new normal.

The conscious decision I've made to accept and embrace is what led me here to write and share. As I was trying to create a name for my blog about this journey nothing jumped out at me. Until recently when I came across this C.S. Lewis quote from *A Grief Observed*, "Grief is like a long valley, a winding valley where any bend may reveal a totally new landscape."

I also looked up the definition of bend and found these two definitions: "Bend-to bring something into a state of tension or to force to assume a different direction or shape."

When I asked a friend what she thought of the name for my blog, she questioned whether bend was a strong enough word for what I had been through. No words are really strong enough to convey my pain and grief. Yet, I write to give words to bends in the road we all face. I write about the twists and turns of fate sometimes bringing us to our knees. Or having us shouting with joy.

There aren't many things guaranteed and unchanging in this world. There is one thing guaranteed and doesn't change. It is God. He is at the end of the road I'm traveling. He's the destination. This God of yesterday, today, and tomorrow was there at the end of Noah's road on earth too. Knowing that comforts me greatly. My final destination has become more inviting. Today's journey is simply a bend in the road.

# Don't take it for Granted

In my son's short ten years on this earth I confirmed many dates and times for him. As many parents know the list was endless. From dentist and doctor appointments, play dates, and practices. After losing Noah Dean I cancelled a number of engagements planned for the future. Conversely, I made and confirmed other undesirable appointments. We set a time to pick out his casket, a time to select a headstone and a time for the service. We even had appointments for meeting with experts to review investigative reports about what in the world happened during Noah's accident. We continue to meet with experts to make sure no one else suffers a tragedy like what we experienced at the lake that July 4th day.

One of my most difficult appointments was setting a date and time to watch the installation of his headstone. I had numbly forged through the administrative aspects of dealing with my son's death.

When I received the call, "We have the monument ready for Noah," I keenly felt the loss of my son. My child was gone way too soon.

From my loss I encourage parents not to take your kids for granted. Don't be frustrated when they cling to you and you can't get on with your day. Don't roll your eyes when the school calls you with a sick child and it interrupts your workday. Let your child know THEY are not the interruption. Your workday is. Find out what they enjoy and immerse yourself in it. Ask questions. Get down on the floor and play. There are a lot of things I learned about Noah and what he liked AFTER he died. It was irony at its finest.

Encourage and help them better their skills. Strengthen what they are good at so they won't feel as incompetent when their weaknesses come up. Find the good in life. From the simple things of bird watching to delivering food and fellowship to a shut in. Teach them empathy and compassion for others and the world we live in.

Don't take a single second for granted. From rushing out the door in the morning to the last goodbye as you drop them off at school. Kissing their forehead goodnight and telling them as you truly looking them square in the eye, how very much you love them. How you are blessed God allowed them to be in your life.

## Faith that Can Move a Mountain

"He replied, 'Because you have so little faith. I tell you the truth, if you have faith as small as a mustard seed, you can say to this mountain, 'Move from here to there' and it will move. Nothing will be impossible for you.'" Matthew 17-20 NIV

This is a verse I have heard my entire life. But I don't think I have ever understood how the verse applied to my life as well as I have now. I take things very literally. In my black and white thinking, moving a mountain doesn't seem to be something I could ever do. No matter how big my faith grew to be. I finally figured out my problem with understanding and applying this verse. It was my focus on having a perfect faith to save me instead of focusing on the perfect object of my faith.

Losing my son Noah Dean, was the most painful and challenging life experience I can imagine ever enduring. The only comparable thing would be losing my daughter, Haleigh Raye. Losing her is a daily fear. At least twice a day I pray to God, "please don't take Haleigh Raye away from me and don't take me away from her and let us live our lives out together." My constant ache to be with Noah and my constant fear of losing Haleigh Raye have been dark mountains I've had to climb.

My mountain is learning to live for now without Noah. It is learning to live for a little girl who did not die and needs to see her momma live, laugh and love. Not just exist. My mountain is covered in grief and sin. It is ebony black. I suspect I will be climbing this mountain for the rest of my life. But while I am trudging ahead I will keep my focus on God and the strides He's taking with me.

Sometimes I still think irrationally. I wonder if he is upset I'm going on without him. Or if going on in life means I love him. I realize these thoughts aren't rational. I'm slowly learning to turn the thoughts around and focus on Jesus. He's the One who is taking better care of Noah than I ever could. He's the One who knows me, knows my heart, knows my intentions and understands my mustard seed faith.

Many times I've said I am on the "Road to Noah Dean." Well, I am. However he's no longer the destination at the top of the mountain. At the top of the washed white-as-snow mountain, I will see Jesus face-to-face. I will see the One who took my mustard seed faith and moved my mountain. He can move your mountain too.

## He Will Restore the Years

"And I will restore to you the years that the swarming locust has eaten . . ." Joel 2:25 KJV

This had always been one of my favorite verses. It meant no matter the strife I faced, the hardships I endured, God promised to restore what was lost. Then one summer it quickly became one of my least favorite verses.

My family suffered an unthinkable loss. We lost Noah, my son, in an unimaginable lake accident. The aftermath was nothing short of complete devastation. I vividly remember crying out, "Please God don't ask this of me; don't ask this of my family!" To this day, I remember calling my dad from the ER trying to tell him through my sobs to come to the hospital. I have imagined him a hundred times enjoying his July 4th when my call came.

A few months after Noah's death, my mind kept coming back to this verse. I couldn't fathom how life without Noah could ever be restored. There could never be a replacement for him. Any kind of restoration seemed unimaginable and impossible.

Yet over time, I realized relationships have been strengthened. I have received lots of encouragement and gained friends both near and far. The gift of these true friends renews me frequently.

After experiencing days when I just wanted to "end it," I've slowly gained more confidence in my ability to make it. I accepted life for what it is today and renewed hope for what it can become. My love for my daughter, Haleigh Raye, revives me. She has a full life ahead of her. She needs me. I choose to be strong for her.

God's grace has and continues to save and redeem me. Ultimately, though, He has given me eternity. In this He will restore the years.

## Living without Faith is like Driving in a Fog

One morning as I was driving my daughter, Haleigh Raye, to school I became frustrated because the windows of my car became so foggy I couldn't see. I pulled over to wait for the fog to clear. While waiting, Haleigh Raye noticed handprints and finger drawings appear in the condensation on the backseat windows

"Mom, look at the fingerprints."

At first, I couldn't look at them.

I was reminded of all the days I had said, "Noah stop writing on my windows."

After a minute, with tears in my eyes I turned around and looked. Noah's handprints, initials and character drawings appeared in the condensation. My heart melted. I was so thankful for the evidence of his life on my windows that morning. I thanked the Lord for the gift He gave me in the moment.

I usually move through my hours as if I am limited by condensation, especially since I lost Noah. I tend to see the negative aspects of life and to let the foggy moments either stress or discourage me. I'm learning to notice the gifts. When I appreciate a child's handprints and drawings on a window or simply allow the fog to give me an opportune moment to pray, I've chosen to see. That foggy morning taught me to CHOOSE TO SEE the gifts from my heavenly Father.

# Chapter 18

# I WILL NOT STAY IN DARKNESS FOREVER

By Kimberly Crumby

I never thought by the age of thirty-four I would have enough experience to write more than a few words about the hard emotion of grief. My first thirty years were fairly light on the loss scale. My parents did divorce. Yet I never considered my home broken. I have precious memories from my childhood, met my husband in high school and went to college to become a teacher. We effortlessly had a perfect baby girl. After a brief struggle with infertility our son was born almost three years later.

We strived to make God the top priority in our lives though we often fell short. While life never was and never will be perfect it was pretty gentle to our little family. One September, as the leaves began their colorful transformation, our lives were also transformed.

As I returned to my classroom after dropping my kindergartners off in physical education class, I heard my phone vibrating. My husband was at the doctor's office with our four-and-a-half year old daughter. She had been a super healthy child. We were stumped when a low-grade fever stubbornly persisted for several days with no obvious cause. She told us neither her ears nor throat hurt. I thought we should let the pediatrician look her over to make sure it was not one of those common illnesses.

I thought it was odd when I saw the clinic was calling. A nurse told me my husband asked her to tell me to come to the office. I asked why he wasn't calling himself. She relayed that he was too upset to talk on the phone. It literally felt like my stomach dropped to the floor as I grabbed my purse and quickly told my teammates where I was going. Upon arriving, the doctor told me based on lab results he believed our child had either leukemia or some other type of blood disease. We would need to go home, pack, and go to the children's hospital in our state. It was three hours away from where we lived.

From the time she was eighteen months old, our sweet pea was a force to be reckoned with. We watched her morph from the world's easiest baby (not exaggerating) to a toddler of terror (maybe a slight exaggeration). She suddenly became a fit throwing, strong-willed ball of orneriness. As she continued to grow we were able to reason with her most of the time. She still had definite ideas about how things should go. She was sassy, stubborn and smart. Her favorite things included digging in her dress-up trunk for the perfect outfit, watching Disney princess movies and harassing her brother. Ironically, her teachers at preschool and church never had too much trouble with her. I often consoled myself with the idea she would be a great adult--if we could just mold her spirit without breaking it and survive her teenage years.

After an agonizingly long drive and several hours in the emergency room, we were told our sweet girl did indeed have leukemia. It is hard to describe how disconcerting it is to have a perfectly healthy child for four years and then in a half-day span try to absorb a cancer diagnosis. We were admitted to the oncology floor and told we would get more information the next day about what type she had, her treatment plan, and prognosis.

I lay in the tiny hospital room that night not able to sleep. I was crying and asking God why my baby was going to have to endure this. I wish I could say I praised God for giving us this trial . . . I never questioned his infinite wisdom . . . but it is not the case. I always thought it was cliché to hear a mother say she wished she could take something on for her child. It was exactly the thought I had that night. I desperately wished I could have been the one to have to fight cancer. Not my child whom I had loved from the first moment I knew of her existence.

In the following week we were told she had the most treatable form of leukemia. We signed what felt like a hundred papers. The oncologist went over the plans for her treatment. She underwent several procedures to begin what the doctors believed would be a two to three year journey to full remission. During the first week she would not speak to anyone. Instead she responded by shaking or nodding her head. She laughed with delight when her almost two-year-old brother came to visit one evening. She watched movies, ate when she wanted to and pulled the cover over her head when the doctors came in. We believed this to be her way of dealing with the trauma of being in the hospital, being poked and prodded, and basically being ripped out of her normal life.

Eight days after we arrived we were able to return home on a Friday. We were scheduled to go back Monday for a chemotherapy session. Over the weekend she was not able to sit up, still did not speak, slept almost the entire time, could not move her right side, and would not eat or drink. I expressed my concern to the oncologist on-call at the hospital.

Monday when we returned for chemotherapy, we again relayed our concerns. The doctor ordered an MRI of her brain to get an idea of what was going on. Late that night, we were told she had brain damage. They were not sure what had happened at this point. We were admitted again and that night, unable to sleep, I asked God why leukemia alone wasn't enough.

A day or two later the doctors and radiologist finally decided she had suffered a stroke approximately a week earlier. This was why she did not speak, could not hold herself up and could not move the right side of her body. No one had any idea it happened. I had a really hard time dealing with the fact I hadn't able to tell something else was wrong. Rationally, I knew all the reasons why no one saw this coming. Rationality can be hard to hang on to when it comes to your children.

The team of doctors reassured us that kids could make remarkable progress after brain injuries. We would now be looking at lots of physical, occupational and speech therapies in addition to chemotherapy. Her treatment plan was to be adjusted. The oncologists would no longer give her one drug in particular. She would not get medication put directly into her spinal column like all other patients with her type of leukemia. As you can imagine, this felt overwhelming to say the least. I never thought I would long to just go back to a "simple" cancer diagnosis.

The next two months can only be described as the worst roller coaster ride you can ever imagine. She went septic which furthered the brain damage. She almost died. She spent lots of time in the pediatric intensive care unit (PICU), but amazingly made some improvement. Our sweet girl eventually woke up and would answer us with head movements. She went back to the oncology floor and she was doing well enough for the different therapists to begin working with her. They were even talking about moving her to the rehabilitation floor.

One weekend she was sleepier than normal. Her lab results were somewhat alarming. Back to PICU we went. She was suffering from hydrocephalus. The fluid on her brain was causing it to swell. The doctors told us the next twelve hours were critical. There was a chance she would not survive the night. She did and eventually she was stable enough to move back to the oncology floor. However, the brain damage was getting to the point she would no longer be a candidate for rehab, at least for the time being. I remember this being one of my lowest moments. I had pinned a lot of hope on her being able to get extensive rehabilitation services in order for her to have some semblance of "normal" functioning.

In mid-November things started going downhill again--our little bald angel started running a fever, slept all the time with spikes in blood pressure and heart rate. One night, she really seemed to be struggling from a respiratory standpoint. Her breaths were coming slowly and the nurse kept using suction on her to try to help her clear secretions in her throat. An emergency team ended up having to rush in, taking her back to PICU to be intubated again. She was taken for yet another MRI. This one had a devastating result--another stroke had impacted her brain stem. The brain can indeed do miraculous things, but the brain stem (which controls all basic functions like breathing, blinking, consciousness, etc.) usually does not heal.

After several weeks of waiting for improvement that never came, we made a decision no parent ever wants to be faced with. With the trusted doctors' advice and lots of prayer and petitioning to God, we felt as peaceful as we could about removing her from the ventilator. Four years later I still cry when I think about this day. She was taken off life support on December 6th. After a terrible forty hours, she was finally too tired to keep fighting. I like to think she went straight from my arms into the arms of Jesus.

No one was ever able to really say for certain what caused the strokes or the other issues. An autopsy did not really shed light on the medical mystery that was our daughter. Ironically, the leukemia was in remission when she died. For someone who likes to know why things are the way they are, this was another bitter pill to swallow. Two and half months earlier we were cruising right along with our boy and our girl. Now, we were figuring out how to live without our child.

We returned home just a few weeks before Christmas. One of the hardest moments, among many, for me was walking into our house full of a thousand memories. Christmas is a holiday so much about children. It was breathtaking to see it through my daughter's eyes when she was old enough to take it all in. Now I was trying to take it all in without her. I really attempted to focus on Jesus and how grateful I was he was born into this world so he could eventually save us. I was mostly just overwhelmed with sadness. And I think it is okay. Her birthday quickly arrived in February, she would have been five. I still could not quite wrap my head around the fact she was gone. It did feel like a dream at times. I think God gave the brain the ability to go into a fog for a period of time as a protection for us.

After about six months the fog began lifting. This also coincided with the end of the school year--which meant lots of unfilled days for me as a teacher. Looking back, this was the hardest time in my grief journey. I really had to accept it was most likely going to be a long time before I laid eyes on my baby again.

I did not really want to go to church. Even so I made myself keep going. I did not want to open my Bible and read. I had devoured the Word and books about grief while we were in the hospital. I had a hard time listening to my much beloved contemporary Christian music. And I think that's ok. People, especially those who truly do their best to love the Lord with all their hearts, don't like to talk about such things. For me, it was a time of deep despair. I did not stay in darkness forever. That's been one of my grief mantras: *I will not stay in darkness forever.* I do visit some dark places, but I have to choose not to stay there. And over time I visit those less and less often.

Working towards a new normal is no easy task. No one in the same family grieves in exactly the same way. It was very difficult to try to help each other and honor how someone else copes when you are barely coping yourself. My husband struggled with anger towards God. We do not believe God purposefully struck our child with these cruel circumstances. We do know he allowed it. He could've healed her but he didn't. It's understandable this could make a daddy angry. I wasn't really angry, but simply bewildered. I just could not for the life of me make sense of what transpired. What mother could?

I had to gift myself and others with lots of grace. I had to ask God to get me out of my bed on more days than I can count. I had to forgive people for their trite expressions and cliché uses of scripture even when they didn't know they needed forgiving. I had to reign in my usual perfectionist tendencies and realize whatever I could do was enough. I had to trust God harder than I'd ever trusted before. Trust he is for me and he truly has plans to prosper and not harm me.

I had to sometimes go with what I knew in my head was true about my Savior. And not what my heart was screaming. I had to go through a season of asking why and then accept I was never going to get the answer in this life. I had to work to honor my daughter's legacy by doing good things for others in her name. I had to accept good could come from her death even when I didn't want it to. I had to keep loving…keep living…keep laughing…keep longing. Longing for the day when I see Jesus and my sweet girl.

# Chapter 19

# FROM THE ASHES

By Heather Blair

Awhile back a home in our neighborhood suffered fire damage. Luckily, it was not a total loss. The fire department was able to contain it to just the master bedroom and bath. Despite the home suffering smoke damage, it could've been much worse. The fire happened during the day and nobody was injured. Really, as far as a house fire is concerned it was one of those best case scenarios.

The family living there however probably doesn't feel the same. Their life has been turned upside down the past few months. They had to move out on a moment's notice juggling all the details that come with tragedy or disaster. Normal life for them has been paused, while the world continues to move forward. They are living out of boxes in a temporary house while rebuilding their home. I'm sure they've had a multitude of decisions in the midst of the chaos.

The home is directly behind ours. I've watched the progress through this transition. One of the things amazing me most is the overwhelming support system they have. It seems the majority of repairs have been done by family and friends. Those friends have worked all hours of the day and night with the first whacks of the hammer always starting at daylight and the whir of the generator humming through the midnight hour.

I was on the deck letting the dogs play in the yard one weekend and couldn't help watching their work. It struck me how symbolic rebuilding after loss was. While their work was physical and progress could be visibly seen, it reminded me of our own home and the rebuilding we've done since losing our oldest son Austin.

Rebuilding after child loss is no comparison to a fire. A home is material and everything under the roof can be replaced. Our child cannot be replaced. There will forever be a void where Austin was and should now be. However, the spiritual, emotional and even physical damage our family suffered is real. It could tear a family apart if not for an effort to rebuild.

Thinking back to those first few days, weeks and months I recall how broken we were. I once described it as a cracked windshield. Still functioning yet to an unknown casual observer it may look the same, even normal. Through the eyes of the family there are only pieces and fragments of what once was. We can't do anything without seeing and feeling the loss. We have felt at times as if our family was floating, forever paused in the pain and chaos. Yet everyone else goes on. Many times I wanted to scream, "We are still hurting! It has not gone away. It never will!"

I retreated. Months went by when I didn't want to leave the house unless it was necessary. To avoid running into someone, shopping trips were scheduled for two in the morning. Emotions would overtake me when I talked on the phone and I'd end up a sobbing mess. Online support was the only way I could speak of our loss. Being a writer helped me survive. My husband was the opposite, he sought out company. He welcomed work, extra hours, anything to avoid coming home where there were constant reminders of the emptiness.

I prayed for my husband, our marriage, and our youngest son. All within the same breath of being angry with God. In the early days, as much as I wanted to push Him away, God clung on evermore. He let me yell, scream, cry, question, and attempt to ignore Him. And then He would hug me with gentle whispers of scripture, send me peace that transcended understanding when we needed it most, and ensured I felt His love.

Over time, I guess I learned to move forward. Or maybe I just learned to fake it better each day because in reality the loss never went away. Days were easier, sometimes. Perhaps I just got busier with life again by finding ways to fill the space so I didn't have to think. That's how I felt for about two years. The pain would come slamming back into me just as if it were the first night all over again. It's been five years now. With each passing year I get slammed with pain less often. For the most part I know what triggers it now. On certain days I expect it. Nevertheless, sometimes sadness just comes. I just have to let it ride its course. Every now and then I just have to cry.

Looking back I can see tremendous progress. Even though the pain is still there, the loss is still felt and our son will be forever missed we've grown and healed. I remember each of our first holidays, vacations and special moments without Austin. We got through it despite thinking it was impossible. I remember being in a fog for so long, not wanting to see another living soul. Over time I returned. Many prayers were spent asking God to heal our family, to pull our ties closer instead of allowing us to stretch apart. We are stronger now. We hug, we talk, we laugh, we pray. We continue to go on with each of us having a piece aching for Austin in the background. And we always will. You don't get over child loss; you learn to get through it.

In five years, we have even seen unexpected changes for the good. Our marriage is stronger than ever. We've added my niece, a year older than our youngest, to our family. Our faith in God is solid. We have not only returned to church, but found a home helping to restore us. Our son's life and story has touched so many-- more than we could've ever imagined.

Our rebuilding, the literal patching back together of our family wasn't as easy as going to the store or buying supplies. Our healing didn't come overnight. It could only be found in one Source. Our continual restoration comes only from the Master Carpenter. God is the only answer I can give to why we've survived this time without our firstborn. Only through Him did we find peace, strength, hope and even joy.

# Chapter 20

# WHEN GRIEF TURNS TO MAGIC

By Cheri Perry

Christmas is now a time of peace for my family, full of celebration and joyful expectation. It wasn't always. Years ago, we were a young couple looking forward to the birth of our daughter. My husband had just lost his father, adding to the other struggles we dealt with as a newly married couple. Expecting our baby girl offered the hope we could lean into.

The pregnancy had been a breeze with each checkup being a reminder we were about to become a family! My husband was very excited about his little girl. We often shared our dreams of how she might turn out. *Would she have blue or brown eyes? Would she be a tomboy and love to go fishin' with Daddy? Or would she be a girly-girl surrounded by ribbons and flowers?* Either way was okay with us.

In the final weeks before her arrival we moved into an apartment with an extra bedroom and began the arduous task of creating a baby paradise on a tight budget. *We pondered the really big questions like disposable or cloth diapers? Should we have her sleep in the crib or with us? How long would it be before we let non-family members hold our treasure?* The normal stuff brand new parents ask themselves I'm sure!

The week before the due date my husband did the coolest thing. He loaded the baby stroller into the car and headed off to the store. I was laughing hysterically as he practiced driving the stroller through the aisles of the grocery store telling everyone he was having a daughter the following week.

On December 19th the checkup went well and our doctor thought we might actually make it through Christmas without our new bundle of joy. We listened to her heartbeat and watched her squirming around in her cushy cavern. When the doctor let us go for the day he assured us everything was fine and asked us to come back one more time right before Christmas just to see how things were progressing. We were happy to set the appointment and tears of joy just streamed down my face as I realized she was almost here; that's when the doubt set in. I imagine doubt is quite common for new moms. *Were we ready? What kind of Mommy would I be? Had I read enough material? Would I be able to get through the birth without paid meds? Would my boobs work?*

When I awoke on December 22nd, something felt different prompting me to call the nurse. I explained how the movement of the baby had seemed to slow down a bit and I was beginning to have some back pain. The nurse reassured me, letting me know that as the baby nestles down into the birth canal movement can either increase or decrease and there was nothing to be concerned about. She would see us the following day during our checkup. That night we talked about how cool it would have been to have her on the 22nd; my husband Dean's birthday.

The following morning we were eager to get the checkup over with so we could get on with the Christmas celebration and our last Christmas without a child. I was still feeling a little strange. Since this was my first full-term pregnancy, I expected feelings of strangeness; still, I was a little scared! *How in the world would my nine-month baby make it through the narrows?*

All of those fears would have to wait as I lay back on the table to have my ultrasound. Seeing her was so surreal. You know you 'have' a baby even though you aren't actually able to touch her. She always seemed so close, so within our reach. That's when I noticed my nurse's facial expression. I squeezed my husband's hand because I knew something was wrong. She said she would get the doctor and be back shortly. When the doctor came in, he too worked the ultrasound wand until he clicked the screen off and turned to give us the news.

He said, "Your baby has no heartbeat."

The room was spinning and tears rolled down my face.

I asked, "What do you mean she has no heartbeat. That doesn't make any sense?"

He said she was gone. We would not know why until she was delivered. I was devastated and could hardly breathe. He asked if we would like to go home and plan to deliver the baby after Christmas. "No!" I heard myself scream. We did not want to go home to celebrate Christmas. Christmas would never be the same again.

She was in my arms thirty-six hours later. The doctors determined the umbilical cord was caught around her little foot when she dropped into the birth canal: suffocating her. Stephanie Suzanne was stillborn on Christmas day. Like her life, our world went dark.

Looking back, it's hard to believe such a tragedy would eventually be turned into one of the most pivotal moments of our life. I think grief is like that. Our hearts get turned inside out until there is nowhere to go, but back to the Creator. No one else has the answers. No one else can heal a broken heart. And no one else can take something as senseless as the loss of a child and turn our grief into magic.

It would take us another five years to reach the nine-month mark again, this time with a baby boy. While many of the same feelings of excitement returned, there was a deep sense of caution and concern. When we asked our doctor to induce early he agreed, based upon the tests he had completed and on our history.

With a sense of guarded anticipation we went to the hospital to await his arrival. Happily, our son was born healthy and a weight was lifted from our shoulders. I couldn't help but think about Stephanie as I held our son. Tyler weighed a little more than our girl, was a little shorter and he had lots of hair just like Stephanie did. I would think of Stephanie often over the years as I watched over our son with the watchful eye of an eagle. Many might say he was overly protected. It would be hard to argue!

The truth is that the loss of our precious little girl made his life seem so much more precious. The struggles and the grief we endured returned an even greater love and sense of gratitude! I knew I would be a good Mommy. She made me even better. I knew my husband would make an incredible father. Somehow losing his little tom-girl made him an even more attentive father then he might have been otherwise.

In between the loss of our daughter and the birth of our son a tremendous healing took place and I personally moved from a place of deep anger to a place of peace and gratitude. The love and patience given to us by our wonderful family and well-meaning friends helped us to recover. But more than anything, digging into the teachings of Christ helped us to understand we will see her again. If we look long enough and hard enough, He will help us find the blessing in any event, no matter how tragic.

If there is any sense to be made out of the loss of a child, for me it's this: Loss makes us hold on a little tighter to whatever we are given and grief makes us a little more capable of putting things into their proper perspective. Ultimately, it brings us closer to our Creator.

*Christmas these days?* We talk to our girl, imagine what she would be doing and we wish her a very happy birthday. Then we go back. Back to Jesus and celebrate the birth of a gracious and Almighty Father who tends to his children when they are stricken with life's greatest blows.

# Chapter 21

# THE GIFT OF ENCOURAGEMENT

By Sharon Steffke Caldwell

"Whispering hope, O how welcome Thy voice, making my heart in its sorrow rejoice."
Septimus Winner

"I don't know, Mom," my twenty-nine year old son, Brian, said plaintively as he slowly climbed the stairs and walked into the kitchen, "Some days I feel like I'll never see thirty."

Brian usually hid his pain with an infectious smile and constant joking. Shocked by his uncharacteristic expression of negativity, I replied with all the mother's wisdom and encouragement I could muster, "People don't die from back pain! You'll get through this. It's just going to take some time."

Brian had recently moved back home after his life took a downward spiral due to an accident with a drunk driver. The crash left him with severe back pain and an unending cycle of doctors, chiropractors, therapy, medications and more medications. The months of taking high-dose acetaminophen mixed with muscle relaxants, tranquilizers and other prescribed drugs culminated in unrecognized symptoms that his liver was being destroyed.

Brian had been a superb specimen of physical perfection since the day he was born. When the nurse brought him in to me just hours after his birth, I marveled at his coordination when he folded his tiny fingers together over his chest as if in prayer. *Thank you, God. I'm glad I'm finally here.* Brian was seldom sick as a child. He had always been inordinately strong and muscular. Even injured, his healthy-looking physique disguised his human vulnerability. Little did we know that he teetered on the brink of an impending health crisis that would result in hundreds of days in four major hospitals over seven months.

Brian died on his younger brother's twenty-first birthday—just three weeks before his own thirtieth birthday.

I felt as if my sparkling crystal-vase existence had smashed into a million pieces that would be impossible to make whole again. At first I wasn't sure I even wanted to be put back together.

A couple weeks after Brian's death I visited my youngest son, Sean, in Philadelphia. While he worked in the city, I lay on the sofa in his condo reading the Bible for hours in search of the strength and will to go on living. I'd been totally immersed for months in my tender care of Brian, watching as the hideous degradation of liver disease unexpectedly robbed me of my oldest son's life. Now, with the battle ended, I searched the Bible hoping for answers to put my shattered life back together.

I clung desperately to the beliefs I'd been taught from earliest childhood about the love of God and His precious son, Jesus. Most of all, I held onto the promise of eternal life because of God's own Son's sacrifice. But at times I felt guilty when my normally strong faith wavered, and sobs erupted with volcano-like force. At the time, dear steadfast friends rallied around me. They listened patiently to my heartfelt renderings, questionings, and added their own memories of Brian to fortify my broken spirit. They endured, encouraged, and suffered my brokenness with a fierce determination to resist my attempts to push them away while I was drowning in sorrow.

Then one night, three months after Brain's death, he came to me in a dream. He appeared healthy, happy and fully restored. He said, "Mom! You've got to quit worrying about me! It's so beautiful here! With flowers and colors like you've never seen . . . please, Mom . . ."

The dream brought me some comfort. Still, it was only a dream.

Several weeks later as I loaded the washing machine, I bent down to retrieve a penny from one of the dust bunnies behind the door. I stared at it as I held it in my palm, remembering other pennies I'd found. I wanted to believe each one was a little hello from heaven. As I studied this penny, my faith bottomed. I thought, *That's stupid!" People throw away or drop pennies all the time!* And then I audibly demanded, "If you're really real God, I want . . . I want . . . I want a quarter! And not just out of my change purse!"

Like an errant child pouting to her father, I had blurted out my demand . . . and even put conditions on it! I felt a momentary twinge of remorse for the outburst, but then with emotions spent, I went on with my day and forgot about it.

Later in the afternoon I picked up my six-year-old grandson, Brent Michael, from school. He asked if we could stop at the library. After carefully browsing, he checked out several books and we headed home. Brent Michael sat next to me in the front passenger seat. As he randomly opened to a page in the middle of a book about space, I glanced over to see what he was reading and gasped as I stared at the full-page picture of a quarter! Tears filled my eyes as I remembered my morning edict given so brashly.

Brent Michael asked, "Grandma, what's wrong?"

I answered, "Nothing is wrong, Brent Michael. I'm just happy . . . so happy!"

As soon as we got home I called my husband, Bill, at work to tell him what had happened. I knew he also struggled at times with his faith and I hoped this might provide some comfort to him, too.

The next morning Bill chaired a large meeting at work. After the meeting, as he cleared his notes from the lectern, he glanced at the empty rows of folding chairs. Not believing his eyes, he walked closer. On the middle seat in the front row lay *three* shiny quarters.

It felt like Brian was saying, *"Hi Dad! I'm here with Jesus . . . and it's all good!"*

When Bill called to tell me about this uncanny *coincidence*, I realized God wasn't mad that I brashly demanded proof that He was real. He wasn't offended that I needed a little extra encouragement and a boost in my faith. He lovingly gave both Bill and me just what we needed, when we needed it most.

# Section Three
# WHEN DEATH PARTED US

Photo by Lisa Rodgers

# Chapter 22

# EVEN THOUGH

By Tom Burgess

My wife, Esther, demonstrated her unique grateful perspective as her last Thanksgiving with us approached. I could illustrate it in so many ways, but one incident sticks out in my mind.

After living for two years with no curtains or drapes hanging on our living room and dining room windows, we had some created by a home decor friend. They spent hours designing, sewing and installing the drapes on those bare windows. The rooms were transformed and Esther was so pleased. She called many friends to ask if they would like to come over and see her drapes. When she couldn't sleep, Esther unhooked her feeding tube, went downstairs and stood with her hands clasped in a thankful gesture as she stared at the drapes. When I stumbled downstairs and asked, "What are you doing?" She simply smiled and said, "I am so happy. I am so happy."

Christ shined brightly in Esther. She never voiced a complaint. Not about the cancer continuously attacking her spinal cord. Or life's curveballs, the doctors, nurses, and hospital stays. Esther looked at life squarely and then lived out Ecclesiastes 3:11: "God makes everything beautiful in its time." During Esther's battle with cancer our friends and family gained an appreciation for the phrase *real positive*. Real positive was not Pollyanna to us. It meant being real about her situation, but positive as well; real and positive.

Our real and positive mindset made every day brighter than if we merely sat around asking, "Why Esther?" or "Why couldn't medicines, surgeries, doctors or hospitals have done more?" I was blessed to be able walk with Esther during this time of our lives. Blessed because I just followed her lead.

Esther reminded me her mom used to say "Cast your bread upon the waters and it will come back to you with butter and jam on it!" She was her mother's daughter. I believe all of Esther's doctors and caregivers saw Christ shining through her. They always lit up when they got to see her or help her with something. Once when we went to see Dr. Hansen, the chief plastic surgeon at Oregon Health Sciences University, she was not able see or check Esther's back wound. Instead her capable associate treated Esther. I e-mailed Dr. Hansen the next day to tell her how well Esther was doing.

She immediately responded, "What great news! Thanks for letting me know; I was unsettled I couldn't see you both . . . Esther looks beautiful and happy in the picture you sent. See you soon, Juliana."

All of Esther's caregivers looked forward to seeing her for each visit. She affected them positively. She was a living illustration of "bread coming back with butter and jam on it."

Our daughter was in town to visit us for our last Thanksgiving together. Jean's visit gave Esther an additional boost of energy. Esther pranced as she shopped, cooked and baked. Esther's spirits were really lifted by all the cookies, cakes, pies and all the meals they prepared together. Not to mention it extended my tummy. Oh well, I suffered with a smile when Esther said, "I want to do what I can while I can." Our family and friends enjoyed a great Thanksgiving.

While celebrating our Thanksgiving, I was also preparing to teach a series in a few months at the church where I served as a pastor. It was on the coming of Christ during Advent season. I prepared to speak on "Hope--Worship Fully." I planned to emphasize a couple of key truths: Our appropriate response to life in all circumstances is praise and worship. And in the midst of life's turmoil, what are people hearing from us?

We often use two words to describe our heart's determination when doing something regardless of the circumstances. We say *even though*. "*Even though* this will not be fun, I will do the right thing." "*Even though* this will not be easy, I will smile." "*Even though* this is not what I prayed for, I know good will come from it." In the midst of a terrible time in the life of God's children, Habakkuk triumphantly penned the *even though* principal. "*Even though*," he wrote, "the fig trees have no blossoms, and there are no grapes on the vines; *even though* the olive crop fails, and the fields lie empty and barren; *even though* the flocks die in the fields, and the cattle barns are empty, yet I will rejoice in the Lord! I will be joyful in the Lord of my salvation, the Sovereign is my strength! He makes me as surefooted as a deer, able to tread upon the heights." Habakkuk 3:17-19

In spite of twenty-plus surgeries on Esther's spine and throat, seventy radiation treatments over the span of ten years, and losing her beautiful singing voice, Esther radiantly lived by *the even though principle*. Esther was as surefooted as a deer *even though* she walked through the valley of the shadow of death. She knew the Lord was with her and rejoiced in Him.

Another verse I included in the Advent series was Isaiah 61:3: "and provide for those who grieve in Zion--to bestow on them a crown of beauty instead of ashes, the oil of gladness instead of mourning, and a garment of praise instead of a spirit of despair. They will be called oaks of righteousness, a planting of the Lord for the display of His splendor." The Lord knew the grief I would endure and the timing of the grief. As life brought its *even thoughs*, scripture became more meaningful! God used our family, friends and church to encourage us to display His splendor.

*Would Esther rather have lived longer on earth? Would she miss her daily and her momentous time with us? Would she grieve she couldn't see her grandchildren grow up? Would she have wanted to sing more days?* Oh, yes! She suffered these and many other losses. Yet she rejoiced in the Lord with a twinkle in her eye, *even though* those eyes were at times filled with tears.

Our time here is not eternal and we know it.

A few months after Thanksgiving our sweet Esther, like the Esther of old, put on her royal apparel and gained an audience with the King. Just like the story in the Old Testament, I believe the golden scepter was extended to her by faith. By grace she touched it receiving not only half the kingdom, but the entire kingdom in all its glory. What she longed for became a reality. I know my Esther sings, rejoicing without restraint.

*Even though* I miss her more than words can convey—*even though* my grief is real, I rejoice in the Lord and hold onto His promises. Not with a Pollyanna perspective, but with one that's real and *positively trusts*.

# Chapter 23

# WHEN PLAN A BECOMES PLAN D

By Wendi Fincher

It didn't work out like I planned. You see, as a teacher, it is all about the plans. *Where do you start? And where does it end?*

Stacey and I started our unlikely adventure in 1994 with a chance conversation at his mom's convenience store. We were a nineteen-year-old girl and a twenty-four year old guy.

Our dating years were full of fun, snow skiing trips, lake trips, beach trips, go-kart racing trips, four-wheeler riding trips, weekly poker card nights, suppers, parties and cruising the town on the weekends with friends. Our circle of friends was big and always growing. We loved our time with them!

Christmas of 1996 Stacey blindsided me by popping *the question* when we were encircled by his family. Having just graduated college, I was making plans for a job, buying a new car and now planning for a future with him. Of course I said yes. But I had to have a job and we had to have a house first.

April 10, 1999 the plan was well on its way to working out as perfectly as possible. The house had been bought and we completed the work on it. Both of us had secure jobs. We were uniting in marriage! We were a fairly young busy couple so children weren't part of the plan yet. We wanted to enjoy our time together as newlyweds and we did. Life progressed fairly well and as planned for the most part. There were plenty of hiccups. We could make adjustments to the original plan to get a new plan. Jobs came and went. Refrigerators went on the blink. Money was tight. Suppers were burnt. But somehow we made it through.

A few years into the marriage the idea of children was starting to show up on our radar as a possibility. So we did what every couple does – we got a dog! Bailey was an energetic yellow lab puppy who loved to cuddle, play and even slept in bed with us. Once we were convinced we had done a pretty good job of raising a decent dog, we decided maybe we would try our hand with a real live person. *Logical, right?*

Well, here is where the hiccups started growing into hills and mountains. For years we did nothing to prevent bringing a real, live person into the world. We were constantly being asked, "When are you two going to have children? You know you aren't getting any younger!" And constantly we replied with our *happy mask* on "If it happens, it happens." The happy mask got harder to wear, but eventually the questions lessened.

After not having yearly physicals for several years, I finally decided this *getting pregnant* thing wasn't working. I made the appointment and it was discovered I had endometriosis. As I saw it, it was bad news on the health plan part of my life, but good news on the child-rearing end. Get rid of the endometriosis, have a child, live happily ever after. We would be a normal family and I could let go of the guilt for not being able to conceive.

Endometriosis removal took place and still months later there was no pregnancy. Conveniently for me my gynecologist also provided artificial insemination services. Our hopes for Plan A with conception didn't work so we moved on to Plan B, artificial insemination. What an emotional roller coaster ride for my Type A personality! I was not in control of my body and the guilt continued right through the failure of artificial insemination.

The *happy mask* was coming back out of the closet. I convinced myself it wasn't in God's plan for Stacey and me to be parents. Not a lot of our friends knew of our roller coaster ride. For my sanity, I decided it wasn't a ride I could do again. It was the End of plan B, the end of being a parent and end of going to the gynecologist too.

Again years passed before I began experiencing so much pain with each monthly cycle. I could no longer take it. I knew it meant the endometriosis was back. I knew it meant I had to return to a gynecologist. Based on my family doctor's referral, I switched gynecologists. With hesitation, I met with her in February of 2011. I really didn't want to hear any of what I thought she would say. To my surprise she was a God-fearing woman who had also been in my shoes! I just broke down in her office! Since she had been there she knew what my emotional roller coaster ride had been like. She also knew my frustration with *being broken*. She had been there! She cried with me! This was part of God's plan, not mine. She explained it to me like this: If you were sick would you take medication? Of course my answer was yes and she went on to explain *my stuff* was still possibly *fixable*. WOW! Now twelve years into our marriage we were given hope again. Skeptical though, we stayed cautious. It was best not to get our hopes up too high after the ride we had been on before.

April 2011, Plan C was now beginning with my gynecologist's referral to an in vitro fertilization specialist who had helped her become pregnant. She had also worked with her while in medical school. Plan C took off quickly. We had IVF informational meetings, financial decisions, testing of both of us. All to discover we were good candidates. Yet still cautious, the medications and injections began to arrive in May 2011. For monitoring purposes the trips to the IVF office became more frequent for monitoring purposes. Retrieval day came for my eggs and I had five. Not as many as everyone was hoping for, but by this time I had turned it all over to God. It was in His hands not mine. I knew this would be my final attempt at this parent thing. My biological clock, age, and hardened heart were all working against me.

The night before we went for implementation there were three fertilized embryos. The next morning we only had two. Both were implanted. I was surprisingly calm for my *planning self*. I didn't know the outcome, but knew I had done all I could to the best of my ability. At the time waiting to hear if it worked was the hardest thing I ever had to do. It was a long few days. The call finally came. We were going to be parents! Through my tears and hysteria I called Stacey at work to share the news. I had not been silent about this plan as I had been with artificial insemination. I wanted others to know what we were going through. What we had been through. We had tried. After all the phone calls to family and friends I was now realizing God's plan was better than mine!

July 2011 came and went with Plan C still in check. The *happy face mask* was back in the closet for I now showed a real and genuine happy face. August 2011 came and went. School started back as Plan C was still moving right along. September 2011 rolled in as a special month because it's my birthday. September 3rd we celebrated with family and friends. I was thirty-six and finally pregnant! At thirty-six and *complete* with a good Plan C. Stacey and I were good.

Ten days later, I was broken more than I ever thought possible. My father-in-law called while I was at school saying Stacey had been hurt at work and was on the way to the hospital. They were coming to get me. In my mind it was nothing serious. We would be home by the afternoon and he would be out of work for a few days. It was a hiccup, not a mountain. Or so I thought.

Little did I know the morning "I love you" and kiss would be the last. Stacey died while we were en route to meet him at the hospital. Nor did I know I would be a widow who was fourteen weeks and three days pregnant. We hadn't even learned the gender of our child yet. This wasn't part of my Plan C.

Our dog, Bailey died the next day.

Friends and family held me up with support. All of them, the trip friends, the poker card friends, lake friends, work friends, neighbor friends, new and old friends each played a part in my support. I heard "You are so strong." My reply was always "I'm only as strong as the friends who are supporting me." And it was true.

It is all such a blur. The visitation happened. The funeral happened. The paperwork for such an event happened. Friends stayed with me. Family stayed close by. And they all kept me busy.

My *happy face mask* came back out of the closet. I returned to work and society. The mask hid the resentment and anger steadily building inside. I wasn't supposed to do this parent thing on my own. I wasn't supposed to be a widow at thirty-six. *How was this part of God's plan? Why was this part of God's plan?* Plan D was now a mountain.

Sixteen weeks into my pregnancy my parents, Stacey's parents, my best friend and the entire gynecologist office discovered the baby I was carrying was a boy. He gave us thumbs up in his ultrasound picture. I tried to accept it as a sign everything would be okay.

It took a long time for me to decide Plan D's path would be ok. I had to make a conscious decision not to fall victim to the *widow* title. I had to decide to accept *single mother* as my new role. I was put in this position for a reason. I had to make the best of it. I would learn to live by myself. I would learn which people to call when something needed to be done I couldn't do myself. I would learn that all of the friends spanning sixteen-and-a-half years of our relationship were true friends in every aspect of the word. I would learn to be the best mama I could be by surrounding my son, Ryland, with the best father figure *uncles* I could.

Wouldn't you think by now I could throw this *got-to-have-a-plan* thing out the window? On February 24, 2012, Ryland Stacey Fincher introduced himself to the world via his own plan. I intended to be induced Monday, February 27th because there was a wedding on the weekend I wanted to attend. I didn't want to be induced on Friday. I had planned for Friday the 24th to be my last day at school for the year. It had been a hell of a school year. With the time I had built up I was going to spend the rest of it figuring out this mama thing.

It was a messy Friday. Horrible thunderstorms were rolling through with tornados to boot. About fifteen minutes before my first class of students was to arrive I decided to go to the restroom. It would be the last time before my next break. I experienced every pregnant teacher's worst nightmare: my water was beginning to break. So began the mama journey.

Two-and-a-half years later I still have no clue for any answers to why my journey took the path it did. I'm ok with it. I'm finally past wearing the *happy face mask*. My plan didn't work out. However, His plan continues. Ryland fills my heart with joy and love, and my days with laughter. I see a spitting image of Stacey every time I look at Ryland. Stacey lives on.

Chapter 24

# AVOID THE VOID

By Kyle Koch

The void in my life has become abundantly obvious to me. My wife Juli was the only person who had the capability to honor and validate me. No other living human being's endorsement can fully validate me. I followed the philosophy, "The best thing I can do for my kids is to love their Mother." Now with her gone, none of the kids collectively or individually fill the void created with Juli's passing.

Now my feelings of self-worth, motivation to accomplish, anticipation for excitement and general hustle have all been dealt a mortal blow. My partner and love-focus, the one who was at the center of my small world, has been removed. And she cannot be replaced.

Everyone close to me is doing his or her best to prop me up. My heart has a real hard time placing a bet. I've lost considerable traction. My clutch slips consistently. My emergency brake is defective. I am a big-time carnivore who even has a tough time getting impassioned about a good steak. What am I doing? Why am I doing it? These seem to be the recurring theme and questions I ask myself.

The cold is colder. The heat is hotter. The tired is tired-er. The distances are further. Everything I lift weighs more. The nights are longer and darker. I am getting older faster. I've been living mostly in my rear view mirror. My appreciation for the beautiful has been dulled. I'm not as punctual as I once was. The problem here is I don't really care. I'm finding it easier to daydream without any real expectations. Guess I'll adopt a procrastinator's approach. With that I don't feel much urgency either. So maybe I'll just put it off for a while. And then there's *a a a a a a a*, oh yeah – my attention span seems to be faulty. It's hard for me to focus with any sort of genuine interest on the everyday mundane matters.

Juli gave my life spice, hope, and purpose. She gave me good reason to do a lot of things I don't want to do now. She had some considerable power over me no one else had. A lot of stuff I liked because she did. For instance watching health food shows, QVC® demonstrations and *Gunsmoke®*. Even watering the flowers was to be with her and to win her approval. Any excuse was useful to be near her, even when she was taking her evening nap after work and before a night's sleep in bed. Apparently napping made her tired.

Not another woman in the world would have spent forty-five years with me. Not one. She wanted so many things she never got; a better lifestyle, a more orderly, secure life and more foster kids. Instead, she stayed with me and tried super hard!

I'd be grateful for some complaints delivered from her in person. As her husband I'd be extremely happy to own up to being wrong on everything if it would help get her back. That's what husbands are supposed to do, right?

Oftentimes, she'd shop for gifts to give the kids or grandkids. After they were presented I'd dutifully ask, "What did I get them?" She filled in my blanks. She covered for me. She stuck with me. She sympathized with me and for me. She often felt sorry for me, I think. She never got a restraining order against me. Although she probably had reason enough 'cause I was, and remain, a Juli addict.

She was gracious with such a sweet disposition through her last days. What a trouper! I gained even more respect for her then. I have a few heroes, especially my kids who nursed her toward the end. She is way at the top of my hero's list and I miss her. I really miss her.

# Section Four
# DEATH OF A SIBLING
Photo by Lisa Rodgers

Chapter 25

# TWINLESS TWIN

By Dorothy Wagner

"I seldom ask for miracles, but today one would do.
To have the front door open and see you walking through.
A million times I've missed you, a million times I've cried.
If love alone could save you, you never would have died.
In life I loved you dearly; in death I love you still.
In my heart you hold a place that no one else could ever fill.
It broke my heart to lose you, but you didn't go alone.
Part of me went with you the day God called you home."
Author Unknown

At approximately 9:50 am on June 1, 2008 my identical twin sister Tracy died from complications of leukemia. I was with her as she took her last breath. With my nose pressed to her nose I remember telling her how much I loved her and she could go. Tracy was so brave through a horrendous life altering diagnosis. As she was dying, I saw her climbing a spiral staircase to heaven, looking back and sobbing. I told her to "go home." She climbed to the top of the staircase where Jesus welcomed her. I know what I saw and what I felt. Maybe it was just intense grief. Or maybe it was the Holy Spirit giving me, us, peace.

It all started when Tracy came home from a two week trip to China where she was adopting a sweet three-year-old boy. She was tired before she left for the trip. Working full time, raising a son and preparing for a long trip to China was exhausting. Being weary was expected. I spoke with her twice while she was in China. She didn't complain. When she arrived home, Tracy was experiencing severe pain at the base of her esophagus which prompted her to see the doctor. After running some tests she called me while waiting for medication for possible reflux. She sounded tired, a little uncomfortable, but good. The next day she received the shocking phone call. They needed to run further tests since the preliminary tests looked as if she may have leukemia.

I will never forget the phone call from her that day. She called me many times in proceeding days. This call was different. My twin sister, my best friend called to say she might have leukemia. I will never forget every moment of the call. Soon she had a bone marrow biopsy. I received a hopeful phone call telling me it may not be leukemia. Only forty eight hours later we learned Tracy had Acute Myeloid Leukemia. Tracy felt she was given a death sentence. I did not believe she would die. I was scared, traumatized and so very sad.

Our lives were forever changed with her diagnosis on May 22, 2008. I remember it was a Thursday afternoon at a little before 4:00 pm. She answered the phone listening intently and quietly. Her son wanted her attention so I distracted him while reading the note Tracy was writing, "Acute Leukemia." I can still feel the warm flush running through my chest with what I read. Tracy was in shock. She cried so hard and said, "Dorothy, I have just been given a death sentence." We had an hour to get to Saint Agnes where a room was being prepared for her. She cried, called her husband, I called my husband and our Mother, and she called friends. It was surreal.

Tracy didn't respond well to the Benadryl® given through the IV. She was also given a blood transfusion. Someone was in her room every fifteen minutes to check on her. We were awake most of the night talking. I told her it reminded me of when we shared a hospital room at the age of five years old as we both had our tonsils removed. I told Tracy I wished I had leukemia too. Or I could just take it from her. She said, "That would be horrible." It was a long night. A night I will never forget. There is NO WHERE in the world I would have rather been.

I was with Tracy at the hospital for the first six days. On the seventh day I flew home for three days. Tracy wanted me to celebrate my son's fourth birthday with him. I had been away from my family for a week. However when I came home I really wasn't home. I was with Tracy.

Tracy was feeling pretty good while I was there. The first night I was away she became very sick. Two days later Tracy was in the ICU with a one hundred and two degree fever. She had developed an infection – the greatest fear for any leukemia patient. On May 30th I talked to her for the last time. She was in the ICU feeling very groggy. We told each other we loved each other. I flew to be at her side on May 31st. On the airplane the steward gave me a sixty-four ounce water bottle and a full size box of tissues. I was a mess.

She had declined greatly by the time I arrived. Her organs were slowly shutting down and she was in a drug-induced coma. We spent seventeen hours in the hospital by her side as she fought for her life. I know she felt our presence even as she was not conscious. The unforgettable moment when the doctor and a nurse told us there was nothing else they could do. The news was followed shortly by her death.

I still have "Aha Tracy moments" every day when something I read or hear connects directly to what Tracy would have told me. I know Tracy is living in me. She is part of me. Tracy would want it that way. She was the most selfless person I have ever known. Every minute of every day her life still teaches me through her courage and love.

There are little things making me feel connected to my twin sister. Tracy only bought Bounty® napkins and paper towels. Even today I do the very same thing. It is a constant reminder of being in Tracy's kitchen where countless hours were spent talking as we fed our boys. The hydrangeas in my backyard remind me of when Tracy cared for me during a 2005 hospital stay. Even my own mannerisms remind me of Tracy. For instance; certain expressions, when I laugh, when I cry, when I look at my feet. We were twins after all. We talked often of savoring and cherishing our time with our children. Time was going way too fast.

Just breathing is a reminder of Tracy. Until June 1, 2008 I had never taken a breath on this earth without her. I discovered even breathing isn't as easy without Tracy. Grieving is a daily choice of emotions - you don't necessarily choose. I miss TRACY and I will talk about her every day. Not because I am worried I will forget her. I choose to because it just makes me breathe easier.

My phone rang off the hook for months after Tracy died. No more. The cards and flowers stopped. For most it was "over six years ago" when Tracy died. For me it was only yesterday. I see Tracy in the mirror, I hear her voice coming from me and I feel her presence in my own being.

I've often wondered how to stop expecting so much from those not experiencing the loss of an identical twin. There are people who want me to have already gotten past my grief. They want me to be normal again. I can't imagine "needing" another friend like I needed Tracy. Without her I truly feel like I don't belong. I remind myself not only do I have a husband who listens, counsels, loves, and holds me whenever I need it. I also have a mother who loves me unconditionally. I have two boys who need and love me "almost up to God." And I have GOD! People will disappoint you. That is life. God is waiting with open arms when I cry so hard I feel it will never stop. He carried me this far.

I never once ever considered, and I mean never ever considered, life here on this earth without my twin sister. We were born together and I expected we would die together. In the normal life expectancy you know you will most likely outlive your parents. Your children will outlive you. I expected, as twins, Tracy and I would die on the same day just as we were born together.

I find peace in knowing in the curve balls of life God carries me through the crazy innings I never expect to play alone. I will always feel different, incomplete and half of a whole. But the good news is I will be with Tracy again. We will share a room, talk and talk until it is so late we can't keep our eyes open, share every thought and every dream. We will be together in Heaven.

# Chapter 26

# GRIEF--THE ULTIMATE TEACHER

By Joyce Bone

Grief teaches us from a school we would all love to avoid. Avoidance is impossible. No one goes through life unscathed. It's only a matter of how, when and to what degree we will tangle with grief. Somehow our undesired education comes as a shock when it commences.

Grief forced me to grow. Once I was happy-go-lucky. Grief threw me into a detrimental response filled with anger, resentment, despondency and depression. I was altogether disgusted by life. Questions like, *"What's the point?"* sabotaged my contented daily life. It didn't turn out as I expected. People I love just up and died. It took me some time to pass through the grief stages. Ultimately I did. It was the darkest time of my life.

My brother died of cancer at the age of forty-one. I was holding him in my arms. One moment he was breathing and the next it was the quietest moment ever. No sound came from him. As I sat next to Joe I looked around the room. I stared at the ceiling looking for a sign from him. There wasn't one. It seemed one moment Joe was with me and the next moment he was gone forever. At least this is how it felt at the time. I have come to learn he is actually closer now--only a whisper of gratitude away for our relationship.

This was the beginning of the darkest period of my life. I was catapulted into the descent into darkness when I told my parents their worst fear had come true. Their beloved son died. I sat on the bed delaying the inevitable. As one of six siblings, I wondered why I was the one who had to do this. We were taking turns staying with my brother to let my parents take showers, do laundry, etc. *Why did he die with me? Why did I have to be the one to destroy my parents with this terrible news?* And destroy I did.

The most sorrowful moment of my life was watching their reaction as they rushed to his side. It breaks my heart every time I remember.

I've decided helping others through their dark night makes it worth feeling my heart squeeze tight from the painful memory. I can now release the pain after learning to accept death as necessary for truly living.

I have come to believe everything happens as it is supposed to. We come with free will. Yet we consider the possibility there may be a theme for our lifetimes. Perhaps a path with specific key points to experience as we grow. How we respond is our free will. Our perceptions and reactions are our own. The twists and turns of life force us to look at ourselves deciding whom we are rather than who we "should" be. Or who we were programmed to be instead of who we are at our essence.

Upon reflection, I think my brother died with me instead of another family member because he knew I was strong enough to handle it. I communicate for a living. I speak. I write. I persuade. It is what I was born to do. Now he continues to live in my heart through the opportunities to write about him. He is in the lessons I've learned and the questions I ponder because of my grief. I wonder if my brother knew something about life I didn't. For example, I remember my mother lamenting about the cancer. He was very sick when he whispered, "Mom, don't worry, this is how it is supposed to be."

As if his death wasn't bad enough, my dad died unexpectedly on Thanksgiving morning two years later. I had finished running my first half marathon with my son. We were getting ready for a big family dinner with my dad. You can imagine my shock when I heard the news on the phone. When it rang I thought I was going to be asked to bring an extra bottle of wine or loaf of bread with me. Instead it was, "Are you sitting down?" I was devastated. I loved my dad so much. I couldn't breathe. I was once again thrown into a complete loop of despair.

It is simple what I learned from these terrible events. Life is too short to be fearful. We must be brave and live out loud. Accomplish whatever is in our hearts to do regardless how scary or impossible it seems. We must grab life by the horns expressing ourselves while we have the opportunity. We need one another's brilliance to shine! I live with as much zest as possible to honor both my brother's shortened life and my father's dedication to family. He sacrificed for us. I thrive to honor him. He made the best of the tough times he experienced. I want to say when our souls meet up again, "See, your hard work had a purpose. Thank you." My goal is to leave a legacy of good works to honor his sacrifice.

I knew I had to let go of the despair, the resentment, and the anger. It was literally killing me. I had to stop masking my emotions. I was on a reckless path ignoring all I formerly held dear. I realized I couldn't continue on this path. Instead I went the opposite route. I began to eat healthy, sleep more, exercise, and I gave up drinking. The joy seeped back in when my mind cleared.

I learned I don't have to lose it, no matter what is thrown at me in the future. I can use it! The key for me was to stop resisting everything. I fought and fought with my reality. I finally gave up, admitted defeat, and cried out, "God I can't handle this anymore. Please send me a friend and help me to heal." He did. This can happen for you too. The first step is to quit resisting what happened. Stop pointing fingers and begin the inner work of rehabilitating yourself. You are where you are. Accept it. Then ask to follow God's will for your life. Give up your ideas of how it should be and accept there is a higher order to things.

Thank God at night you made it through another day. Gratitude matters. These are the tactical actions helping me survive the dark times. I am not naïve enough to think I won't be tested again. Next time I will know there really is a reason for my pain. I felt so very alone, so very sad. I feel for where you are right now. I would give you a hug if I could. Heal yourself, and then go prosper. It is what your loved one would want for you. Honor him or her by healing and shining your light to the world.

# Section Five
# GOODBYE TO THE GREATEST GENERATION
Photo by Lisa Rodgers

# Chapter 27

# BRIMMING WITH LOVE

By Kayla Fioravanti

In my first moments alone the day after my grandmother took her last breath, my clearest memory of her flooded my mind. The image I had was of her outstretched arms reaching to hold my face in her hands. Her face was wide open as if she could engulf me in her smile. A kiss sat ready on her lips as she pulled me towards her and kissed my face. Her greeting was never complete until she had held me just inches from her round full face and absorbed my round full face into her smiling eyes.

In all my visits with my grandmother I watched as a twinkle travelled from her heart to her transparent eyes at the mere sight of those she loved. My grandmother's voice always said, "Come in, come in" each time we went to visit her. Her open arms said, "You are welcome here." Her expressive hands would reach out almost as if in a reflective memory of holding our faces in her hands.

When my parents last visited her after her dementia set in, they brought pictures of me and my family. Each time my parents showed her a picture of my youngest daughter she chimed, "Oh, Kayla!" Even when they showed her pictures of me with my children, she still pointed to my youngest child and declared with renewed delight, "Oh, Kayla!" She no longer remembered me as an adult, but she remembered the child she loved. She saw me in the face of my own little one.

I wasn't there, but I can imagine the scene. I can picture her face brimming with the love that only a grandmother knows. If my daughter would have been there, grandma's hands would have reached for her face just as she did mine years ago. Her kisses would land on her face to say, "You are loved." Her smile would say, "You are special." The twinkle in her eyes would say, "You delight me." Her round open face would say, "You belong to me, we are family."

I will always treasure the image of my grandmother in her housedress welcoming me into her home from her front porch. I can only hope I inherited the same twinkle in my eyes to travel from my heart to my eyes when I see my loved ones.

I hope my smile will always say, "You are special."

# Chapter 28

# GRANDMOTHER

By Mary Humphrey

I had been called to your bedside several times, which ended up being several short hospital stays that were washed from memory when you regained your snappy vigor. Your laughter, voice and words, are etched in the depths of my mind. Each time you returned to your extended stay room to rehabilitate you happily chatted about your puppy, your priest Father Paul, and your husband. You lovingly expressed a longing for my grandfather, your faithful late husband whom you missed with an ache I could only imagine through your tears and words. You left a standard for me to follow with the example set forth through the prior years, as a steadfast wife who respected and adored her husband.

I had a beautiful visit with you just days before I received the final call. You talked about me, the granddaughter named after you. You told me you loved me without realizing I was the one sitting beside you. I received a blessing that day, the gift of hearing how you really felt about me, directly from your soul. When you placed a soft goodbye kiss on my cheek you told me that I was a sweet lady. You asked me to come back. I assured you I would.

Then the call came. I knew it was the last time I would be by your side.

I thought the ground would let loose of my feet as I walked through the sliding glass doors of the hospital and saw Father Paul waiting for my arrival. He was legally blind. He could not see me, but he knew me. I did not know him, yet somehow I knew who he was. The moment I came within hearing range he spoke to me. Without knowing who he was there for, I sensed it was for me. As a blind man, he took my hand and led me through the doors and down the twisted hallways. It felt as though God was holding my hand, and was whispering in my ear, "Be prepared. I am with you."

You often spoke lovingly of Father Paul. In fact he told me you asked him to come and pray just a few days before falling ill. In your life God came first. Love extended outwards through your beautiful faith. That afternoon, after Father Paul left me alone with you, we prayed. You could not speak, however you heard and prayed in the Spirit. What a glorious spiritual ability and gift God gives us when we accept his son Christ as our savior!

I held your hand, your breathing slowed. I turned down the lights. The time was nearing. I whispered in your ear, "Jesus is waiting for you." You had somewhere to go; a place with no pain. Where you could feel the same amount of joy you felt while working in your garden, sewing your aprons and quilts, playing with your puppy, singing praise to God, and as you wrapped your arms around the man you so very much adored. In your last hour, you had joy to spread. You gave it to me.

I felt your tiny hand in mine. So warm, so soft, so delicate with age. You gave birth to my father. I was a part of God's plan. You made it all possible. I am honored! Your breathing continued to slow, as did the beat of your tired heart. I watched and listened as peace enveloped me. One beat . . . two beats . . . one beat . . . silence. You left. I held your frail hand as Heaven received you, a beautiful vivacious woman who loved the Lord.

Now I open your jars of buttons, snaps, and pins. I allow my mind to imagine it contains the same air you also breathed. I look at the brightly colored aprons and remember the grandmother who wore them in her younger years fixing breakfast several hours before daybreak for my grandfather. He had to deliver the milk, of course!

Beyond the fond memories, you instilled in me the most important gift of all. I have a love for the Lord, our Father God. He is the one Father who heals. He is the Master Designer. I adore Him. I trust Him with faith that sustains my life. He has given me work to do and I am ready.

Our Father, the Lord who heals, has given me the ability to find joy in all sorrows. Through sadness and longing I learn to gain wisdom while carrying the torch for Him and all good. I light the torch for others who may be on a darker path. It is love that spreads from life to life, from soul to soul, from spirit to spirit.

In our darkest hour we cry out to Him, "Why me Lord? I can no longer do this!" God hears our wailing and speaks to us in a comforting steadfast voice He says, "Yes, you can continue on because I am here. Give your pain and fear to me. I will take it from you. Now, carry on with the torch. Share the light I have given you."

# Chapter 29

# HONORING GRANDPA AND SITTING SHIVA

By Loral Robben

I heard a message at a women's retreat about the Jewish tradition of Shiva where family and friends of the grieving sit saying nothing. Listening to the speaker, I was intrigued by a sense I was learning something important. I didn't expect the opportunity to engage in this practice would present itself so soon.

After the retreat, my roommate and I enjoyed a gorgeous fall drive through the back roads to my home in Franklin, Tennessee. I then took a peaceful nap to catch up on sleep from the fun-filled and somewhat sleep-deprived weekend. I was grateful to have enjoyed such a beautiful day when my mother called informing me my ninety-year-old Grandpa has passed away at 5:45 p.m.

The next day began my journey to Grandpa's funeral and ultimately sitting Shiva with Grandma. First I flew to Kansas City to be with immediate family, and began my part of the funeral preparations. I wrote reflections to read at the service about my Grandpa and his faith. I made a video with family pictures set to his favorite song, *Happy Trails*. I gathered the supplies to assemble a picture board complete with cowboy and farmer decals. My dad, sister and I then drove seven hours to Meade, Kansas where my Grandparents lived their entire lives. My mother had arrived the day before to be with my Grandma. She had been my Grandpa's step-daughter since the age of thirteen.

After we arrived at the funeral home for the visitation my mom, dad, sister, and I began sitting Shiva with Grandma. We sat in front of the casket where my Grandpa lay decked out in a snazzy suit. To honor his military service in both the European and Asian theaters of World War II a perfectly folded triangulated American flag was placed next to his head. We were comforted as we hugged and conversed with other family members who visited throughout the day and evening. Tearful moments were experienced at the casket, individually and as a family. I led a time of family prayer. We were also deeply touched by the people from the community where he had been a member his entire life as they stopped by to pay their respects.

As I sat in the funeral home with Grandma, I recalled some of my best life moments with family. At holidays and after family dinners my mom, sister, Grandma, Grandpa, and I sat around for hours. We would enjoy the comfort of each other's presence with intermittent talking. Occasionally Grandpa would join my brother and dad who were usually watching a game of some sort in the other room. He wasn't gone very long as he was always happiest being with his bride.

The funeral took place the day after the visitation. I was the only family member who spoke. While I am the writer in the family my experience with public speaking, especially in emotional situations, had been limited. I was determined to honor Grandpa with my tribute. I prayed God would give me the strength to speak clearly and loudly. Later many people thanked me for sharing by saying my words really encapsulated Grandpa's life and faith. I felt like the fear of sharing or publicizing my words was broken that day.

Grandpa was buried with full military honors. It was a bright mild day for November. On the drive out of the cemetery we paused to take pictures of the flagpole with my Grandpa's name on it. We had a nice lunch at the church's fellowship hall and where able to look at Grandpa's confirmation picture as a teen. I wondered what he was thinking about when the picture was snapped. I can't wait to be reunited with him in Heaven to ask him and to hear him singing or joking like he did in his younger years.

After the luncheon when friends and some family had left a few of us sat around in the nursing home with my Grandma. The only stirring happened when my sister and I began a little sibling rivalry over who would sit in Grandpa's electric recliner. Every time either of us went to the bathroom or to get some water the seat was relinquished to the other.

In Jewish custom the family sits Shiva with the grieving for a period of seven days. Coincidentally I stayed with my Grandma in Meade, Kansas for a period of seven days even though I wasn't aware of that detail at the time. Five of those days and nights I stayed in the nursing home with her. I slept in the bed where my Grandpa spent many nights when he wasn't at the hospital in his final months.

I let my mom and sister stay with Grandma the first two nights because I was honestly scared to be there. Frightened to face the reality one day we could all end up in the seemingly unfriendly confines of a nursing home if we are blessed to have a long life. I feared seeing the people living there might depress me.

I think I was also grieving the difficulty of aging, and how this lonely fate could one day be mine, especially since I don't yet have a husband or a family of my own. However, I discovered I liked being there when I stayed at the nursing home with Grandma. I helped my crippled, blind Grandma eat, go to the bathroom and get dressed. But most of the time I just sat with her. For an hour or so each day I played an audio book--a classic title called *The Little Princess*. It was fun to see her listen intently to the beloved tale. I also enjoyed seeing her laugh at the amusing parts and seeing her engaged in a world outside of her own. A woman who couldn't remember her last meal and was fearful about the rest of her days alone was transported to the enchanted life of a girl growing up in an English boarding school.

The story helped her recall the memories of her own life. She asked if I would type these memories so they could be read to her. She didn't want to forget her life. I gladly put my journalistic skills to use. What a treasure trove of information for our family! When details didn't make sense a brief discussion with my mother and uncle helped piece the events of Grandma's life together.

I learned taking time to be silent and remember is what sitting Shiva is all about. It helps the grieving and those in their company to take stock of the events in life recalling the blessings of everyday occurrences. When we remember what we have gone through in the past, it helps reassure us we can survive what we are going through now. For believers in Christ it can be a time when we sense His presence and His hand in our lives. Slowing down can clear our thoughts and create meaning.

Sitting Shiva helped me realize just how fleeting life is. Life isn't about hurrying from one experience to the next. It's about connecting the dots to see the beautiful tapestry being woven between our lives and those who have influenced us. It's about beholding the masterpiece of our life, embracing our stories and reengaging in our purpose. *What will my color and shape in the tapestry be? How will I influence someone else's journey?* These questions began to burn in my mind as I was sitting Shiva. This time of reflection helped me to intentionally live out my purpose and to be more mindful of my own limited time on this earth.

In a way sitting Shiva also prepared me for eternity. Although I won't be grieving as I bask in the light of God's presence someday I will have unlimited time to really *be with* everyone. How sweet it will be to have more than an hour or two to catch up with an old friend over coffee. What a gift it will be to take all the time I want to swap stories with people from other eras to learn what their lives were like.

Even though I know my Grandma wishes she still had her husband by her side she is grateful for her fifty-two years with him. Grandma's health has gone downhill in the months since Grandpa's death. I am forever grateful for the time sitting Shiva with her. I am grateful for the chance to honor my Grandpa both by sharing sentiments and memories at his service and by being with his beloved wife during some of her darkest days. I am also grateful God taught me through sitting Shiva to take stock of my life, to cherish moments, to live for His purposes and to look forward to the life to come.

# Chapter 30

# GRIEF WITHIN GRIEF

By Chuck Hagele

Looking back I think I did everything I could that night twenty years ago. Even so there are times I'm not sure I did. My memories are like worn and faded pictures. The images are always the same, but I'm affected in different ways each time I look back. My confidence in whether I truly helped my grandma twenty years ago waivers.

At the time my grandma was battling bone cancer. I really wanted her to get to know my fiancée Kelly. During a long weekend visit, Kelly and I had picked up my grandma to spend the evening with her at another relative's home. After an enjoyable evening the three of us began the winding hour long drive back to my grandma's house. We were half way there when our conversation suddenly stopped. Headlights glared directly in front of us. I slammed on the brakes and pulled our car as far off the road as I could without hitting the cliff on my right. I never saw the other car, only the headlights that kept coming toward us. Even though we made it to the shoulder the other car hit us head on.

It is at this point I remember feeling my first wave of dread and fear. Kelly was gasping for air. I had this sense things were terribly wrong with my grandma. I tried to open my car door but couldn't. It wouldn't open. I jiggled the lock and tried again. I realized the door was jammed. Somehow, I kicked out my door glass and crawled out. I opened the back door to check on my grandma only to find she had passed out.

From this point on my memory is blurry. Grandma was in and out of consciousness. I tried to talk to her and offer comfort. Paramedics arrived and took over. I argued with them about my treatment. Although I was in pain, my concern was for my grandma and not my own injuries.

First Responders were focusing a lot of attention on the other car. I don't have any memories of the people who were in it.

At some point we went to the hospital and waited. Kelly and I were treated for minor injuries. The relatives we had dinner with just hours before the accident joined us at the hospital. We all waited together. Eventually we were brought into my grandma's room to say goodbye. We were informed she was dying and the doctors and nurses were making her as comfortable as they could.

Memories of what followed play like a broken record in my mind. Most times I get stuck on two memories. First, grandma kept complaining about how thirsty she was. I think this was the first time I'd ever heard her complain about anything. She was an eternal optimist who could ride a bus for three thousand miles with a smile on her face and wave goodbye to her new friends as she got off the bus. Yet, when I was trying to give her peace she was complaining.

The second and harder memory was that she snapped at me when I was holding her hand. So I let go of her hand. Shortly after, she died.

Even though I hadn't slept much, I felt like I needed to keep my commitment to preach at grandma's church the next morning. I was in a fog. My chest and shins were terribly bruised making it hard to move. I wore the same clothes I had worn throughout the previous night. Even though I didn't have my Bible I shared the very sermon I had planned before the accident.

I preached from John 19:28 about some of the last words Jesus spoke from the cross, "Later, knowing that everything had now been finished, and so that Scripture would be fulfilled, Jesus said, 'I am thirsty.'" I remember reading the verse aloud and saying that I had never really understood Jesus asking for a drink until now. That morning, as I read Jesus' words I heard grandma's same plea for a drink. It relieved some of the sting from my grandma's uncharacteristic complaints just hours before. I realized even Jesus, when He was physically dying, had longed for a drink. If thirst was on His mind, I accepted it could also be on my grandma's.

Family arrived over the next days from all over the country. They loved on Kelly and me in an urgent way. My grandma's family inherited her optimism. Even though we lost her suddenly, we were all relieved she wouldn't suffer from the bone cancer that had been devouring her spine. Everyone was careful to make sure I didn't feel responsible for her death. At times, I almost felt like they were over-compensating and maybe I should be feeling some guilt about not being able to evade the oncoming car. But I didn't.

The funeral and burial were a celebration of her life. It was the last time I remember singing a solo. I sang *Home Free* by Wayne Watson. The days after her funeral were full of stories, laughter, and memories shared. I took two pictures and a small figurine of a polar bear home with me to remember my grandparents. Back home Kelly and I did our best to get back into reality and continue living. We were especially surprised by our fear of driving at night, and I experienced night terrors.

Even twenty years later I don't know why I wake up terrified at times. Each nightmare has something to do with lights coming toward me. Recently, I thought about her irritation at my touch when I was trying to comfort her. I just wanted her to know I was sorry, I was a good grandson, she could trust me, and I loved her. She seemed to reject my efforts. I hate that she was irritated with me when she died. This is a personal wound I haven't revealed until now.

I've learned there is usually grief within grief. There is the obvious grief that is comforted by family, funerals, and time. Then there is the other grief, the deeper unseen grief that comes from regrets and doubt. My mind was quick to accept the blessing of her quick passing without suffering. My heart hasn't accepted my inability to bring her comfort in those last moments. I replay ways I could have communicated better or served her better. The replay always gets stuck when I remember her irritation.

In my current job, serving troubled teens at the Project Patch Youth Ranch, I've met many teens who also have a grief within the grief. One in particular was a fifteen-year-old boy who arrived with a page full of behavior problems in his file. After a long time of working through the program and developing trust, he shared a vivid memory with me. He was in the first or second grade when his dad told him his mom had died. What was torturing him years later was that he had laughed when his dad told him the news. He regretted not reacting like he thought a typical kid who loved his mom would respond.

Over time I watched the young man release his grief within the grief. He learned, as a little guy he wasn't prepared to process and react to such devastating news. He forgave himself and re-processed the loss of his mom with the emotions, maturity and understanding of a young man. I remember watching him hang a plaque on a tree, wiping tears from his eyes, and his dad giving him a huge hug as they remembered a special woman together.

I was so proud of him. Now as I write this, I wonder whether it's time I follow the young man's lead. I need to forgive myself for not being able to comfort my grandma twenty years ago and for being human in my response. I need to accept I had responded the best I could and in the middle of it all I did give her my love and total selfless attention. Maybe it's time I stop grieving my perceived inadequacy and begin properly grieving the loss of an amazing, optimistic woman who lived and enjoyed more life than I could imagine.

# Chapter 31

# LET GO AND LET GOD

By K.A. Croasmun

When I was seventeen I thought the saying, "Let go and let God" was ridiculous. How could I let go of the fact the woman I loved more than life was gone? How could I let go of the pain? I was shrouded in misery, making it hard to breathe.

My grandmother had been my life. She'd raised me from the time I was three years old until the age of eleven. When she moved away I was forced to live with my stranger of a mother. Grandma promised me I could come live with her when I was eighteen. I counted down the days until I could be with her again. Her stern but gentle ways were a comfort to me. I felt safe with my grandmother, safe and loved.

On the other hand, life with my mother was chaos. She brought a man into her life who was a drunk and loved to beat her. When she was at work he loved to put his hands all over me. When I finally told my mother what her boyfriend had done to me, she beat me and called me names. The one name I felt stung the most? Liar.

Mom threatened to send me to live with my dad if I didn't apologize to her boyfriend. I realized if I were sent to my dad's I would probably never see my grandmother again. I made the ultimate sacrifice. I apologized to Mom's boyfriend for hurting me. It was worth it to keep my grandmother in my life. I kept ticking away the days in my head until I would be able to live with her. I prayed to God for strength to make it through. Then I got the news she died. My world was rocked.

My grandmother had been my sanctuary, my love, and my escape plan. Now all of it was gone. I was beside myself. Much to everyone's shock I skipped the funeral.

"Are you *sure*?" My mother asked. She knew how special my grandmother was to me.

"I've never been more sure in my life." I said. "I can't see her like that." I didn't want my last memory of her to be a cold lifeless form in a casket. Some people need it for closure. I didn't need nor did I want it. My mother told me I would regret the decision. To this day, I haven't.

However, what I did regret was the way I acted after my grandmother's death. It seems after living my life for someone else, I was lost. I fell into a deep depression, began smoking, was thrown out of school and even cut myself. I ran away from home twice. The second time was for good. By then I was eighteen and free to do what I wanted. I ended up in the same situation my mother had been in. I was living with an alcoholic who was physically abusive to me. During the time he was at work I would quietly ask God once again for guidance. I couldn't stop mourning the life I should have had with my Grandma and mourning her loss. It was like my life became a spectator sport. I was sitting back watching life go on around me. I wanted to be the game changer. I didn't know how.

I saw a sign outside of a church once saying "Let Go and Let God." Before, I would have rolled my eyes at the sign and laughed. But this day, this particular day, something clicked. I had to let go of all the pain and guilt I had been feeling and trust God would help me somehow. My grief put me into a very bad place. I had to trust God was going to extend his hand and help me out of the dark place. I had to have faith.

I remembered how I loved to make my grandmother proud of me. It was such a simple thing. It helped me feel loved. Couldn't I still make her proud of me now? Heaven knows I hadn't been doing such a great job of it lately. If I tried really hard perhaps she could still be proud of me. The thought of her smiling down on me from Heaven was comforting.

I started small. I got my GED in hopes eventually I would go to college. Grandma was big on education and college was an absolute necessity in her eyes. Next I left the alcoholic boyfriend and found my own place. A few years later I graduated with my Associate's Degree in laboratory science. After writing a poem to the Queen of England, I received a thank you letter from her lady-in-waiting. I wrote poetry for three United States presidents. Each new victory was a stepping stone on a path to peace. I knew Grandma would be proud of me. Though I still missed her terribly I knew I was on the path she wanted for me on all along. The path to peace was a long one. I learned when you are willing to make the journey the jagged rocks of despair don't cut you as deeply.

Grief changed me. It forced me to look inward and become more self-aware. As my grief evolved, I think I did too. I was able to look within myself and know my grandmother would want to see me happy. I wasn't doing myself or her memory any good by shutting out the world. I needed to get back out there and live once more. With God's help I was able to do it. I let go of my pain and let God pull me up from the depths of despair to a place bright with possibility.

It can happen for you too. If you let go and let God.

# Section Six
# SAYING GOODBYE TO EXTENDED FAMILY
Photo by Lisa Rodgers

# Chapter 32

# HISTORY'S KIDNAPPER

By Kayla Fioravanti

Something was different. I could sense it even in the air I breathed. For whatever reason my Uncle Tom was on my mind this particular morning. He had been dying for some time and we knew the end was imminent. When my phone rang with my parents' phone number flashing on the screen, I knew what was different . . . Uncle Tom was gone.

Because of my dad's career our family lived all over the world. Wherever we lived, Uncle Tom always came bearing gifts, stories, games, and laughter when he visited. Each one of our homes, as a child or a young adult, holds memories of my Uncle Tom I cherish to this day.

I vividly remember the first sign of Alzheimer's I encountered.

Wanting to have a chat, I called him from my kitchen phone, "Hi Uncle Tom! It's Kayla."

"Kayla who?" he responded.

My heart skipped a beat. I prayed it was just age temporarily stealing a moment of his memory. At first he tried faking it by pretending he didn't hear my name. It was clear he couldn't pull me up in his memory. As many miles away as he was physically, I was even further away in his memory. Years of visits, phone calls, and letters already started to slip out of his history.

Two years later, and before his official Alzheimer's diagnosis, our family spent Christmas with Uncle Tom. It was clear the disease had already kidnapped him. He was different man. Quiet. Reserved. Withdrawn. All the qualities would betray my outgoing, vibrant, and generous Uncle Tom. The laughter booming from his voice and the personality sparked by his smiling eyes had been stashed away.

My Uncle Tom's Irish heritage ran thick in his blood with the gift of gab, as if he was born and raised in Ireland. His eyes glowed when he recalled the stories from his past where every day sounded like the most glorious adventure. He could make the mundane seem like a major motion picture. I grieved when he could no longer remember the characters of his lifetime. It is my theory he lived his life so fully he simply used up all of the words needed to retell his adventures. His allotted vocabulary was spent early. Like running out of storage space before his story ended

Always ready to come to the rescue, kindness oozed out of Uncle Tom. He loved the most unlovable stray cats. He served through the generosity pouring from his spirit. During some difficult years for me, when money often ran out before the end of the month, he always knew exactly when to deliver help. He never asked, he never offered. He simply sent checks miraculously arriving in my mailbox just as my bank account reached zero. Generosity was never a chore for him.

Needing to say goodbye, I went to see him the summer before he passed. In his place I found the man who stole my Uncle Tom's future. For a moment, his eye's connected with mine and . . . they smiled. I let him know forever stored in my memory's treasure vault were the exploits with his siblings, the McFenney brothers, the adventures of his Navy life and our lifetime together. It was a long decade when Uncle Tom stopped faking he knew who I was. His stories dried up as one by one he forgot everything. He became a remnant of himself. Alzheimer's finally stole the last memory left. The very essences of how to live, breathe, eat, and drink. Now, I have to be the keeper of the stories for the greatest storyteller I ever knew.

Alzheimer's isn't a robber stealing life overnight. It's a kidnapper taking a victim hostage. It steals the victim's identity and diminishes history at an agonizingly slow pace, tiny bits at a time. It is a very cruel and heartless captor. There was no ransom we could pay to set Uncle Tom free. No. This hostage taker offers only goodbyes until finally; the captor sets his victim free. In the end Alzheimer's gave us the opportunity to mourn Uncle Tom's final breath.

Always walking a just few paces in advance of us, showing the excitement of the next step of his walking tour, we couldn't help being propelled forward in his journey of life. Uncle Toms' stories where the link between the past, the present and the future we will all share someday when we reach heaven's gate--where history's kidnapper ceases to be the captor for eternity.

# Chapter 33

# THE EBB AND FLOW OF GRIEF

By Shila Laing

It's been over twenty years now. You'd think my memory of you would be nothing more than a whisper in the wind blowing away. Instead there are torrents of tears pouring down like rain. I'm so grateful for your love, patience, and care. I still remember you telling me you would always be there as much as possible. I wish you were still here so you could see me now. I keep hoping you'd be proud of who I am and who I became. You helped shape me from the very start.

You were my great uncle. You held my hand as a frightened girl who was exposed to all kinds of violence. As a young girl I would run away. I would cry at the drop of a hat because I was scared. I didn't understand. I did not know my world was not *normal*. I could not verbalize much. Nothing stopped you from loving and believing in me.

You and Aunt Mimi would visit us at our home in Maryland. Or we would visit you sometimes four times a year at Ohio State where you taught economics. As a little girl I remember sitting in your lap as you read to me from Agatha Christie, Shakespeare, Robert Frost, or the latest economic magazine report. You asked me questions about subjects completely over my head. When I didn't understand you took the time to explain it to me. You assured me one day I would get the hang of reading.

Over a fourteen year span of time, each and every time we got together you taught me all kinds of things I now finally appreciate. You taught me the joy of listening and discussing music, books and art. Along with it came an appreciation for the richness of reading, writing stories, poems, and plays.

I wrote my first poem when I was thirteen years old. You and Aunt Mimi were among the few people I shared it with. I felt safe with you. As I grew in my writing you sent me letters of encouragement to keep going and never look back. You taught me to keep moving forward in my journey as a writer no matter what turbulence came my way. The key was to put one foot in front of the other and push ahead. As time allowed I kept writing for the next ten years. You continued to love me simply for being me. Not for what I could give you, do or how I performed something.

When I was seventeen years old you passed away. Your death sent my world crashing down. It swept my heart away into a sea of grief. I felt like I was drowning and lost for a few years. I kept in touch with Aunt Mimi for a while. She was worse off than I was. Each time I saw her face it looked like she had just spilled fresh tears. Her eyes were frequently red and swollen, and her voice cracked. She was totally lost without you. Our phone conversations were rich with stories of the life we shared together. We reminisced about our times of watching movies on the floor, walking around Ohio State University, and of the hours when we sang silly songs while she played the piano.

At about the second or third year anniversary of your death people asked us when we were going to *just move on* and *forget you*. I've discovered grief never really dies. It just fades and withers away slowly. In time it's replaced with joyful and grateful memories. But there's always some sadness. In our case there is sadness we didn't have more time together.

Grief has no defined timeline, it ebbs and flows like the sea. Sometimes grief crashes into the beach of my life and erodes away joy. Sometimes the same wave of grief can uncover deep memories of joy, grace, and gratitude. I've learned to be grateful for what time we had and for the love shared. No one can live without experiencing sorrow, joy, and grief.

# Chapter 34

# YOUR WAVES ECHO FOREVER FROM YESTERDAY

By Kayla Fioravanti

Sometimes people come in and out of your life
Like ocean waves.

Sometimes their lives lap gently up
onto the shores of your life.

Sometimes they are powerful rolling waves
that inspire you, touch you deeply
and then settle into gentle consistent waves that comfort you.

Sometimes the tide is out and they seem distant.
Other times the tide is in and their presence comforts you.
All the time their lives are an undercurrent of movement
that shifts the sands below your feet,
and you can still feel their lives touching you,
even when you can't see them before your eyes.

Your life has touched my life in many ways.
You have been beside me to hold me up during rough seas.
For many years you have been at a distance I can't see.
Yet even today I can feel your life shifting the sands
below my feet, because your life is forever intertwined with my life.

I can feel the impact of you leaving even at this distance.
I think I will hear your gentle rolling waves
forever from yesterday even as you say goodbye
From so far away.

## Section Seven
## GOODBYE MY FRIEND
Photo by Lisa Rodgers

# Chapter 35

# AUTUMN AND THE BREVITY OF LIFE

By Kayla Fioravanti

When the leaves change colors each year, I'm reminded of the outdoor celebration we held to honor my friend's life. Just a few days prior, I had passed Troy in the cafeteria as I rushed out the door. I waved at him. The look on his face told me I should spend a few minutes. In fact every fiber of my body told me to stop to talk to him. But I was in a hurry. I pushed aside my instinct and rushed out the door. I never saw him alive again.

He had leukaemia. Because he still lived on campus the reality of the disease never set in for me--until the word spread he had died.

I cried out into the void his loss left in my life, "If only!"

The painful lesson reminds me we don't know the number of our days. It is easy to get caught up in the busyness of life and rush past a moment where instead I should linger. Now it's my mission to stop and savour important moments. Sure life is packed full with the hectic activities connected to being a wife, mom, daughter, and friend. Even so, I try to tell my children I love them every day. I strive to live my life in a way telling my husband I love and respect him. I now always listen to my instinct to call someone or pray for him or her when they suddenly come to mind. Now, I try to never ignore a look saying I need you to connect with me. There are days when my humanness shows and I fail at my daily mission. But, with each sunrise, I embrace my mission anew.

I remember almost everything about the moment I rushed past Troy without stopping to talk. The sounds I could hear around me and the cafeteria smells. I remember clearly the look on his face asking me to linger for a moment. I remember the feeling I had as I rushed away. The one thing I don't remember is what I was rushing to do.

Autumn always reminds me of the brevity of life. I still feel a lump in my throat in response to the opportunity I lost. Although now, crimson leaves also remind me to slow down and enjoy every golden moment of life.

# Chapter 36

# ONE PERCENT

By Zachary Fisher

I heard a voice, strange and familiar. It floated through the office and winnowed down the hallways. It disrupted the dull litany of fax machine and talk radio. It announced the presence of someone who didn't belong here anymore. And it was welcome because no one sounds like our beloved Walter.

Walter had been diagnosed with a malignant brain tumor almost one year ago, not long after his retirement. How unfair for a man to earn a reprieve from one curse only to walk right into the snares of another. I honestly did not believe I would ever see him alive again. News of this kind seems to have such an inescapable finality. Any hope was long buried in the numbing sands of busyness and daily routine.

But here stood Walter with a remembering smile. We clutched hands as I tried to shake out a dumbfounded, "How are you doing?" It was an obvious, if not silly, question considering the softball-sized crater in the side of his head. His words poured out like molasses through his trademark southern drawl. Doctors were pleased with what they saw; encouraged by what they did not see.

As others gathered, I turned to his wife Ruth. She explained the removal of brain matter had damaged his memory. The next three months were a time for him to heal in preparation for radiation and chemotherapy. Tumors like Walter's have a ninety nine percent chance of recurrence. My mind raced to craft a consolation when her enlarged eyes interrupted me. She declared that they were believing in God for the one percent option. Immediately something in me woke up.

The gentle brush of Ruth's faith alongside Walter's journey was powerful enough to awaken something more imminent than death. These resilient people did not deny their terrible circumstances, but they were not consumed by them either. This wasn't just wishful thinking. The empirical evidence my mind could not fathom before was now standing here in victorious defiance of the odds. At once I became willing to trade all that knowledge, my calculating, my doubt and my busyness - all for the honor to learn from them how to be hopeful again. It was a holy moment.

We all need help digging out from under the lies we've believed for years. These lies tell us God is not moved by our diagnosis, or only the dispassionate words of science have ultimacy in our trial. Jesus once asked, "When the Son of Man comes, will he find faith on the Earth?" I believe He was asking us to think about who (or what) has the final word in our lives. Will He find a people paralyzed by the inevitability of death? Or will He find a community waiting for the possibility that makes all the difference in this world - and the world to come?

People like Walter and Ruth help shake us from our despondency and show us how to believe in miracles again. They are willing to stare down the ninety-nine percent believing for the one percent in the expectation of one hundred percent. Their faith becomes ours. It is faith in despair. It is hope in a dark place. It is life in the desert.

Chapter 37

# A LIFE WELL-LIVED

By Kayla Fioravanti

When I met Esther she easily made the list of women I admired most in life. We met about two thirds of the way through a ten year battle she was having with terminal cancer. Her beautiful singing voice was silenced to a whisper when her vocal cord was accidentally paralyzed during surgery. She suffered chronic pain and faced more surgeries knowing the cancer would eventually take her life. Yet there wasn't a bitter bone in her body. She faced everything with humor and radiated peace, joy and love. When I heard the jokes she made as her doctor delivered bad news, I laughed so hard tears streamed.

While looking forward to heaven Esther cherished every moment with her friends and family. In response to the nurse grimly explaining the hospice process Esther said, "You don't have to worry you can't scare me with heaven." Her husband, Pastor Tom, inundated the doctors with questions as they tried to describe her choices, prompting Esther to break the tension with a joke. Then she told them what to do next.

My mother was going through heart surgery around the same time. I observed many similarities in how each of these beautiful women used humor when facing surgery. Maybe it is why I felt so comfortable in Esther's presence.

Valentine's Day was the last time I spoke with Esther. I was running around the church preparing last minute details for the Steve Green concert the next day; I rounded a corner where she was standing in the doorway giddy like a school-girl. I stopped running to enjoy a few moments with Esther. Years ago I learned the hard way about not rushing past people. She was so happy she almost seemed to float away. Waiting for her husband to take her to the store for his Valentine's Day card, she joked about making him look away as she found a special one. Being madly in love with her husband she looked forward to writing a love note to celebrate their forty-sixth Valentine's Day.

I have been deeply touched by watching Pastor Tom and Esther's love story play out before my eyes. Up until the very last moments, Esther was serving Tom and Tom was serving Esther. They both found great joy in doing so. I loved being a witness to the life they shared.

We chatted a little more until she couldn't remember what she was saying. Making a joke about the medication she merrily changed the subject to her daughter's upcoming visit. This was our last one-on-one conversation, an encounter precious to me.

Esther loved tremendously. She served sincerely. A smile always came easily to her whether she enjoyed good times or struggled. She poured her life into everyone she came in contact with, her husband, her children, her ministry, and missionary work in India. She died peacefully with her family and friends singing *Amazing Grace* around her bedside. Nothing could have been more fitting for her departure.

During Esther's memorial service I pondered the giant footprints she left on earth. I wondered what would be said at mine. Will it be said I lived well? As we celebrated her life it made me consider how I would live the rest of mine.

If only I could live…

with half her courage,

with a portion of her smiles,

with a slice of her faith,

with an ounce of her servant's heart,

with a smidge of her humor

My life will have been well-lived.

Esther's example will always pull me forward and upward.

# Chapter 38

# THE LETTER

By Lynn McLeod

I wrote a letter on the afternoon I realized my sweet friend might die. I say "might" because no one, not a single person, believed it would happen. I'd heard her pray a hundred times since the diagnosis had come. Each and every occasion she thanked God for the opportunity to carry the cancer in her body so she could glorify Him through it. And that she did!

There were literally no outward signs of the battle going on inside her. It wasn't simply the gusto in how she took each step or breath, but in her genuine nature for making everyone else the center of God's world. Nothing slowed her down. Not chemo or surgery or the darkness she rebuked.

We shared the same second row church pew for years. This particular Sunday was no exception. Her skin was lightly browned, healthy as evidence of the cruise she'd just returned from. During the second song of the worship service, singing her heart out with hands in the air and tears dripping from her cheeks. The lyrics hit far too close to home for me as she sang about her strength failing, the days drawing near and how her soul would sing God praises forevermore.

The Holy Spirit has a way of grabbing your attention in subtly profound ways. Front and center of a traditional southern Baptist congregation, where posture ruled over emotions she openly wept as she praised God. It wasn't unusual in the least for her. This time the contrast pricked my heart as I wondered about the last time we would worship together. I know now how illogical it sounds, but I believed we would have many more times together just like this one. Yet, I knew it wouldn't be enough.

So I wrote the letter and placed a copy in her mailbox, then forgot about it.

*My beloved Linda,*

*If your time were my time, you would know how much of it has been dedicated to you. Random thoughts have gone in so many directions and landed ever so sweetly in a place where our lives would have been different had we met and become friends as children. Our imagination is a gift from God to fill in the gaps where reality in this world falls short. Rather than give a place for regret it didn't happen, I've written a little story about the day we would have.*

### Linda's No Da

*Frankly I can say with utter certainty, it's impossible to forget when Linda and I first met. As if it wasn't bad enough starting a new school in the middle of the fourth grade, I carried a* companion monkey on my back squealing a sense of dread mixed oh so completely with honest fear it would not go well . . . again. You see I had been the "new kid on the block" often. Even so, I hadn't quite mastered the art of a smooth transition as each new school ended in another stumbling act of awkwardness.

Usually the days before and leading up to the teacher's introduction kept me craving for it to be easier. It was as if the actual first steps into the classroom erased my hope as easily as equations were wiped from a blackboard. Sadly each experience ended with similar gnawing aches of self-doubt. The newness lasted a couple days while other kids tried to get the scoop on who I was and where I came from. I learned very early being vague was much easier than the slightest hint at truth. So the ties didn't bind and the initial curiosity routinely turned into an exercise in unintentional isolation. In other words, the kids soon moved passed me onto the next intrigue du jour. Perhaps it was my fear and perhaps it was their distracted nature. Either way, first days at a new school did not hold the optimism a new adventure might.

If you remember the teacher's voice in the Charlie Brown cartoon sounding an irritating "Wha wha wha" void of distinctive words, then you know exactly what I recall about Mrs. Castle's introduction of me. Standing at the front facing the other students I could see what you might expect, an assortment of young bodies jostling around their desks with energy reserved for nine and ten year olds. A couple with cowlicks left in their hair, several pony tails with ribbons, an assortment of mix and matched clothing, some fumbling with books and papers, with one or two whispering together behind an imaginary shield of protection. And just a hint of curiosity on many faces as they listened to what I didn't.

Then there was Linda! Tiny, smaller than the others, with brown curly hair cut close to her face making it shorter than any of the other girls. Her clothing remarkably sophisticated in its simplicity, timeless. With a white cotton blouse, crisp and neat topping a pair of black trousers cut slim at her ankle reserved to compliment her black patent leather slippers. Gracefully draped around her neck was a pearl necklace with a golden cross, centered just above the first button of her blouse. Yet it was her smile that was far too generous to be contained in such a small classroom let alone her petite frame. The light in her beaming brown eyes shaped her expression of boundless joy creating an aura I hadn't seen before. And there from the last desk in the last row on the right side of the room, Linda began waving with her open hand tossing back and forth into the aisle so her "hello" wouldn't be mistaken. She was a force of nature unto herself.

I wasn't sure what to make of everything, so I slipped quietly into the seat the teacher pointed to. I opened my book in hopes to continue slipping into it even deeper, until I disappeared. My solitude lasted only until the bell rang marking time to break for lunch. As was my pattern of behavior, I began shuffling papers, pencils and books to delay my departure thus intentionally positioning myself in the rear of the bustling pack of students. To my astonishment Linda paused standing next to my desk waiting patiently for a break in my *shuffling. "Hi, I'm Linda. I'm so glad you picked our school. You will really like it here. It is the best school ever, you know! Let's have lunch together so I can show you." She didn't leave room for a polite "no thank you." Instead, I felt myself nodding with sheepish approval while she slipped her arm in around mine locking tight a friendship that would sustain beyond what any fourth grader could imagine.*

*Lunch was a continual wave of chatter between two little girls nestled inside a bubble created amidst a combustible cafeteria full of incessant adolescent vitality. We didn't share the typical curiosity often resembling a job interview, but rather an easy-natured give and take laced with sporadic giggles. Linda's interest wasn't in finding out the details of my story as much as it was about sharing a bit of fun in a new way much like two lifelong friends would. Somehow the details didn't seem to matter to her. I would even go so far as to guess she may have innocently read the nature of them in my face before she waved.*

*Every few minutes someone would stop by the table where we were seated to exchange niceties with her. As they did, she didn't miss a beat in making my introduction. "Hey, this is my new friend Lynn. No 'da' . . . get it? Linda and Lynn No Da!" Many of the others didn't understand her joke. I loved it. And I loved her claiming my place in her life as a new friend so easily and without qualification. When it was time to return to class, with heads up, chins out and a spark in our steps together we skipped down the halls with our arms locked in a confident statement declaring we would be inseparable. You could say I fell in love with her that day!*

*As time passed, the details of our stories unfolded naturally as they should have. I found while many people truly liked Linda, still many others truly loved her. Yet, she still had room in her heart for a special someone to be close in a rare and unpredictable way. There is never enough time to do all the things we dream about. Magically there is always enough time to love each other well. Indeed, anyone who crossed paths into her life can attest, Linda loves well. And as she would be the first to tell you, it was because God taught her everything she knows.*

*I love you!*
*Lynn*

I loathe voicemail. I rarely listen to it. By the time you put in your password, listen to the instructions and move past old ones to the one you are waiting to hear, you could've called the person. I missed a call from Linda, which then turned into a missed call to her from me. We played the "tag you're it" game often in our daily chats. And sometimes it meant we would talk to each other the next day. I wanted to hear all the details about her cruise since we had both scurried off in opposite directions after the church services ended.

Tuesday morning the email blast came explaining she suddenly began experiencing trouble breathing, had gone to the emergency room where she had an MRI, and was sent home with hospice. Wednesday was going to be reserved for family and friends, while others could set an appointment to visit starting on Thursday. My time slot was 11:30 a.m. for fifteen minutes and then she would rest before the one scheduled for noon.

As people describe surreal, it never quite encompasses the reality one is feeling. Reality mixed with surreal. After reading the email I couldn't function at work, went home, prayed and paced. Paced and prayed. Fretfulness turned into urgency for making those last fifteen minutes count. They would be the ones to define our love for each other. I had to glorify God in these moments, just as she had taught me. I continued to pace and pray.

When I walked into her otherwise cheerful living room it had been rearranged by hospice as a quasi-comfort zone marked with a hospital bed where she lay surrounded by family who prayed. They stepped aside as I approached leaving us a place for intimacy. She recognized my voice as I drew near to kiss her, said my name and clung to my hand. Only someone who has stood in a place so close to death knows the comfort and peace one can find there. I had one last thing to share with her . . . the story. I began to softly read it to her as she gently nodded her head. She heard me.

Exactly like air bags unexpectedly exploding in a car, a blonde woman from Georgia interrupted me. Took Linda's hand from mine, stepped in between us, described the food being delivered, and mumbled something random about how she changed her life. She was a distant friend who hadn't seen Linda for over three years. She persisted in her dribble while she poached our last few minutes. Then the fateful hand on my shoulder said, "Your time is up, she needs to rest."

Without a word I left.

Anger is an insidious cohort, leaving no place for anything beyond itself. I was scarcely recognizable as anger danced so vehemently with hatred in the battle of my grief. The blonde woman stood in my danger zone. It was anger's most prized intention to slip the following letter to her at Linda's funeral.

TO THE SELFISH BLONDE FROM GEORGIA . . .

YOU STOLE THE LAST FIFTEEN MINUTES THAT WERE SUPPOSED TO BE MINE TO SAY GOOD-BYE TO MY DEAR FRIEND. YOU COULD NOT HAVE LOVED HER MORE THAN I DO AND REGARDLESS IF YOU HAD KNOWN HER LONGER OR NOT WHETHER SHE "CHANGED" YOUR LIFE OR NOT OR EVEN IF YOU BELIEVE YOUR PLACE WAS TO BE BY HER SIDE AT THAT TIME OR NOT . . . YOU ARE WRONG! WHAT YOU DID

WAS SELFISH AND TOTALLY UNCALLED FOR. YOU TOOK A PAINFUL SITUATION AND TURNED IT INTO A MOMENT OF ANGRY REGRET. YOU CERTAINLY WOULD HAVE MORE CHANCES TO SHARE WITH HER OVER THE NEXT COUPLE DAYS--EVEN IF THEY WEREN'T ENOUGH-- THOSE FIFTEEN MINUTES WERE NOT YOUR LAST. THEY WERE MINE. I WAS STUNNED AND SPEECHLESS WHEN YOU INTERRUPTED US. NOW I REGRET I DIDN'T DROP MY GOOD MANNERS AND SAY SOMETHING RATHER THAN LETTING YOU JUST DO IT. PEOPLE LIKE YOU ARE CARELESS AND STEEPED IN AN IGNORANT LACK OF UNDERSTANDING AS IF IT MAKES YOUR BEHAVIOR ACCEPTABLE OR WITHOUT CONSEQUENCES TO OTHERS AROUND YOU. IT DOESN'T.

I stopped when God's mighty, powerful and unfathomable hand reached into the safest places of my heart to say, "What was it you were looking for? Haven't you already had the best of Linda?" I quietly closed my computer and gently wept for the sweetest place my dear friend would be going. Into the arms of our Savior for the kiss we both longed for.

A couple hours later as I walked into the grocery I ran into her husband. It baffled me why he would be there and I told him to go home, to be with her, I'd do any shopping they needed. Before "Hello" or a word about groceries he told me how sorry he was my time with her had been stolen. He saw! In the tender words only God would fashion, I explained even though I'd been hurt and angry God reached into my heart to share peace only He knows how to give. Linda's husband didn't need distractions by others. Yet in his grief he was. It was an odd exchange I doubt he remembers. However, for me it was unmistakably providential.

The next day, on All Saints Day, my beautiful sweet friend said good-bye to this world skipping into the Heavens waving with her open hand tossing back and forth singing God's praises.

I miss her. Seventy-one days later, without any cause or warning I was checking a voicemail message from a number I didn't recognized only to hear the following recording:

*"Next message sent Sunday October, 27th at 6:30 p.m. 'Hey Lynn, this is Linda. Jimmy just brought in the mail and we read your story. It is so precious we have pouring tears. I don't know where you come up with the words. They are so wonderful. The way you normally write is so very beautiful. Nobody writes better than you. I love you, call me back."*

# Chapter 39

# LIVE OR DIE

By Kayla Fioravanti

"Your eyes saw my unformed body. All the days ordained for me were written in your book before one of them came to be." Psalm 139:16

I was standing at the local gathering place when I heard my mother calling me home at an unusual hour. Heading towards her I saw something I didn't recognize in her countenance. Apprehension engulfed me.

Her words tumbled out, "Robin is dead."

It was there in my front yard at the age of ten, where I was first introduced to death. It greeted me awkwardly as I stumbled behind mother and towards our first meeting just three doors down from Robin's house.

It had been an ordinary day at the gathering place. The place where all the kids on base belonged. There were no outsiders inside the gates of our military housing. Once transferred to the base you automatically belonged to our not-so-secret society where the password to join was always, "Hello, I just moved here from . . ."

I was truant of the knowledge of death before my mother broke the news to me. Robin was still the vibrant girl who walked in front of me to school. She was still the high school student who was my fifth grade teacher's assistant. She was still my neighbor and I was still working on the picture she asked me to draw.

Robin's death wandered in and out of my reality until a few days later when I found myself sitting in a pew at her funeral. My bottom lip quivering, I did not know how to express my grief. Death would become an all too familiar acquaintance after Robin. As I learned through loss, only God knows the number of our days.

In remembering those who have gone before me I am reminded of the frailty of life. Death confronts me with the truth we are not in control of our tomorrows. Therefore I must live completely each day. Death taught me to never waste a day doing anything less than my best; thinking anything other than positive; or being anything other than genuine.

Live or die each day. A good day is absent of regret. It is one in which I am present and accounted for in the service of our Lord.

Chapter 40

# DARE TO HOPE

By Tom Burgess

Daring to hope is not crossing your fingers and trying to imagine there isn't a problem. Daring to hope is looking at reality in the face while staring it down . . . it is daring to hope when all looks hopeless. Daring to hope is acknowledging a portion of my world has just collapsed, but I will discover and recover the strength to live the future with renewed vision.

Daring to hope is the story of a twenty-one year old young man from India. The future looked bright for him. Fifty-one years ago, in 1963 John Gabriel headed to America from Kerala, India. He arrived in New York with wide-eyed wonder. He came to America for a job with Georgia Pacific Corporation in Samoa, Northern California where he planned to learn the lumbering industry. However he learned his student visa wouldn't allow him to be employed. All was falling into place very nicely as God opened the door for him to change his visa.

He obtained a Greyhound® bus ticket from New York to California. He spoke little English. He read little English. With about eight dollars in his pocket he made the journey. Even though he was often quite hungry, John was anticipating a great future. For him there was a remarkable back-story bringing him to America.

To quote Paul Harvey, "the rest of the story" goes back to 1947 when John was a little boy of six in Southern India. A cousin of John's father became a Syrian Orthodox priest and was transferred to the area which would soon become the state of Israel in 1948.

At the very same time, a young Bedouin shepherd was herding his sheep in the Judean hillsides by the Dead Sea. While looking for lost sheep he hurled a rock into a cave hoping to hear bleating from any sheep wandering into the cave. There were no animal noises just the sound of cracking clay pots.

The shepherd and other members of his tribe returned to enter the cave. They found ten clay jars about two feet high containing leather scrolls with writing on them. They knew archaeologists digging in the area might be interested in them. They took some of scrolls and tried to sell them with no success until the scrolls were shown to an antiquities dealer in Jerusalem by the name of Kando. Thinking the writing looked Syriac, Kando showed them to Athanasius Samuel, the cousin of John Gabriel's father. By now he had become the Syrian Orthodox Archbishop of Jerusalem. Athanasius Samuel recognized the writings as Hebrew. Therefore he thought very possibly, they were a potentially significant find. It turned out to be a huge understatement!

Athanasius Samuel made the decision to come to America where he also had the scrolls shipped. After years of many experts studying the findings, it was determined the scrolls were one of the greatest discoveries of ancient Old Testament manuscripts! You may have heard of them? They are, indeed, The Dead Sea Scrolls!

As it turned out the young man from India needed someone in America to sponsor him before coming to the U.S. It was Athanasius Samuel, the Syrian Archbishop to whom the Dead Sea Scrolls were given, who also sponsored John Gabriel! All things were looking bright for the young man now landing on the west coast after a bus trip across the country. However, with his limited English, he was a bit taken back as he arrived at the bus depot in San Francisco. He was very hungry and shocked to see a sign saying "Hot Dogs." John couldn't imagine eating dogs in America—he thought it was only done in India!

John started working for Georgia Pacific when he finally arrived in Samoa, California. One of his supervisors was named Erville Buck. Erville had a high school aged son named, Gary who was writing a paper on India. His father suggested they invite John to dinner for Gary to interview him.

Gary and John struck up a great friendship and Gary invited John to church. Some of the workers at the jobsite discouraged John from going to church. They told him it would be a *weird* experience. Skeptical and worried John cautiously went anyway. He sat in the back in case he wanted to leave at any time!

Week after week, month after month, John listened and learned. He would spend time with the Buck family becoming close to the preacher, Doyle Farnsworth. Everything was wonderful for John during the next two years. He spent time with his new family of friends in America. Then it was time to return to India. John continued to correspond with Doyle and the Buck family.

In a letter he told Doyle about wanting to start a church in India much like the one he attended in California. He asked Doyle what was needed to begin a church. Doyle wrote back telling John before starting a church it would be best if he committed his life to Jesus and became a Christian. They continued to correspond while John pursued the reading of scriptures. He told Doyle he couldn't sleep very well. John made his decision. He was ready to commit his life to Christ and accept Jesus as his Savior. John immediately taught his friend, Kurian. They read in the scriptures that followers of Jesus were baptized. They agreed to baptize each other by immersion. John continued his business pursuits and concluded from reading scripture he was supposed to talk to others about Jesus. As a result the first little group of believers became a church in India.

This reminds me of a passage of scripture in when God was predicting the rebuilding of the temple. Zechariah 4:6 of The Message: "Then he said . . .'you can't force these things. They only come about through my Spirit, says God-of-the-Angel-Armies…..He'll proceed to set the Cornerstone in place, accompanied by cheers: Yes! Yes! Do it! Does anyone dare despise this day of small beginnings?"

Doyle made a number of trips to India for encouraging John and eventually others came from America as well. John happily observed God working in his life for the next several years. The Lord even provided a wonderful wife for John. The young lady, Kunjamma, prayed throughout her teen years for God to bring her a husband who loved the Lord. John and Kunjamma married and had two beautiful daughters. John was happy in his business pursuits and the group of believers was growing. By 1979 John was preaching in two locations while maintaining his occupation. He thought it was what Christians did—you became a Christian and you taught others!

In 1982, in John's eyes, his world collapsed. He received a devastating message. His friend and mentor, Doyle Farnsworth, died suddenly of a heart attack! John was emotionally torn apart and upset. Over the next few months he became angry and bitter. "Why did you let this happen, God?" was the cry of his heart. "I am committed to you, Lord. I was living for you. What will I do without Doyle to help and encourage me?" These were dark days for John. It was hard for him to dare to Hope.

John prayed but heard no answer. He fasted. He mourned. Then, with his heart broken, God spoke softly and tenderly to him, "John, I have been preparing you for this time. I want you to give your life full time to ministry in India." John listened and then reached out to Doyle's daughter, Charlotte. Charlotte Hoff was my secretary at Crossroads Christian School in our church in Portland, Oregon. John said, "Charlotte, would you ask Tom and the leaders at Crossroads Church to consider ordaining and setting me aside to do ministry in India." Charlotte made the request. We agreed to partner with Kerala Christ Church Mission and John Gabriel. We joined hands and hearts and dared to hope for the future! We began this journey together because we believed the scripture "Not by my might or power but by the spirit of God these things would happen."

In 1984 John began to dare to hope again. God has been faithful and encouraging far beyond what we could have imagined.

*****

The two little churches have multiplied into over forty churches including churches in two neighboring states to Kerala—Tamil Nadu and Andrha Pradesh.

*****

Crossroads English School was begun in 1985 with thirty-five, three-year-old pre-school students. Kunjamma approached John with the idea saying Doyle suggested it before he died. People in their community in India laughed saying it couldn't be done and wouldn't last. John felt incapable and very busy. He said, "With nervousness I told Doyle I couldn't do it so it was easier for me to tell my wife, 'no.' But then Kunjamma responded like wives in America. She cried! I said, "O.K. if you will get the education you can lead the school." Kunjamma got the degree because she dared to hope. Today, in 2014, the school goes up to the twelfth grade and has twenty-one-hundred students enrolled. They are receiving an education in English with a Christian influence. John and Kunjamma's oldest daughter, Lynn, has been teaching in the school. She received her Master's degree and last year took on the responsibilities as principal.

******

A few years ago the needs of orphans and children in dire circumstances became a heartfelt burden. John and Kunjamma's youngest daughter, Liz, heard the Lord speaking to her about this. She now heads up the Children's Village as part of the ministry, providing a home for forty to fifty destitute children. A big expansion of the vision is now in the prayer and planning phase. John *dared to hope*. His mission now provides support for several hundred children in the village areas. Churches are established as a means of providing help for the hurting and opening the door for them to hear about Jesus.

With over one billion people, India is fast becoming the most populated country in the world. It is a country one third the size of the U.S.A. with four times the population. Many are open to hearing about "The Living God."

John Gabriel did not walk away from life when it collapsed. He *dared to hope*.

We should never despise small beginnings. Allow the Lord to bring beauty from ashes and to make a message out of your mess. *Dare to hope!*

Chapter 41

# AUTUMN MEMORY

By Kayla Fioravanti

You have been alive in my dreams lately,
all fiery red, orange and for some reason, green.
Your laughter has been echoing
through the chambers of my mind
like it used to when it could still carry down the hallway,
around the corner and into my room.

I suppose it could be because it is Autumn now
and something about Fall reminds me of you.
We celebrated your life one crisp day after
you died. I remember that we were surrounded by
colorful trees as we sat in the damp grass.
Through tear-flooded laughter
we waved goodbye to you in unison.

I keep dreaming you back to life,
and when I wake, I expect to find you sitting
beside me, waiting to finish our conversation.

Our times together are too precious now
to wake willingly some mornings.
The last time I saw you in real life
I thought that I was too busy to answer
the expression in your face that asked me
to linger awhile in your presence.

That moment haunts me. You knew you were dying,
and I didn't. I just waved and walked away forever
….forever, I learned later.

Fall always reminds me of your laughter,
so I keep dreaming you back to life.
I spend the long hours of the night
in deep conversation with a man I once called my friend.
Every time I see you in my dreams I tell you
how you taught me to show my love more often,
to answer a hungry stare, and to tell my children,
"I love you," over and over again, each and every day.

# Chapter 42

# MOURNING 2.0

By Rachel Turner

The last of the nail polish wore off today. It was a dark glittery gold I chose because it reminded me of red clay dirt. The polish made my toes look like they had been dipped in a cosmic mud puddle.

Alice painted my toes the night before my wedding. We sat on the hotel bed catching up on all the things we'd missed and admired the rings on each other's left hands. We laughed. We sleepily promised to stay in touch more. She touched me for the last time when she cradled my ankles and painted my toes.

I've now been married for three months which means Alice has been gone for two months and three weeks. I haven't repainted my nails because I want to remember her in as many ways as I can. I want to think of her when I look at my feet, when I scroll through my phone and when I see movies we saw together. But for every flake of nail polish coming off in the shower, I feel like a tiny piece of her is disappearing from my life.

I was on my honeymoon in Europe when I received a text message Alice had died. "We wanted to wait until you were home," it said, "but we thought you'd see it on Facebook®."

And I did. I noticed the profile photos of so many friends changed to photos of Alice. There were photos of Alice from my wedding, photos of Alice from high school and photos of Alice wearing silly hats. Our friends changed their profile picture to a photo of Alice to remember and honor her. Those photos were a testament to the world, "Alice was a part of my life and she was important!" Her digital village had come together from corners of the country to mourn together online.

Alice's Facebook® page became a wailing wall. People from her past and her present paid their respects with memories, songs, videos, and tears. I replied to her husband and to her sister on Facebook®, sending my condolences. I proclaimed my love for this vivacious woman, wishing I could have been with her, and we could've had more time. And we all supported each other in our mourning, in our solitude.

Alice is gone. Now everyone's profile picture has gone back to photos of children or a New Year's champagne toast. But Alice's Facebook® page still lives. Occasionally it will pop up in my news feed with some newly posted memory from a friend or family member. I'll see her smiling face, feel my love for her a little, miss her a little and tuck her away in the place right behind my heart.

Last week was Christmas. I dreamed of Alice every night. I no longer had to keep these happenings to myself. I went to the confession booth of her Facebook® page, and I posted. I was surprised to see how many posts were there. I assumed after her funeral the activity would die down. It hadn't. There were posts dated mere hours before mine. Almost every day someone comes to the page to lay down memories at her digital memorial.

I realized because of this new way to mourn I would be reminded of her more than I ever would without Facebook®. I get glimpses of her while I'm at work, while I'm scrolling through my news feed on my couch and while I'm checking messages. I've got a far more permanent reminder than glittery nail polish. I have her family and friends at my fingertips to mourn with. We will continue to lift her up together and hold her there.

# Chapter 43

# EMPTY SHOES

By Kayla Fioravanti

I could not believe
that you were dead
until I saw the empty shoes
that you had removed only yesterday.
They looked so lonely without you.
The shoelaces fell to the side
like weary tears always do.

I could not say goodbye to you
until I saw the emptiness
of your life, without you.
Your books spilled over with words,
crying in silence for your eyes
to fall once again upon them.

I could not believe
that you no longer breathed
until I touched the silence of your room
with no heartbeat, but mine.

# Section Eight
# GRIEF OBSERVED
Photo by Lisa Rodgers

# Chapter 44

# GRIEF FROM THE OUTSIDE, LOOKING IN

By Duane Bigoni

I've been intimately associated with grief for forty-one years and conservatively observed over thirty-thousand expressions of grief. You could say I have a unique perspective. The first ten years of my career path were spent as a paramedic and first responder to medical emergencies. It led to spending the next thirty-one years as a death investigator at the Multnomah County Medical Examiner's Office, in Portland, Oregon. I've witnessed thousands of death victims, interacted with as many survivors and been involved in numerous follow-up investigations. Additionally my office personally notified surviving family members upon as request from other law-enforcement jurisdictions from around the world. Most of my interactions were limited to a few hours. However it wasn't unusual for a case to require extended involvement. A couple of cases lasted for years.

In my line of work you don't have to be an educated scientist of the psychologies to become, as I have, an astute observer of human reactions. I've met survivors who exhibited grief from one end of the spectrum with no detectable expression all the way to the other end where they wailed in a caliber as portrayed in the Bible. I have interestingly found the grieving process varies according to ethnic background as well as gender, age, religion, and biblical knowledge. The outward signs may vary in length from short to very long. On certain holidays or days of importance, such as an anniversary or birthday, the grieving process can be triggered to start all over. Not a single lost victim is forgotten completely, even over time. The grief for a child of any age will last as long as the parents live.

Grief is not limited to just family and friends. For example as a paramedic, I had a partner quit after we were dispatched to our third Sudden Infant Death Syndrome case on a single Christmas morning! Another time as the Medical Examiner, I had to dig up a baby who was only a few months old after she had been killed by her father during an illicit drug psychosis. She had been dead only a couple of days. A photo of me carrying her made the front page of *The Oregonian* newspaper. The expression on my face moved a reader to write a poem conveying her impression of how I must have felt about the case. She continued to send poems annually for the next dozen years. Even though I never spoke with the writer, I so appreciated her words each time they arrived. I normally professed to be abnormal because I didn't seem to be an emotional person and hadn't felt grief. This particular case proved me wrong.

An especially grueling case lasting months, involved a traffic incident (note I don't call this an accident because it involved a drunken driver) where six people were killed. It occurred on the tall I-205 Bridge over the Columbia River separating Oregon from Washington State. The victim's car held five adults and a newborn as it was catapulted off the bridge and into the river. Two bodies were recovered quickly. However, the remaining four were recovered over the next several months. One body actually traveled thirty miles into the Kalama Boat Basin in Washington. The newborn was the last one recovered. As the point of contact for the surviving family it wasn't unusual for me to talk to them daily. Sadness engulfed everyone who worked on this case. As for me, with the sadness I also felt a deep sense of anger. We were grateful when the final victim was found.

In another case, the Oregon State Police were in a quandary. This case did not fall in my jurisdiction, but I offered to assist. A fisherman in a boat on the Columbia River found a fancy decorative urn floating in the water. He brought it to the shore and turned it over to Oregon State Police, who then turned it over to me. The urn contained cremated remains sealed in plastic where they stayed dry. It took me only a short while to learn the name of the man whose remains were inside the urn.

I called his wife. When I reached her she had been crying for a full two weeks. She explained her husband of fifty-plus years had passed away. She was trying to follow his wishes to be cremated and have his ashes spread onto his favorite fishing grounds, the Rainer-Longview Bridge overlooking the Columbia River. Being extremely emotional upon arrival, she accidentally dropped the whole urn, still unopened, into the river. I offered to return it to her so she could complete her husband's request. She started crying anew saying she was unable to do the task. We later met and I assisted the wife in completing her husband's final wish.

As I mentioned, I carry a unique perspective and could easily continue to share many more stories. I've found there is no natural setting for grief. To work with grieving families, as I did daily, you have to provide support. Perhaps if it can be of help to share your foundation of faith with grievers. I found that in my profession it was necessary to have a solid footing in reality. My foundation is my Christian faith.

# Chapter 45

# GOD'S ASSIGNMENT

By Linda Reinhardt

One Christmas season I managed to get some extra time off of work before and after the holiday. I was in dire need of a vacation and planned to shop for presents on the first couple days. After enjoying the holiday celebration with family I planned to stay home to finish up some remodeling projects in our new home.

I was pretty grumpy the morning of my last day at work. With coffee in hand, a present for a co-worker for the Secret Santa party, and a dish for a potluck, I was already overwhelmed when I got into my car. The day was just getting started.

I almost reached my destination when suddenly I heard a loud and horrible noise. The only thing I could see was a white mass. My car kept moving, despite anxiously pressing down on the brake pedal repeatedly, until I realized it was the accelerator I was pushing and not the brake. Still blinded by the white mass I stomped my foot onto the brake causing the car to finally stop. I opened my door and quickly got out of the car. The front of my car was completely shoved in like an accordion.

It was hard to breathe. My chest hurt. I wondered if I was having a heart attack. I didn't exactly know what happened yet, except I had been in a car wreck. Another car was parked in the middle of the road. I ran over to help the driver out of the car. He was passed out and someone was in the car trying to help him.

The driver behind me was one of the witnesses to the accident. It turned out he was a doctor at a clinic where I was a patient. He later explained to my husband what happened. I had been driving east going through a green light. The other driver was traveling west running the red light as he turned left in front of me. We hit hard enough our cars both spun into opposite directions.

Before the paramedics arrived wonderful people came to help me. I told a paramedic I felt like I was having a heart attack. My chest hurt and I could hardly breathe. He poked at my chest. When I said, "Ow!" he determined I wasn't having a heart attack. Rather it hurt from getting hit by the air bag. He then informed me he needed to strap me down to a board on the gurney to prevent me from moving until I had x-rays.

I get extremely claustrophobic and was adamantly against this. I don't remember how the guy got me on the gurney and strapped me down. Then he put me in the ambulance where another paramedic laid his clipboard on my legs causing so much pain, I cried out.

Then I heard the most beautiful voice calling my name, "Linda! Linda…" It was my mom. I wondered how she heard about the accident and how she had gotten there so fast. Even as an adult I get emotional whenever I'm in a situation where I'm hurt or tired and hear my parents' voices.

"Mom!"

My mom poked her head in. It was so good to see her. I didn't realize how scared I was until I saw her face.

I had called my husband on a stranger's cell phone to tell him I had been in an accident. I didn't tell him where I was, nor did I even hang up the call. I just handed the phone back to the stranger. My poor husband yelled into the phone wanting to know where I was. He wasn't heard. He hung up the phone and called my parents who knew I was driving in the direction of my job. My parents hurried to search for me. Traffic was backed up as they arrived at the scene so they parked their car on a side street and ran to the accident. My dad said they saw pieces of my car on the road.

My mom rode with me in the ambulance. I don't remember being carried into the hospital exam room. I do remember another doctor laying his clipboard on my legs. It was so painful and I couldn't move. When my dad went to my sister's place of work to tell her I was in an accident he was pale and could only say my name and maybe I had been in an accident. When she followed him to the hospital she didn't know if I was dead or alive. As she got out of her truck she looked at my dad and asked if I was dead.

I felt claustrophobic and didn't like being at the mercy of those around me. To top it off a migraine developing in my eyes made it hard to see. They wouldn't release me from the straps. I began to assume there was something terribly wrong, but no one wanted to tell me. My sister bent down whispering in my ear. "No one is keeping any secrets from you."

The people I loved were going through emotional turmoil while I lay wondering what on earth was going to happen next. Finally they took the necessary x-rays of my spine. The results determined they could release the strap on my head. They shot a picture of my legs. Nothing was broken only bad bruising.

When they released me from the hospital I went to my parents' house for the day to rest and relax in a recliner as they lovingly cared for me. My husband left to go clean out my car.

I was stuck in bed at home for the next few days. I did get up to go to church after having a friend come over to do my hair since my shoulder and hand were injured.

Following church my husband informed me he had something to do and arranged a ride home for me. For some reason I had anxiety about being separated from him. I poked and prodded until he finally admitted he was going to the hospital to see the other person in the accident. I insisted on going along.

By the time we walked the hospital corridors to the ICU I could hardly stand. We rang the bell and a nurse came out of the big locked doors asking whom we wanted to see. Of course, normally she couldn't let anyone but family into the ICU. Given the situation she would see what she could do. She also said I shouldn't be standing and got me a wheelchair.

While we were waiting for the nurse to come back a young lady and an older woman walked up to us. I knew the young lady as the clerk in the pharmacy unit where I frequented. We would chitchat a bit whenever she was my cashier. My husband immediately perceived the people were family of the other driver. He was correct. They were his daughter and granddaughter.

They hadn't heard any information about the accident yet. I was the one to tell them he ran a red light and we collided. It was not a fun moment. It's quite an uncomfortable situation when you have to divulge a person's loved one is at fault for something. The man had emergency surgery and hadn't woken up yet. The family hadn't even been allowed to see him.

The doors to ICU opened and the nurse returned with a wheelchair to bring me into ICU. My husband and the two other ladies followed along behind us. She left me at the side of his bed. We asked if we could pray for him. They were excited about it. They had been praying for him to become a believer for years.

So, I reached over laying my hand on him, and began to pray for his salvation. When I came to the part about believing in Jesus his body moved. I looked up at his face seeing his lips were trying to move around the tube in his mouth. We were all excited. Believing he agreed with my prayer because right after it he relaxed again.

Throughout the next couple of weeks my physical therapy was draining. Going back to work was even more draining. My memory didn't serve me right. I had a lot of physical problems. My mind was always on the other driver.

Then one day while Ben was driving me to work I prayed for the man. I felt like the words, "He is home" went through my mind. I told Ben I thought the guy went home. I suggested we look up his address to visit him.

Ben acted a little strange so I dropped it. One of my co-workers called the hospital and learned he was no longer a patient there. I found his address and planned to see him. That night Ben told me the driver was indeed home, in heaven. He had died a couple of weeks earlier.

I began to shake. It felt like I had nothing to hold on to. As if I was standing over a great big hole. Ben was afraid I would go into shock and led me to bed covering me up with blankets. I kept shaking and tried to fathom the thought I had been in a situation where someone had died. I also thought, "What could I have done?" and "Could I have prevented it from happening?" Ben read a devotional story, which brought me peace for the moment. My body finally settled down. My thoughts didn't.

I struggled with why I had been in that place at that time during his last moments of his life. Why it was in such a violent way. I thought about what his family must be going through emotionally.

To help me deal with it I tried to convince myself it wasn't my fault. There was always the question, "What if?" I played different scenarios in my mind. I would end up back at the same place. No matter what I thought, it happened, and I couldn't change it. I had to somehow accept it.

During this time I was involved in a Bible study that taught about viewing life's circumstances as God's assignment. One day a few blocks from where the accident took place the word "Assignment" went through my mind.

*God's assignment? Is this why, I was there on that day, at that time?*

I thought about the connecting threads. A family praying for someone they love to come to know Jesus, the One who knows our beginnings and our endings. Before, the accident without knowing them or their prayers, I developed a little bit of a connection with his granddaughter at the pharmacy. My husband has the heart of a pastor. He often visits the sick in the hospital to pray for them and their families. God knew my husband and I would end up at the hospital. And Ben would be given access into the ICU even though family was still deterred. We prayed for the man's salvation and he responded.

Everything about the accident changed from that moment on. Yes, it was awful. But I truly believe it was an assignment.

The prayers of a family who loved the man were answered.

# Section Nine
# GRIEF FOUND BETWEEN THE CRACKS
Photo by Lisa Rodgers

# Chapter 46

# MATERNAL ECLIPSE

*Escaping the Shadow of a Narcissist Mother*

By Mandalyn Rey

Most forms of grief, however devastating, tend to fall into general categories that help us wrap our minds around them: *death, divorce, bankruptcy, illness, natural disaster, and so on.* While these categories bring no particular comfort in themselves, they do help describe the particular type of grief we're experiencing—which gives others a general idea of what we're going through and makes it possible for us to connect with those who are enduring similar pain.

Yet other forms of grief are more "between the cracks." To the naked eye, they're utterly invisible. No one knows they're there, so no one knows to comfort you.

In fact, those who suffer from invisible grief may even find themselves feeling shamed for their pain—because to the casual observer, they're "getting upset over nothing." This adds insult to injury and piles a second layer of grief on top of an already broken and overburdened heart.

I know this all too well, because I've suffered from invisible grief my whole life. I was born into it, like others are born into royalty or poverty. This insidious pain began in infancy and continued to send shockwaves through my life for decades.

My mother held powerful sway over my life for as far back as I can remember. Before I was born she dreamed of having a little girl much like me: one with blonde hair, blue eyes, and delicate features. *A porcelain doll to complete the fairy tale.* My father tells the story of watching her play with me like I was a doll. A real live doll of her own who would finally love her back. She was barely twenty.

I did my best to fill the role. I memorized nursery rhymes, wore pretty clothes, and did whatever I was told. But I soon discovered that the doll she'd dreamed of was only *part* of who I was. I had other parts she'd never imagined. I had a mind of my own. I thought outside the box. I liked things she didn't like and questioned things she took for granted.

*And the rage against the doll began.*

Any attempt on my part to differentiate from her was greeted with disapproval or hostility—as if she'd been personally insulted. I soon learned to stifle my "stubborn" tendencies whenever possible. I held them in as long as I could, but periodically the impulse to say what I truly felt got the better of me. There was usually hell to pay.

It didn't help that we were polar opposites in many ways. My mother was always on the go. Things like cooking, cleaning, and gardening were the real stuff of life for her, as opposed to writing or study, which she'd always found difficult. She loved being active and considered anything less a sign of weakness. I, on the other hand, was a bookish little girl who loved to sit. Reading, writing, and thinking were my favorite activities. I had no interest in housework or cooking and could easily spend a whole day just pondering a really interesting thought. This too was unacceptable. From early on, I was deemed "lazy" and still have vivid memories of her injunction *"Don't sit while you fold the towels!"* as if to do so revealed a deep and obvious character flaw.

On the other hand, being different also had its compensations. When my mother's own unhappy childhood backed up on her, she often reached out to me for solace. Strange as it may seem, these were some of our closest moments. Suddenly my disagreeable nemesis was replaced by a weeping, wounded creature who desperately needed my understanding and protection. I listened to her stories, felt her pain, and offered what comfort I could. And quite unexpectedly, I found that the same qualities in me which usually brought disdain now brought high praise. She called me wise beyond my years and showed a deep respect for my opinion. And for a brief moment, we were friends.

Except for one thing. It didn't last.

Once my mom's tears subsided, life returned to normal. She would resume her role as angry mom while I once again became the flawed porcelain princess. As many hundreds of times as I've watched this switch occur over the years, each one feels just as jarring as the first. As if a rip in the fabric of the universe had torn my soul along with it.

Thus began an internal "double bind" of colossal proportions: a daughter's inescapable resentment pitted against a confidante's undying loyalty. *Should I hate her . . . or protect her?* Most days, the loyalty won out. Or the fear of provoking her anger. Or both. Occasionally, when my frustration couldn't be held in any longer, it erupted toward my mom in ugly outbursts. This was followed by groveling and profuse apology on my part – which she usually rejected as insincere – and the cycle continued.

On the face of it, we must've looked a lot like the Brady Bunch. I even looked a bit like Marsha, with my long blonde hair and miniskirts, while my mom's frosted hair and toothy smile bore a striking resemblance to Florence Henderson. But under the surface, her heart was like a black hole that could never be filled, no matter how desperately I tried. Meanwhile, the hole in my own soul slowly festered, while the real me became increasingly unreachable year by year. *All I knew was I felt deeply flawed all the time, even when I wasn't doing anything particularly wrong. I also began to feel more and more invisible.*

This bizarre pattern between my mom and I continued year after dysfunctional year, well into my adulthood. Like a tired but well-rehearsed vaudeville act, we each played our parts without question. Meanwhile, my true self faded more and more into the shadows, decade by decade. For what seemed like an eternity, I found myself alternating between the shameful suspicion that my real self was "too much" and the deep conviction that I would never quite be "enough." I couldn't shake the feeling that even if I screamed at the top of my lungs, no one would ever hear or see the real me—or if they did see me, I would turn out to be horribly flawed.

Through the years, it's been difficult for most people to understand the extreme emotional vulnerability which was simply "standard issue" for me. They'd never encountered anyone whose identity and sense of self were quite so fragile. I, on the other hand, had never experienced life any other way. I'd spent my growing up years literally eclipsed by a mom whose every thought and emotional need took center stage over mine. Even her strong maternal instincts in practical areas left me feeling overshadowed, as I internalized her belief that I was weak and helpless and could never survive on my own in the "real world." During my formative years when I should've been discovering who I was, I instead was learning that my only value came from mirroring back to my mom who *she* was—in the best possible light of course. If something about me was useful to my mom, it mattered; if she didn't find it useful, it was tossed aside like so much garbage. I felt like someone who'd had the marrow sucked out of them, and all that was left was the dry bones of my hollow personality, as I tried desperately to function in day-to-day life.

When asked what my favorite color was, I'd answer blankly: "I don't know." When pressed for my opinion, I froze like a deer in the headlights; anxiously trying to guess what the person in front of me *wanted* me to say. Other times, I stubbornly clung to trivial viewpoints or opinions in a desperate attempt to finally be taken seriously. I felt like an emotional amputee who could feel her fingers yet for some reason could never quite use them. Deep down, I longed to be creative and adventurous and resilient, yet when I reached for those qualities all I found was this weak, flawed version of myself instead. I now realize that after years of seeing myself through my mother's eyes, I mistakenly believed that this tossed aside "dry bones" version of myself was the real me. It was a horrible way to live, and I grew more despondent with each passing year, until my late thirties when I finally grew suicidal.

*I'd like to pause at this point and say something very important.* My motive for sharing my story is not to vilify or make a monster of my mother. I love her dearly. I want her to thrive. And in her heart of hearts, I know she loves me too. Yet there comes a time when the truth simply cannot be held back any longer. For far too long I lived in a mental and emotional prison designed by the enemy of my soul to steal, kill, and destroy my identity, creativity, joy, purpose, and even my very life. But let me be clear: *My mother didn't design that prison. In fact, she lived in one of her own.* My guess is, more little girls than we'd like to think live in their own version of a generational prison, handed down to them by their parents, grandparents, or even great-grandparents. Sadder still, many of them have never broken free. And many little girls—both young and old—are still living there, even as we speak.

As I reflect on my own journey, I'm grateful beyond words that God has broken me out of the internal prison I grew up in and remained in for the next two decades—because I believed lies masquerading as truth, both about Him and about myself. I can honestly say the day-to-day joy of my release far outweighs ANY loss I may have suffered as a result.

And believe me, I don't say that lightly.

Because the way out for me has not been pretty. It's been littered with a shattered identity, a wasted youth, decades of relentless depression, and an aborted suicide attempt. It's also involved therapy, anti-depressants, "loving mirror" friends and mentors, and a tenaciously devoted husband. It has taken years of renewing my mind in Scripture and immersing myself in the love of God to get back to square one: *truly loving and accepting the person God made me to be.*

In the long run, it also cost me the ability to have my own children—because the brokenness I experienced all but deadened my maternal instincts until well into my forties when I'd finally experienced several years of healing. Then in a strange twist of fate, once the dormant desire finally awakened, I was overwhelmed by the "mother-lode of mother love" which flooded its way into my heart—then devastated beyond words when I realized the opportunity to bear my own children had passed me by. Not only that, but unlike most women who wait until later in life to try and start a family, I didn't have a thriving career to show for it. I was eventually faced with the stark reality that due to years of paralyzing emotional trauma, I had virtually nothing to show for half a lifetime of living—and the branch of the family tree I was sitting on would most likely begin and end with me.

These are not small losses. They're the sort that can open old wounds, reactivate childhood trauma, and send you hurtling into a second wave of bottomless despair. And in all honesty, for a while I teetered on the brink.

Yet this time, I didn't go over the edge.

*Why?*

Because by this time, my heart had truly become grounded in God's all-encompassing love for me—the kind of love which really and truly, beyond a shadow of a doubt, works all things together for good. *Words can't express how freeing it is to finally be able to walk out into the clear light of day without shame or apology for who I truly am.*

I still have to work a little harder than the average person to stay centered in God's view of who I am. It's absolutely non-negotiable for me to converse with Him often, meditate on the truth of His Word, and take daily steps of active obedience—or I quickly find myself frozen in place or headed toward depression. I used to consider this a handicap, a shameful weakness I hoped others wouldn't quite notice. Yet now I realize God has slowly but surely been transforming this area of vulnerability into a strength—a surprising portal to deeper dependence on His power and love than I ever dreamed possible.

As if that weren't enough . . .

Recently, after over a dozen years of walking out my healing, God showed me a vivid picture of what He's done for me, and what He continues to do every day of my life. He revealed that during all those excruciating years of feeling invisible to others, His inexhaustible love—so wide and long and high and deep—remained as constant as the sun during a solar eclipse. *His radiant life-giving power was not even slightly diminished, but was only temporarily obscured by a much smaller something—or someone—which got between Him and me.*

He also revealed that as long as I keep my eyes on Him, no one else has the power to eclipse my view of Him, or His of me. A quick mental step to the right or left is all it takes to restore my line of sight to His "all-knowing" love once again. In fact, over time this panoramic view of His love has the power to finally, imperceptibly . . . *ECLIPSE the eclipse!*

His constant, steady love has transformed me into a person whose identity is distinct, durable, enjoyable—and wonder of wonders, resilient. All those seemingly endless years of renouncing unbelief and returning my gaze to Him have finally taught me to put my full weight on His full-orbed view of me, rather than the tiny "eclipsed" view I'd mistaken for reality for so long.

I'm daily amazed as He continues to restore "what the worm has eaten and the locust has destroyed" and often feel like a newly-released POW rescued at the last minute—who's grateful to be alive and ridiculously happy to finally be living the life she was meant for!

Chapter 47

# THE DAY I LEFT HOME

By Steve Green

I suppose the trip to Cerrillos was inevitable. My older sister and brother had already been at the missionary boarding school for two years. The time had come for me to enroll. I would be the only student in third grade. I was a homebody, however, and didn't at all like the idea of living away from my mom and dad. I had completed second grade at the national school in our small town of Tartagal, Argentina and had gotten used to the idea of being the blond, fair-skinned kid in a town of dark-skinned people.

My folks had mentioned I would soon be living away from home. Secretly I hoped nothing would come of it if we didn't talk about it. An eight year old doesn't really have the necessary tools to deal with such dread.

The seven hour drive seemed interminable. I sat silently in the back seat of our Jeep®, except for the two or three times I was overcome with nausea and had to ask my dad to pull over. My parents said I was carsick. It felt like much more than that to me.

There had already been a lot of change in our young family. While pastoring a church in Portland, Oregon my folks, still in their late twenties, had sensed God calling them to Argentina as missionaries. With remarkable determination they set out for language school, with five small children in tow, ages nine-months, two, four, six, and eight years old! Upon arriving in San Jose, Costa Rica the rigors of learning a new language demanded most of my parents' time, so they hired a maid to stay home with the three youngest kids while they attended classes. Our maid's name was Bienvenida and although she wasn't Mom, she did provide a measure of comfort.

One year later we left Costa Rica to travel south to Salta, Argentina, the hub of the mission. I was only six, but I remember our arrival very well. No one knew we were coming. We waited at the small airport until word could reach the mission leaders. When two missionaries finally arrived, there was a lengthy discussion and then the mood turned somber. The missionaries had suggested to my parents that it would be best for them to leave immediately for their new post in the northern part of Argentina and that the two older children should be placed in the boarding school that very afternoon. I don't even remember saying goodbye.

One of the missionaries drove my parents and my two oldest siblings to Cerrillos, a small town thirty minutes away, while the rest of us were taken to a mission home to wait. It was dinnertime when my parents returned. Kids can feel trouble even if parents act like everything is fine. Our family was fractured and I felt unsafe. We began our drive north at dusk. Although tired, I was wide-eyed from the upheaval.

We arrived after midnight, once again unexpected, at a missionary's home in Pichanal. The sleepy missionary opened the door to find a frazzled family on his doorstep. We waited outside while they put their guard dogs in the back. They told us not to be alarmed by the strange sounds coming from a deranged lady who was staying in their shed. The couple set up wooden cots for us in the living room. Even though I was the oldest now and supposed to be brave, my cot was too far away from my parents. The shadows on the high ceiling accentuated the strange sounds. I was still awake when I heard my dad's steady breathing across the room. That night I wet my bed.

Two years later and just minutes away from the boarding school, I felt a strange mixture of emotions. As with most things in life there is usually some sweet mixed in with the bitter. I did look forward to seeing my older brother and sister. Like any little brother, I looked up to them and wanted to be with them. They had acclimated well to their new life. When they had been home I was surprised they didn't seem to feel the anxiety and fear that gripped me.

As we drove through the gate and made our way along the winding gravel driveway, I spotted a few kids playing on the concrete basketball court. Friendly collies ran alongside our car and barked excitedly. The setting was idyllic. We parked at the entrance and as we got out, someone yelled into the house that the Greens had arrived. My siblings ran to greet us. After visiting with my parents for a while they appeared anxious to get back to their friends. I felt out of place. The only certainty I had known in this foreign land was my mother's presence. At the very moment I needed her comfort the most she showed no sign of emotion. Later, I would learn that my parents had been told it was better for the children if they appeared stoic.

After moving a few belongings into the room I would share with another boy and getting familiar with my surroundings, a cow bell announced it was time for dinner. As the children hurried to the dining room, I could already feel the strange transfer of power. My parents were present, but now there were rules that trumped their authority. Someone else was going to be in charge of me. There was a regimen that I was not used to.

The children had to eat what was put before them and could not leave the table until their plates were clean. Each room was inspected in the morning to see if beds were made properly, clothes put away and shoes shined. There was study hall after school, chores on Saturday, and letter-writing time after the Sunday afternoon nap. At dinner that first night I was told I would have some free time, followed by cleanup, then devotions, and finally bedtime.

My parents decided to leave right after dinner, before the evening routine began. While the other fifteen children were playing, my mom and dad gathered us to say goodbye. After hugs and kisses they lingered a bit, talking with the house parents. I slipped away and went to my room to watch through the window, my face pressed against the screen. They got into the Jeep®, started the engine, and then I watched the taillights move slowly down the driveway. I still remember the smell of the screen. It smelled like dust mixed with tears. Eventually someone found me still standing by the window and told me it was time for devotions.

It took several decades along with some helpful counseling sessions to realize God was not absent in those early years. He was very present and was tenderly authoring a unique story that would ultimately be for His glory and my good. The very thing that caused the most pain is what God used to bring me to the end of myself. I don't think it's coincidental that the year I entered boarding school, I also began to recognize my need for Jesus. On a Sunday afternoon following a sermon on the gospel given by a visiting pastor from Arizona, I knelt by my bed and called to Jesus, the One who knew loneliness and grief. I received comfort from the One who had suffered to take away my sin.

I think everyone would prefer to be whole, strong, and free from frailty. But it is precisely those things that God uses most in our lives. I agree with author Dan Allender that people who lead from strength are inspirational, but those who lead with a limp, point to the greatness and power of their Redeemer and Sustainer.

# Chapter 48

# LAUGHTER THROUGH THE DARKNESS

By Kayla Fioravanti

Everyone has their valley of darkness stories. There are simply times in life we all spend in a dark valley feeling as though we're swimming against a current. It is the ebb and flow of life. There were times in my life when I simply didn't know how to take the next step or if I was even moving forward.

~ ~ ~

Like the time when . . .

    . . . I knew I'd be answering a call from my mother's brother shortly after the holidays. I was reaching for the phone before it rang. I knew with all certainty the sound of the phone would pierce the darkness to inform our family that Grandpa had just passed away. With tears of loss already stinging my face I brought the phone to my mother knowing I was handing her heartbreak. I was expecting the news that Grandpa had folded his hand and left me to play solitaire all day.

Like the time . . .

    . . . the terrorist attacks hit closest to home for me. I planned on going to Oktoberfest in Munich, but decided at the last minute I just didn't feel like going anywhere at all. I was all alone at home when the phone rang and frantic voices on the other side of the ocean were calling to see if we were okay. I could feel my body go numb as I realized I could have been at the Oktoberfest when the terrorist bombed the area where Americans frequented.

Like the time . . .

    . . . I burned down my kitchen one. I learned sometimes life displaces you and yet you still have to go about the business of living. I was living life at a million miles a minute. Seconds after leaving the kitchen I realized my mistake. I turned towards the kitchen to face a wall of fire. In a flash our very first house and brand new kitchen was on fire.

In my darkest valleys and times of crisis I try to find a way to laugh, hard, like my dad. He is gifted at spotting the one kid in a stage performance picking his nose. It sends my dad into restrained hysterics. His attempt at holding his laughter makes it even funnier. Tears stream down my dad's face in between snort-filled laughter and trying to hold it back, which only makes him laugh harder.

~ ~ ~

The ability to find laughter in the midst of dark valleys is a gift. Embrace it. Search for the little things in life making you smile. Life can take the wind out of your sails.

Sometimes the air feels dead around you and the emotional crisis steals the actual strength to get out of bed. Laughter can be a universal language of healing breaking through the darkness and helping you move forward in my life. And the wonder of it all is that laughter is contagious.

# Chapter 49

# A GARDEN FULL OF GRIEF

By Ginger Moore

"You intended to harm me, but God intended it for good to accomplish what is now being done, the saving of many lives." Genesis 50:20

My grief was planted with an early seed of rejection, watered until it grew into a thick and sprawling plant with deep and hidden roots. It was planted deeply, but had no boundaries and spread into every area of my life's gardens. The bitter roots invaded my every thought, decision, emotion, and relationship. My grief seemed all encompassing, sometimes debilitating and almost insurmountable. It has literally taken me a lifetime to process it moment-by-moment, day-by-day, one life event after another. God's grace and unconditional love cut layers of grief away, pruned dead branches and plucked the weed-like roots.

My grief was born from absence rather than loss. It grew from the lack of basic fundamental needs being met by my mother and father. They failed to love, nurture and accept me. They failed to provide the safety, security, and significance that are absolute fundamentals for every human being. The very needs God, our Creator, ingrained in my being from the word go were never provided. My personality, mental stability and self-worth formed without a parent's loving touch or nurturing guidance. The prism my parents created for me out of their rejection distorted my view of God. The seed of rejection planted even before I was born was fertilized by their emotional neglect. The sorrow burrowed deep inside my soul and affected every single part of my life.

Let me set the scene. I was born during the summer of 1967. My mom and dad were both seventeen years old and unmarried when they discovered I was on the way. In the 1960's, teen pregnancy was not as common or accepted as it is today. As a result, my mom had to drop out of high school. There it was - the seed packet of rejection was in my mother's hand. She opened it. My unplanned existence meant she would not fulfill her dreams. The seed was taken out of the packet when my parents were forced to marry. They became two married kids who were not in love and had an unwanted kid on the way. My dad drank regularly and I've been told he was controlling, verbally, mentally and physically abusive. Some family members on my mom's side who were overly involved in their marriage compounded my parents' volatile equation. Disaster was inevitable.

After a second pregnancy ended in a stillbirth, my mom divorced my father. I was about two years old. My mom was a divorced nineteen year old with no high school diploma and a small child to care for. She was stuck working menial jobs for meager pay. Her life had been set upon a course she did not want. And here I was, this little thing looking at her, clinging to her and needing her every day. I was a living reminder of the path she felt stuck on.

I don't remember any of these events during my formative years, but I've heard them recounted repeatedly. What I remember most from my childhood are the looks, actions and the tones toward me in my mom's voice. I remember the resentment and hatred my mother harbored toward my father and anyone associated with him. This included me. And with this, the seed of rejection was planted in fertile ground, watered and took root within me.

Growing up I knew I was not wanted, accepted, cherished or important in my mother's eyes. I did not hold a place of prominence in her heart. I felt it every day in varying degrees. I couldn't put a name or description on it until years later but I knew. I was a burden and an obligation. I was tolerated for the sake of appearances. It became even more evident with the arrival of my brother and sister, twins who were born when I was four years old. They were treated in completely different ways than how I was. I cannot remember my mom ever telling me she loved me or showing love in any recognizable form. There was no affection, no encouragement and no affirmation.

I remember her criticism and control. I felt constant pressure to perform and do well in order to gain her acceptance. I wasn't given loving guidance or hope. In fact, it was quite the opposite. What I was given was a long list of do's and don'ts with standards I couldn't possibly live up to. And yet, no matter how good I was, how smart I was, and how hard I tried the acceptance never followed.

My mother criticized me until I became exactly the person she repeatedly accused me of being. I believed there was something wrong with me. Other mothers evidently loved their children. I saw what it was supposed to look like from my classmate's moms, on TV and everywhere I turned. With my child-like understanding, I believed there was something horrible about me making me unlovable. I believed I was worthless, incapable, a problem, always at fault, and responsible for everyone's unhappiness.

I was told from the beginning my dad didn't want to see me. This heaped the plate with double rejection and super-sized side of grief. I never saw him, talked to him or heard from him. I later learned he wasn't allowed around me. I actually didn't meet him until I was about sixteen years old. I didn't have the opportunity to get to know him until I was out of high school. By this time he had accepted Jesus Christ as his personal Lord and Savior. He had gone through many changes and had learned how to love with the real love of a father as a child of God.

To my knowledge my mom on the other hand has never changed. She still hasn't learned to love. I say "to my knowledge," because she promptly disowned me when she discovered I had contacted my dad and was developing a relationship with him. I think she was actually relieved to have an excuse to let me go. Just after my eighteenth birthday, she kicked me out of her home and her life. She looked me in the eye and told me I was dead to her. With such a final rejection, she shoveled a good bit of fertilizer on the growing, blooming plant of rejection already consuming me. Many years later, she and most of my maternal family continue to have virtually no contact with me.

In my early teens I accepted Jesus as my personal Lord and Savior, but had not walked in my salvation for most of my teen years. Soon after graduating high school, I found my faith again. In my mid-twenties I met and married a wonderful Christian man. As God often does, He had a plan. During the early part of our marriage my husband and I ministered in the small church where we were married. After a short while, we followed the Lord's leading to a large church with many avenues of participation, as well. But I was still a hot emotional and mental mess.

My deeply planted seed of grief had grown into a hearty weed with no boundaries. It easily spread into every single area of my life's gardens. I was still battling the ever blooming, heavy bearing fruit of rejection. I was overrun with feelings and mindsets from my past including childhood sexual abuse and the finality of my mother's rejection. The grief nearly took over completely.

I grieved for the lack of love and relationship with the one who gave me life. Every turn, every event brought up a new branch of grief growing from rejection. At every normal life event I had a big seeping hole sucking the joy and hope right out of me. I had gotten married without my mother being there. I battled issues with infertility without my mother to cry through it with me. I was trying to learn to be a wife without my mom's example. I was trying to be a woman without my mother providing an example. I was facing life, my roles in life and everyday living, without my mother's love and acceptance.

Unfortunately, I didn't take hold of the assurance of safety, security and significance God had for me. No matter how much I tried I still felt worthless and thrashed about in a thicket of grief and sorrow almost daily. Every area of my life suffered in some way from the seed planted within me long ago. While on the outside, I may have looked well-groomed and presentable, the reality was that I was struggling constantly on the inside as this weed nearly strangled the life out of me.

Thankfully, against my will, God led us to the church I mentioned earlier. This place, this wonderful body of believers and leaders became my healing place. God's plan for my life was at work in a church flowing with the Holy Spirit. They emphasized who we are in Christ, our true identity. They taught about the finished works of the cross, the power of the blood and the Father's love for us. Suddenly, there were words in my ears about this great love and who God said I was. I had never heard this love and identity before, much less experienced it. There was affirmation, hope and a focus on personal relationship with the Lord. Christianity was no longer about rules or performing for acceptance. And there was an ever growing circle of friends and mentors the Lord placed in my path to sow godly seeds in me.

I slowly began to see myself differently, but definitely through new eyes. I was receiving everything I had been denied by my earthly mother and father from my Abba Father. I came to the revelation I was accepted, loved, and cherished by the very One who had created me and planned my existence long ago. Wow! I was of great value to HIM, very much loved, planned, accepted…. and wanted!  With this revelation of truth, the roots of rejection began to wither. Their food was cut off and they were being plucked up.

I'm grateful for every lesson I've learned in the process. I know He will use every lesson in ways I cannot begin to imagine at this moment. My mother may have planted a bitter seed of rejection and watered until it grew into a hearty plant with distorted roots. But God is transforming the weed into the most glorious bloom. My tears along with His grace have created fertile glorifying ground. He plants seeds and I am growing new roots--HIS ROOTS. He becomes the thresher who removes the chaff. He offers me shade to hide when an old or never before seen wound surface. He comforts me when the pain is so deep I cannot see through my tears.

I really can't say that I'm totally free yet, but I am growing with the light of the Son. I have access to the love and grace of God, which I now fully embrace. In Him I have found that our bad things will turn out for good. According to Romans 8:28: "And we know that in all things God works for the good of those who love him, who have been called according to his purpose." More importantly and gloriously, 1 Corinthians 2:9 promises the best things are yet to come, "What no eye has seen, what no ear has heard, and what no human mind has conceived' the things God has prepared for those who love him."

# Chapter 50

# LOVE WITHOUT A DOUBT

By Shirley Logan

Baby brother's got a belly ache
He hasn't eaten in at least two days
But he's smilin' at me, as he falls asleep

Town to town tryin' to settle down
He holds a pebble like a treasure in hand
My favorite part is at a long days end

**CHORUS**
When it's just you
When the lights go out
It ain't never been easy
But you're my solid ground
It's just me
When you're feelin' down
I'm holdin' all those pebbles you saved
Love without a doubt

Single Mama with a big heartache
They make it easy to escape the pain
Always kissin' on me, givin' hugs for free

I work real hard; I hope they know I love them
I miss a lot don't wanna let them down
My favorite part is at a long days end

**CHORUS**
When it's just you
When the lights go out
It ain't never been easy
But you're my solid ground
And it's just me
When you're feelin' down
I'm holdin' all those kisses you gave
Love without a doubt

They cry at night, turn out the lights and hold them
I will never make them understand
Daddy's never coming back he said he's never coming back

**CHORUS**
And it's just you and I can't break down
It'll never be easy
But there's a peace I've found
And it's just me
When you're feelin' down
I'm holdin' all those tears you shed
Mmmm
Yeah it's just you and me kids
Love without a doubt

# Chapter 51

# RESPLENDENCE

By Carol Wilson

*Life…*
*begins with innocence,*
*teems with dreams*
*and potential—*
*That's the design.*
*Yet…often,*
*innocence is stolen,*
*dreams are crushed,*
*potential bullied.*

*And, many…*
*self-sabotage.*

"You're pregnant."

Delight surged when I first heard these words. Motherhood was *the* dream of my life. Yet, my emotions mimicked the twists and turns of the relational roller coaster I had ridden for several months. One day my boyfriend and I climbed towards intimacy; the next, we spiraled down in withdrawal.

Our relationship idled in January after the holidays so I planned a Valentine rendezvous to revive the romance. The nice hotel, candles, wine and chocolate would surely carry us to the top of the romantic track. Unfortunately, rain pounded outside while passion sputtered inside. Even so, a tiny Valentine life was conceived.

Now, emotions seesawed.

Hope – despair; excitement – fear; joy – shame; love – hate.

When I told the baby's father I was pregnant, he was thrilled—until I rejected his marriage proposal. Our relationship wasn't secured with the depth of committed love. Nor was it loosely latched with shallow physical attraction. It was fastened with loneliness, a clasp too weak to hold in tumultuous times. After rejecting his crisis proposal, runaway emotions and a fast track of poor choices sparked fiery pain.

The financial hole I dug for myself months before compounded the crisis. Fortunately, promotion opportunities at my new airline job extended a rope that could pull me out of the pit. How could I jeopardize a potential financial rescue? I was also a caretaker for my ill grandmother who raised me. She was proud of me because she thought I was finally doing things right in life. How could I break the news to her? I felt I had to keep the pregnancy a secret to preserve my reputation at work and at home.

The baby's father threatened my cloak of secrecy with my grandmother when he drove in front of my home and yelled, "You'd better get an abortion, or get a good attorney!" *Get an abortion? Get a good attorney?* I guess he figured if we weren't married he didn't want fatherhood responsibility. Anyway, those words yelled out of a car didn't exactly convey the sentiment a woman desires from a Valentine's Day lover. I kissed the relationship goodbye and opened the door, once again, to loneliness.

I received counsel from impersonal parties. A friend of a friend told me about her choice to have an abortion: "Abortion is not a big deal. I'm glad I did it." In an attempt to find clarity, I met with a nurse and a counselor at the clinic where I took my pregnancy test. After the examination, the nurse told me I would have a difficult time having a baby. Then, she ushered me next door to see the counselor. The counselor seemed to assume I'd have an abortion.

I didn't have a basis for my belief, but I told this woman, "I don't believe in abortion."

I will never forget her response. "You'd be surprised how many Christian moms bring their daughters in for abortions." I wasn't a Christian at the time. Why did she say that?

Persuasive words rush onto the mind's landscape when we're caught in unexpected and unwanted circumstances. In my crisis I listened to words—my own self-talk and others' coaxing—that appealed to my immediate desires and fears.

*I don't want to marry him; I don't even want to be with him anymore!*
*I can't face my family. They already think I'm messed up.*
*I will lose my opportunity for promotion.*
*I can't afford a baby right now.*

***

"You'd better get an abortion, or get a good attorney."
"I had an abortion; it was no big deal."
"You're going to have a difficult time if you have this baby."
"Christians have abortions, so it must not be a bad thing."
"It's just tissue."

The more I listened to these seductive words the less inclined I was to acknowledge my deeper feelings, desires, and convictions. I also neglected to evaluate future consequences of various options.

I didn't consider the fact that I was thirty-one years old and had always deeply desired children. I didn't determine if financial and practical assistance might be available. I didn't learn about fetal development. I didn't learn about the abortion procedure and the possible risks. I didn't seek to understand how my physical, emotional, and spiritual components intertwined or how abortion might affect me in each of these areas. I didn't seek to understand why I would tell a counselor I didn't believe in abortion.

I did allow seductive words to chart my path. I scheduled an abortion.

\*\*\*

When we plunge into a choice that denies our deepest desires or opposes our core values, we often repress memory and the emotion attached to the memory. I believe this explains why I remember little about the day of my abortion. I don't remember leaving home in the morning, driving to the clinic or signing forms. I don't remember most of the actual procedure. I don't remember my activity for days afterwards.

Only three snapshots of the day etched into my memory. I remember the surrealistic lunch with a friend who drove me to and from the clinic. Lacking sensitivity, she arranged for us to meet one of her guy friends at an outdoor café. Only minutes before, the abortion doctor had inserted laminaria[1] to dilate my cervix, given me a tranquilizer, and told me to return in a few hours. My friend savored her food and laughed with the man I had just met, seemingly oblivious to my lack of engagement. Back at the clinic, I remember a nurse held my hand during the procedure, but she failed to convey genuine compassion. The sharpest image of that day depicts my body curled into a fetal position in the back seat of the car for the ride home.

Even though I yearned to be a mom, I had extinguished an opportunity to realize that dream. Grief and remorse surged but then went underground. Self-destruct mode mushroomed. I latched onto another guy. Alcohol and pot entertained us nightly. After a while, I brilliantly realized drinking and smoking every night yielded destruction instead of entertainment. I admitted to myself that addiction serves as a wobbly foundation for a relationship, so I ended it.

A year after the abortion, I met a man who introduced me to Jesus. Within a few months I gave my heart to Jesus and also to that man. He was already a father, but said he wanted a child with me too. A few months after we spoke our marriage vows he decided he didn't want to have any more children. He told me I should leave and find another man with whom I could have children. I maintained my devotion to the marriage; yet, sadness and regret smoldered within me when I realized I aborted the only baby I'd probably ever conceive. He divorced me a few years later.

During this time I grieved the loss of motherhood, but eventually laid the desire down and focused on my relationship with Jesus. My spiritual growth was boosted exponentially when I started volunteering at a pregnancy resource center. It was here where God also began to heal the wound festering within me.

He opened my eyes to the biology of fetal development and to relevant scriptures. I was overcome with remorse when I learned God intimately formed the eight-week old baby in my womb. I was horrified when I saw the fetal development images.

"My baby had fingers and toes!"

"My baby's heart was beating!"

"Why didn't I know this?"

"I should have known!"

"If only one person would have told me, I wouldn't have done it!"

Before I saw those pictures, I hadn't sought healing from my abortion. Life was gratifying in most every way. Almost pristine. I was flourishing because of my daily discoveries from the Bible about Jesus and because of my new friendships with other Christians who helped me understand each new discovery.

But, the fetal development discovery caused me to feel like a cross-country skier caught in an avalanche. One minute I enjoyed the pleasure of striding across pristine terrain. The next minute it felt like I had tumbled down a mountain and slammed into a tree just before being buried under a mass of snow that weighed on me like concrete. I ached in every way and was forced to capture what breath I could from a small pocket of air.

> I felt pulverizing regret.
> I felt suffocating shame.
> I felt crushing grief.

I had experienced numerous reasons to be buried emotionally during my life. My mother and her whole family slipped out of my life when I was two. My alcoholic military father ditched my brother and me and left us in the care of his parents. Both my father and grandfather stole my childhood innocence. I also grieved the loss of too many relationships.

Most of the pain from these experiences was the consequence of others' harmful behavior and hurtful decisions. This anguish was different. It came from my own depraved behavior. I killed an innocent person! I had taken the life of my own baby!

I had two choices: asphyxiation or airlift.

I could lose hope and suffocate under the crushing weight upon me.

Or, I could be like the prepared skier who wears an avalanche beacon that transmits signals to other skiers wearing transceivers. I could believe the Lord had received signals from my soul's "avalanche beacon," and trust Him to airlift me to a place where He could administer specialized healing treatment.

I perceived His airlift and specialized care could be a significant stage in my spiritual journey. I transmitted a cry to Jesus for rescue.

G.K. Chesterton stated, "It is always simple to fall: there are an infinity of angles at which one falls, only one which one stands."

Because of the restorative grace and steadfast love of Jesus, I stand. He administered healing through Bible studies written for women who suffer from abortion. I moved out of the deepest pain into joy when the Lord led me to believe my baby was a girl and His Word led me to believe she was in heaven with Him. Shame gave way to tender maternal grief when I had the privilege of naming her and creating a memorial in her honor. Jesus continues to inject doses of healing to me through my ministry to other women who bear the same crushing weight after choosing abortion.

Life is almost pristine now. I compare it to the scenery I marveled at while on an Alaskan cruise. I sat on the promenade deck while the ship cut through the narrow passageway of College Fjord in Prince William Sound. Numerous glaciers cascaded down the mountainside into glassy emerald and turquoise water. Alongside the icy glaciers, black stripes of rocky debris and sediment, called moraines, also snaked down. I only saw magnificent beauty, though. It was as if the moraines existed to accentuate the resplendence of the glaciers.

My abortion will always be a moraine in my life. I will always regret it. But the stripe of debris doesn't dominate the landscape of my life anymore. It exists only to show off the resplendence of Jesus and His sacrificial grace.

When I was in a vital stage of my healing journey the Lord led me to read I Peter 1:3, 4: "Blessed be the God and Father of our Lord Jesus Christ, who according to His abundant mercy has begotten us again to a living hope through the resurrection of Jesus Christ from the dead, to an inheritance incorruptible and undefiled and that does not fade away, reserved in heaven for you." [2]

It is by the mercy of my Father in Heaven that I have been born to a living hope. Because of the death and resurrection of Jesus, I will receive an undefiled inheritance in heaven where no personal moraines exist.

I love imagining my daughter in this undefiled existence. Even though I never got pregnant again and missed the joy of being a mom on earth, I rejoice in the sure hope that I will meet my daughter in heaven. I named her Genevieve DeAun, which means: *Victorious heart, pure; Beginning anew, praise.*

One day, Genevieve and I will praise our resplendent Lord together.

---

[1] laminaria – Any of a genus of kelp, applied to the opening of the cervix in order to stimulate dilation. The Free Dictionary © 2012 by Farlex, Inc.

[2] Scripture taken from the New Kings James Version®. Copyright © 1982 by Thomas Nelson, Inc. Used by permission. All rights reserved.

Chapter 52

# BROTHER FOUND & LOST

By Debbie Richards

Thanksgiving Day in 1967 seemed like every other Thanksgiving. Mom was basting the turkey. My sister was peeling potatoes. Dad was reading the newspaper in the living room. An absolutely normal holiday until the phone rang.

The caller asked to speak to my dad. I didn't know who it was on the other end of the phone. I could tell they gave my dad bad news. The caller told him to turn on the TV to watch the breaking news. The four of us gathered in front of the TV. We watched without saying a word to each other. There were some *"oh my God"* whispers from my dad and occasional gasps from my mom. There may have been tears, I don't remember. My twelve year old brain did the best it could to piece together what I was hearing and seeing. Mostly I was confused. I did not ask for clarification and neither did my older sister.

We tried to absorb and comprehend this terrible news as we watched it unfold on television. "Twenty year old biker gang member is shot and killed. Identified as local man, Hank Skelley." We didn't look at each other. I felt very alone, scared and brokenhearted. We were interrupted by the phone ringing again.

There were many phone calls throughout the day and the days to follow. I have no memory of this Thanksgiving beyond watching the breaking news. I'm guessing we ate turkey and sat around in silence. I was in a fog. I was grief-stricken because the TV informed me not only did I have a brother, but he'd been killed by a California Highway Patrolman. A growing sense of betrayal was incited by the unspoken rule of silence regarding this tragedy and the facts surrounding it.

*A brother? I had a brother? How was it possible my parents had kept the existence of my brother a secret?* I had always had a deep longing for a brother. I was envious of friends who had brothers. I pretended to have a big brother who protected me. Who loved me. And on that day I found my brother and lost him all in the same moment. I felt a deep sadness inside me. It felt like a terrible injustice to discover the brother I longed for actually existed and died in this very public way. He was taken from me before I ever met him. I was cheated out of the chance to have a relationship with him.

I was also dismayed when he was touted as a member of a local biker gang. Hearing the news that he had attempted to steal a highway patrolman's motorcycle troubled me. He had been shot in the back as he rode away from the patrolman. *My brother.* Before I even had knowledge of his existence, my twenty year old brother had been alive that very morning and dead by the afternoon.

Later, I listened to the answers my dad gave to my sister when she mustered up the courage to ask a few simple questions. *How? When? Who?* It was even more confusing to uncover the hidden truth my dad had been married before. For twelve years of my life, I was unaware divorce had touched my family. My dad had been married before I was born and he had a son. I asked myself a million times, how could *my* dad disown his first born son even as he had proven to be a model dad to all who know him?

My world was shaken. My personality changed from being light-hearted, giggly and out-going, to shy and hesitant. I sat in the back of my sixth-grade class terrified to raise my hand. I wandered alone on the playground. My confidence was disrupted. I struggled to trust again. My grief was severe as it combined with emotional turmoil. The details continued to live on as a secret. There was no closure. I couldn't tell anyone, "My brother died," because his existence had been a secret. There was horrible shame attached to his death. *Who would sympathize?* To all my friends he was merely a stranger whom the media portrayed as a bad person. But I couldn't believe him to be a bad person. Compounding the grief was the broken relationships within my family. A wedge of mistrust inserted itself into my heart in place of the unconditional love I had previously enjoyed with my parents.

Part of the difficulty in attempting to comprehend the facts came from my dad being adored by all who knew him. He was always outside with us and the neighborhood kids flying kites, playing baseball, or sitting on the front porch laughing and sharing stories with neighbors. The phone continued to ring in the days following the Thanksgiving Day discovery. One caller asked my dad to help pay for the funeral. My dad declined. *Who was this man I thought I knew so well?* Horrible people make choices like these, not *my dad*.

Later in the year my dad surprised me with a puppy he found on his construction site job. He also finally caved and bought me a horse. I had begged for a pony since I was a tiny child. I drew pictures of horses before I learned to write, hiding them in his lunch box. I begged and pleaded. We lived on a shoe-string budget and couldn't afford the expense of horse boarding. Somehow he found a way and my heart slowly began to mend. Even so my inability to trust combined with unresolved grief periodically returned to haunt me.

Forty years later the opportunity to make peace arrived with another life-changing phone call. The voice on the other end of the phone introduced himself as Robert, my nephew. To my surprise my brother had an infant son when he died. My brother had named his son *Robert*, after our dad. Robert was forty years old. He recently uncovered his own family secret. His biological father was killed by a cop when he was an infant. He wanted to meet his biological family. He desperately wanted to meet his grandfather, my dad, if he was still alive.

I was stunned. I thanked God this person existed and chose to find us. I remember the exact moment I got the call. It is permanently etched into my memory. Within a few days I made arrangements for a meeting. I flew to California where my eighty-year old dad lived. Robert and his wife drove in from Arizona to meet the Skelley family. At first Dad denied Hank had a son. "It isn't possible," he said. He was skeptical, but reluctantly agreed to meet under his terms. Dad chose the place and time. Breakfast at Denny's®.

My dad stared at Robert without saying a word. Halfway through the meal he looked at him and said, "You look just like my brother, George." My dad then asked me to trade places with him so he could sit next to Robert. Dad proceeded to tell him story after story about the Skelley family. Sadly, he had nothing to share about my brother. It was heartwarming Dad wanted to share his life with his grandson, Robert. I thanked God for the chance to reunite with a part of my family I'd longed for but never knew.

Robert and I clicked. I felt like I was getting to know my brother. Yet it was confusing to keep reminding myself this is my *nephew*, not my *brother*. We shared pictures and he had copies of newspaper articles from Thanksgiving Day 1967. We filled in some of the blanks for each other. It was healing. Both of us had grown up with family secrets. Finally the truth was exposed. A family connection was made and because of it I was filled with joy.

We said our goodbyes and exchanged hugs. He said, "Call me when you get home!" I felt peaceful as I boarded a plane to come home. Thrilled at the prospect of getting to know this important new part of my family, I pictured our families enjoying Thanksgiving dinners together. We spoke a few times in the weeks to follow. Sadly my nephew told me he had realized after returning home he already had a family. To be honest he was content with that. There was no room in his life for a new family.

It felt like my heart had been ripped from my chest again. The old wound was reopened and I relived the sadness of losing a brother I had never known. At the same time, God whispered in my ear, "I've given you a gift. A part of your brother is alive and well. You have seen him, talked to him, and heard his stories. Accept the gift I gave."

Even though our families won't be sharing Thanksgiving meals, I know a little about who my brother was and I'm grateful God performed a miracle by bringing us together after forty years. My dad passed away four years later. He took the rest of the secrets with him. I'm okay with that.

# Chapter 53

# JOINING THE RANKS OF THE UNEMPLOYED

By Bruce Fong

One spring Saturday I was driving down the freeway on a route I had driven hundreds of times. It had been such a routine often I did not remember driving on several parts of the particular commute. This time, however, was very different. This journey had the uncertainty of my new reality hitting me like a semi-truck. After investing a decade in a not-for-profit ministry this would be my last commute. In the back of my pick-up truck were forty collapsed and bundled boxes ready to be formed into moving containers. It was time to begin packing.

I joined the growing list of unemployed Americans. Since my first paying job I had been gainfully employed for thirty-one years. Over the years I walked alongside several men through the dark world when their economic life deflated like a bum tire. Now, it was my turn. So much of my life had been about intellectual pursuits. This time it was about my feelings.

While driving alone I participated in long conversations with myself. *Who knows how to think through such an unwelcomed world? How does a person prepare for this mental, emotional and spiritual sinkhole for the day and days to come?* Doubt, fear, and sadness were frequent visitors to the conversation.

I had invested so much of my life. My loyalty had been deep to that ministry. I struggled with the abrupt halt of my vocation. Like any sudden loss there was a grieving process. Tears threatened to overflow my eyelids. They almost broke through the surface tension. For a few moments I let the emotions run free. There are no shortcuts through this transition. The ending of my vocation hurt with feelings needing to be purged. Loyalties would find new partnerships and true friends would be kept for the rest of life.

It was difficult to be friendly with myself during this conversation. This world of uncertainty touched deep strains upsetting my personal tranquility. On the one hand I second-guessed my decisions. I wondered about people I thought I could trust. I seethed when the face of antagonistic people come to mind. I shook my head at the innuendo and laughed at the ludicrous allegations. On the other hand, I was seeking a change. I had been experiencing a tug to return to my family, to seek a new challenge and pursue a long-term goal.

Still lost in thought I rolled into the parking lot that would no longer be a regular destination in my life. I was contemplative as I carried a bundle of boxes into my office. In a deeply reflective moment, I played through many of the historic events marking a decade of investing my life in this ministry.

There was a lot of nostalgia connected to the items I packed away. Pictures, reminders of past blessings, and monuments to God's grace at key times often gave me pause in the packing process. The symbolism of closing each box, one after the other, pushed the feelings of this tiresome work further into the vault of my heart. I let out a long sigh knowing a new end had begun. I still deeply loved this ministry. But, bringing this chapter of my life to an end was my choice. It was time for a change. Saying goodbye was sorrowful, but I did it and never returned.

Afterwards it was time to act. The tyranny of the present did not allow for self-centered mourning. Pouting would not pay the bills or put food on the table. Big decisions about the house, moving to a new place and consolidating expenses demanded my attention. Most importantly serving as the leader of my house and assuring my wife God would take care of us was paramount.

Losing the house was a simple reality to me. It was far more emotional for her. Economically, we lost everything we earned over decades of ministry. The downturn in the economy and the loss of work took a massive toll on our lives. It was not the perfect storm, but very close to it. Sorrow was poised to hit us when we were down, steal the vestiges of hope and pressure us into doubt, discouragement, and personal pity.

I am used to long hours on any given day. I continued to wake at five-thirty in the morning without the need for an alarm clock. It was right on schedule for me. In my normal routine the early digits on my clock were normally the first images to fill my retina. My time in the Word and prayer were also the same. Even my writing continued chugging along during the wee hours of the morning. A big part of my day had been planning my calendar. Forward thinking was my *modus operandi*. Scheduling my upcoming speaking and teaching sessions was thrilling. I loved being busy preparing for events, looking forward to meeting people, or cheering others on in their lives. Now I was unemployed, things had changed.

My wife left for her work as usual. That was when things got really weird. My schedule was no longer on a high plain of planning. Instead, I did the dishes. There was enough time to empty the dishwasher and fill it again. Then, I cleaned up the kitchen and had my bowl of cereal. The whole day still stood ahead inviting me to fill it with something. Research filled my morning. I was corresponding, organizing information, and updating my plan for a job search. By the time lunch rolled around I was done with all of my administrative chores for the whole day. That was very different for me.

I met a good friend for a meal. He picked up the tab. I did not like it and missed treating others. I love being generous just to bless others. Besides, I believe deep down inside, the Lord honors a quiet unassuming spirit of giving to others. Checking my desire to be generous was different. *What did I do after lunch?* I went grocery shopping. That is not unusual for me; I often shopped for our groceries. But, I was not used to doing it in the middle of the day when it felt very different to be there.

While my days were different I was determined to make them stimulating. I still kept studying. Besides my contacts for a new position I kept up my discipline of hard work. Prayer was intense. Time with friends was a priority. Faith steps were relentless. My days were different but the same God I have glorified in all I have ever done remained the same.

When my bride came home from her work-day we would enjoy a pleasant meal together. I rehearsed my day's activities to share with her. Without getting her hopes up, I spoke about possible opportunities around the country. Several contacts were thrilled I contacted them. There were even tentative interviews scheduled. My wife smiled. We planned to get the house ready for sale. That was especially hard for her. When you have to leave a home it is the homemaker who feels the loss the most.

After the house sold, we started to count our blessings. A good friend stored our earthly valuables. Another good friend made it possible for us to live in one of his apartments. Still another made sure her church got my contact information so they could consider me as their interim pastor. In the meantime, another friend had their board contact me to serve as their guest speaker for a month. Suddenly I was working again and when we worked over our modest budget, we realized without a mortgage payment we were debt-free.

Our new digs were made possible by a wonderful friend and still have a special place in our memory as one of our favorite homes. Life was simple and joy was restored. Joyous prospects for several ministry opportunities came along and eventually contacts led to a "sweet spot" career move that was never before in our imaginations. The temporary experience of being unemployed was brief and sad. Nevertheless, it was ultimately used by God to lead us to an amazing ministry where we are enjoying the thrill of thriving in His wonderful grace.

# Chapter 54

# VETERANS HANDS

By Prevo Rodgers, Jr

They walk down the street with a loaded gun
Nowhere to hide, nowhere to run
Not knowing today who's wanting to take your life
Going nights without sleep and days without a bath
Warm water to drink, dried food from a bag
They hold their head up high, and they just drive on

'Cause no matter how cold, hot or dry
They go every day and put their life on the line
They do it for your freedom; they do it for the flag
Next time you think you've had a bad day
Go shake a Veterans hand

Well they see the smoke and they feel the blast
Their stomach knots up as you check your men
And Thank God for surviving another roadside bomb
You hear the shot and you see the flash
You hear the thump as your gunner shoots back
Just another day on patrol in a foreign land

And some of you know what I'm talking about
Saying a prayer every time you go out
We do it for the freedom; we do it for the flag
Next time you think you've had a bad day
Go shake a Veterans Hand

Well I've been there and I know what it's like
To be awaken by mortars in the middle of the night
And I've seen a lot of things I hope I never have to see again
So remember next time that you go out
The choices that you get or things you pick out
It's freedom that you get, 'cause somebody made a stand

The next time you think you've had to sacrifice
There's some falling soldiers who paid the ultimate price
And next time you think you've had a bad day
Just remember them

# Chapter 55

# HIDDEN LOSSES

By Melodie Tunney

Often when we think of grievous situations, our minds immediately go to tragic accidents or deaths and illnesses. And while those incidents definitely fit the category of loss and grief, there are also *happy moments* which can cause us to experience grief feelings. When we aren't aware of all of the possibilities, we can find ourselves blindsided by unpredictable grief symptoms and not know where they've come from or why they have happened.

This was my story several years ago. I looked at my *current life* and things seemed to be smooth. My husband and I were settled into the world of empty-nesters. Both of our girls had married and we had a new little granddaughter. We were enjoying ministry related jobs and our health was good . . . there was no outward reason for me to be feeling like I was. Yet during those days, I would find myself sinking into a heavy-hearted, restless, and desolate place. These feelings were particularly puzzling since I'm generally a *glass half full* person.

As I was driving to the airport to pick up my husband one night, I began to cry out to God, "What is wrong, Lord? Why do I feel like this?" After my prayer, I felt led to call a dear friend who had dealt with some of these feelings when she was diagnosed with clinical depression. She had an immediate response after I explained it to her. "Mel, you have experienced so much loss in the last few years. This doesn't surprise me at all."

I began to recount the past thirty-six months of my life. In a nutshell, it began in the month of December when our oldest daughter was about to be married. Two weeks before the wedding my mom had a mild stroke which prevented her from attending. After I knew Mom was going to be okay, I pushed forward. Neglecting to grieve the fact my mother would not attend her granddaughter's wedding. Mistake number one.

My mom passed away suddenly the following June. I grieved her loss, while I was in the throes of preparation for our other daughter to be married in August. So again I pushed ahead, believing my precious mom, who knew the Lord and was in Heaven now, would want us to celebrate this second wedding and not be sad. In hindsight, this was not necessarily the *wrong* way to approach it. But again I did not grieve as I should have. Mistake number two.

The following October, both my husband's father and my dad were diagnosed with cancer. My husband's father had surgery and recovered. My dad's cancer was stage four. He lived thirteen more months and also went to be with the Lord.

In the midst of those thirteen months, our youngest daughter and her husband learned they were going to have their first child. Wanting to be there for the birth, I purchased a ticket to fly to their home in remote southern Oregon with a scheduled arrival date ten days before the baby was due. Our daughter went into traumatic labor a month before the baby was to arrive. Ultimately all was well after an emergency C-section. Nonetheless I still missed the birth and wasn't able to physically be with my daughter during this difficult time.

In summary, there was a lot of change: two weddings, both of my parents passing away, and a grandchild who was born under distressing circumstances. A lot of change. A lot of loss. Some of the losses were very obvious. And others were hidden. For example, when both of our girls married we were excited about adding wonderful sons-in-love to our family. As a very tight-knit family of four, I neglected to realize I would grieve the loss of *what used to be*. Our family would never look the same again.

There also was a realization I should have spent more time grieving the losses of both of my parents. Because I knew they were both in heaven, I moved ahead with the pressing issues of life at a quicker pace than I probably should have, without dealing with the heavy, complicated feelings that needed more attention. Now I was beginning to see how it piled up and pushed me into a pit. Taking time to grieve is important for many reasons. And grieving takes time.

The good news? Nothing in God's economy is wasted. He uses all of our life challenges to increase our faith and draw us closer to Him. Eventually, I spent wonderful time with a Christian counselor. Spilling out the details of each of these life experiences began the necessary healing process. When we delineated through the timeline, it became apparent I had not properly dealt with my losses. There came a point where the weight of them pushed me into the pit where I found myself that night in the car.

I've found since then, facing these experiences – reliving them, sharing them, and not rushing away from them – has been a catalyst for the Lord to heal me and help me move ahead. I have come through this season with a deeper relationship with my Heavenly Father. A better understanding of who He is as our Comforter and Prince of Peace. I also have more insight about the circumstances of our lives that may not even seem like losses, yet need to be dealt with and experienced. Psalm 34:17-18 says, "The righteous cry out, and the Lord hears them; He delivers them from all their troubles. The Lord is close to the brokenhearted and saves those who are crushed in spirit."

Chapter 56

# THE POEM

By Beverly Brainard

The jangle of the telephone broke the still quiet of the early fall morning. The executive director of the agency for troubled youth where I worked was calling.

She said she had to let a counselor go the day before, "Can you come to work full-time?"

I said, "When do you want me to start?"

She said, "Today, right now."

I shoved down my bagel, finished my latte, and was soon being briefed on a stack of client case files. I learned one youth was scheduled to leave the next day, partly because he was unwilling to work on his issues. I was told he wouldn't even make eye contact with the counselors.

Like a simmering headache, empathy for the young man pricked at my concentration all afternoon. *He's too young to be so crushed by life!* I wondered what would have caused him so much grief. As I reviewed my day in front of the fireplace that evening, waves of sadness buffeted me. Going to detention would make life even worse for him. With overflowing eyes, I scrawled blurred lines onto a yellow pad:

**A Piece of Ice in His Heart**

There's a piece of ice in his heart,
that's why he can't get off restriction.

There's a piece of ice in his heart,
that's why he can't put down his guard.

There's a piece of ice in his heart,
that's why he can't allow hope into his world.

There's a piece of ice in his heart,
that's why he can't laugh.

There's a piece of ice in his heart,
that's why he can't trust.

There's a piece of ice in his heart,
that's why he can't love.

There's a piece of ice in his heart,
that's why he glares at the ceiling day and night.

There's a piece of ice in his heart,
but is he willing? Willing
to let tears,
hot, scalding tears
melt that heart of ice?

When I was spent conviction hit me, I had to share the verse with him. The next morning I learned he was at the agency waiting to be transported. It was time to speak with the director. Not sure of what she would say I told her about the poem asking if I could share it with him. She said I could--if he was willing.

I did not know the young man and he had no reason to trust me. I asked if I could speak with him for a couple of minutes in private.

He said, "Okay."

We went into my office. Balanced on the edge of the chair I explained I would like to read him something.

"Do you want to hear it?"

"Yes," he said in a low voice.

I read the poem and then gazed his way. He met my eyes.

I blinked, "You are the only one who can melt the ice in your heart."

He nodded slowly. "Can you read it again?"

I said, "Sure."

Once more I recited the few short stanzas. I looked at him and saw dark, luminous eyes glistening.

He said, "Can I take it with me?"

I said, "I wrote it for you," and handed the paper to him.

He folded the crisp sheet into a small square and slid it in his front jeans' pocket. I opened the office door for him. Back in the lobby he slumped onto one of the green corduroy couches and stared at the floor. I don't know what happened to the young man after he left the agency. I do know those few words held within them the potential to bring the tears needed to melt the ice.

# Chapter 57

# LIKE A FATHER WOULD

By Shirley Logan

**VERSE 1**
I came to you when I scraped my knee
Little girl with little dirty feet
Broken heart, an open wound
You know I looked up to you

Innocent and full of need
A little scared to share my plea
You stood so tall I was wondering
If you'd bend down to see
You gave me

**CHORUS**
Father heart and father hands
Father feet in shifting sands
Heal my wounds with tender eyes
Much to my surprise
You loved me like a father would

**VERSE 2**
Came to you barely seventeen
A little woman broken and unclean
A shattered soul, I took the hard road
Learned my lessons on my own
Ooohhh

I lost the girl and felt the fool
I knew I could turn to you
So ashamed for you to see
But you knelt down to pray with me
With a

**CHORUS**
Father heart and father hands
Father feet in shifting sands
Heal my wounds with tender eyes
Much to my surprise
You loved me like a father would

Chapter 58

# WHERE ARE MY GIRLS

By Mary Humphrey

I look in their eyes. I see love and beauty. I look at their expressions. I see grace, carefree lives, and jubilance. They live in my soul. I feel an ache in my heart from a missing link that seems larger than life itself. My goat barn is now empty. I have an entirely different role in life to fill. My throat compresses. My body aches. My head feels as if it could explode. Tears begin to build behind my eyelids. *I can't do this,* I voice into the emptiness. I feel the pain is more than I can bear. *What did I swallow?* I cannot breathe.

I am trying to choke back grief, sadness from loss, something that cannot be seen, and my fingertips cannot touch. Yet, the sorrow leaves as if the wind picks it up and carries it off, and later returns with a direct hit, a stunning blow when I least expect it. I cry out, with only the trees and wind to hear me. *I cannot do this! When will this pain end?* I ask myself as my pen scratches out words on paper. God steps forward to answer, "Keep on writing, my daughter. You will see." He knows writing is the way I express myself freely. It is the way I reach out to others. In the beginning were the journals I wrote speaking only to myself--therapy.

The eyes I see are not in my own pasture. Kid goats kicking jauntily off rocks and tree stumps are not calling for their mothers or bottles from my barn. The tight udders needing milked are not within my reach. There is no milk to feed my future kids or to be spun into soap. Instead, the soul-searing reflections of eyes go into my stories. I, the goat keeper, help others raise their own. God keeps the animals I care for in His pasture of choice.

*Where are you, my girls?* I miss you so very much. Can you still hear me on the frosty mornings when I am reminded how I cupped your long ears in my hands and kissed you on your nose? You are in safe quarters. I know you are. I made sure of that. None-the-less, your care-takers are no longer me. Through me your character lives on in the stories I tell. The secret conversations I imagined you having when I was not in the barn are being told to the world. Your voices are being heard through mine. When God said to me, "I have plans for you," I picked up my cross, despite the weight that seemed to draw my shoulders down to the very ground steadying my feet. I said goodbye to you one by one. I still see you. I still hear you crying out.

Through my words, I promise to share your loving head butts, whirly gigs, warm nuzzles, nibbles on my nose, and constant companionship with others who, also needed to learn and experience you. This is my promise. This is the design my Father set for me. His will is to be done.

Someone once said to me, long before you left my care, "I believe there are people on this earth who will take care of God's animals in heaven. I believe you are one of them." I will be honored if his words come true. For now, I'll joyfully accept the waves of ache helping me to gain strength, knowing the tides fill my human heart and will never stop rolling in. They will eventually take on the look of beautiful still waters with only a gentle reminder from time to time, just a ripple.

# Chapter 59

# HE CARES

By Linda Reinhardt

When new construction projects declined in our area, my husband Ben got laid off from work. It was pretty stressful trying to pay bills and get Sarrah, our daughter, ready for starting a new school. Thankfully, when we were at the end of unemployment benefits and stretched financially as much as we thought we could handle. He was re-hired by a company where he worked formerly.

When Ben started he received a small sign-on check. It enabled us to almost catch up on our bills. A month or so into the job he heard the husband and wife who owned the business arguing. He overheard his name being used.

What he found out was the company was four million dollars in the hole. They couldn't afford to have another salaried employee. The husband came to Ben's office to let him know he would immediately be put on full time commission; the sign-on check would be his only paycheck for the month.

*Uh, excuse me, Mister!* The check was spent before we ever made it to the bank. We had enough left in our account to pay a few bills and the next month's rent. That was it. And who knew how long it would take to build up enough sales to support our family.

*Ana guess what?* It was December. *Another thing?* I learned this information the day my husband planned a surprise fiftieth birthday party for me. I put on my ugly sweats and curled up on top of my bed in tears. Unbeknownst to me, people were waiting for me to show up at a restaurant to celebrate.

I was so concerned about what we were going to do. Jobs were really hard to come by in our area. It seemed hundreds to thousands would apply for the same job. We had no idea if we were able to obtain unemployment benefits again.

And it was the holidays.

My husband somehow got me to the surprise party. I endured it, but couldn't wait to get back home.

When we finally did come home I put my daughter to bed and climbed into my own. I lay there in the dark wondering why this happened to us again. Why Christmas? My heart normally hurt for children whose families couldn't afford things for them. Now we were in the same place. *How would I explain to my daughter Santa couldn't bring her presents this year?* The same weekend my daughter wanted to decorate for Christmas! Ugh! I put my smile mask on and we started the decorating process. It was hard. I wished for Christmas to just pass so I didn't have to deal with it. I felt pressured by all of the expectations coming with Christmas. Even buying cards was out of my reach.

I felt deserted and bewildered God would allow this to happen again. I still hadn't gotten over the fact I prayed fervently for the last company my husband had worked for to succeed in spite of the recession. I prayed there wouldn't be any lay-offs. But it didn't happen. There were lay-offs.

I had also prayed for my neighbors. The husband needed a job and couldn't get unemployment. They lost their home and lived in a trailer.

I was afraid this would happen to us.

In the midst of all the fear and pain I watched other people I knew prosper. They were living my dream of a steady income, a house, and no worries about bills.

While decorating with my daughter, my sister called to inform me she was coming to pick me up to go shopping. I adamantly said, NO! *Didn't she get it?* We didn't have an income. *Why would I want to go to the store and see the things I couldn't afford to buy for my daughter for Christmas? How could I watch people stand in those long lines buying things for their loved ones?*

I hung up. She called me back a few minutes later telling me she was almost to my house to pick me up. I felt angry. I explained I did not want to go to the store. We were in the middle of decorating. She ignored me and again informed me she would be at my house shortly. I can't tell you how frustrated I became.

Then there was a knock at the door. Surprise! It was my sister.

I was a complete grump. I ended up going with her to the store. We stopped at Starbucks® for a coffee. *How rude right?* I mean I couldn't spend money at Starbucks®.

My sister placed her order. I didn't really pay attention. Ever since she picked me up she had been saying how God told her to do this.

Whatever, I thought.

When she got her drink she turned around handing me a drink too. She also handed me a gift card saying, "God told me to give this to you."

*Wow!* I thought this was cool.

Sipping on our drinks we walked over to the store across the parking lot. I still felt sad, but was touched by what just happened. When we entered the store my sister told me to start picking out the things on Sarrah's Christmas list and to hurry because we had some more stores to go to. She pulled out some gift cards telling me God told her to take care of Sarrah's Christmas.

Tears filled my eyes--just the night before I had felt so alone and afraid. We spent the next couple of hours getting Sarrah's presents. I hid them in the garage and couldn't believe her Christmas was all set.

I was able to go into the house actually putting aside my concerns about our future and enjoy decorating a little bit.

My concerns didn't rest long. Monday's routine put things back into perspective. I was upset about dealing with the repercussions of the recession. I was so discouraged I spent almost an entire day crying.

Then a thought went through my mind. *What am I crying for? What's it going to do? Who cares if I cry? It's not going to change anything.*

Not too many days later I was looking in the empty fridge. *Lord, I'm going to need to go grocery shopping.* I didn't want to spend any money because I didn't know when or if money was coming in again. I wanted to hold on to it as long as I could.

I needed to go get my daughter from school. I had about five minutes. The doorbell rang just as I was preparing to leave. I opened it to a friend from church and other social groups. We were friends but not close enough to visit each other's homes very often. I felt a bit awkward because I needed to leave.

I invited her to join me on my errand. She said, "No, I have groceries." I asked if she wanted to stay until I came back and she said, "No, I have groceries and some of them need to get in the fridge." I didn't know what to do.

She explained she had been to Trader Joe's® and felt she was to buy groceries for us. She had groceries for us in the car. I stood there in amazement. I had just prayed about groceries. Our families don't normally eat together, but she purchased food my family likes. And not only that, but I had a few events I was committed to where I was required to bring *something*. The bags contained things I specifically needed for the events. After we brought the bags in and put stuff in the fridge, I thanked her profusely. I had to leave immediately to pick up my daughter.

When I started to pull out of my driveway I didn't hear an audible voice. Instead I clearly heard some words in my mind. "Remember when you asked, who cares? I CARE."

I knew beyond a shadow of a doubt whose voice I heard.

GOD CARES!

He really does!

I wish I could say the struggle was short lived. But I can't. It went on for quite a while, stretching my faith beyond what I thought I could ever handle. We lived by faith in a way I never thought I would be required to do.

Yet, despite our bank balance God provided. Our church paid all of our bills for entire month! He provided in ways beyond what I could imagine. He is GOD.

In the beginning, God spoke . . . And day-by-day the earth was created through the words He spoke. I've learned on this scary empty-looking road God still speaks. What He speaks happens.

I just need to say in those moments where you feel alone and cry unseen tears. God never sleeps. He never slumbers.

He watches over us night and day. He CARES.

# Chapter 60

# BEAUTY LIVES IN BROKEN PLACES

By Gary Forsythe & Rex Paul Schnelle

Beauty lives in broken places
Hope is found on desperate faces
Healing comes as grace erases the shame
Tears are joy when mercy falls like rain
Let it fall

Glory shines through clouded spaces
Wisdom's found through foolish chases
Hate is lost as love calls out our name
Peace is born as mercy falls like rain

**CHORUS**
Oh. Let it fall
Let it fall on us
Oh, let it fall
Let it fall on us

**BRIDGE**
It may be a paradox
A kingdom unorthodox
But those crushed beneath the rock find life
Let it fall

Beauty lives in broken places
Jesus fills our empty spaces
Healing comes as mercy falls like rain

**CHORUS**
Oh. Let it fall
Let it fall on us
Oh, mercy fall
Oh, mercy fall on us

**ENDING**
Beauty live in my broken places
Beauty live in my broken places
Jesus fills up our empty spaces
Beauty lives in my broken place.

Chapter 61

# THE FRACTURED HEART

By Cathy Koch

The floral heart-shaped box was tied with a filmy raspberry sherbet colored ribbon. It was small enough to fit neatly into the palm of my hand. As usual I tried to guess the contents. *Jewelry? Scented soap?* The box felt a little too heavy for either. My curiosity was piqued.

Quickly removing the bow, I lifted the tiny lid, removing the fuchsia tissue-wrapping that carefully cradled a glass aquamarine colored heart. My favorite color!

Holding it up to the light, the color captured my imagination reminding me of the translucent sea green waves you see at the beach on a sunny day. I studied the heart's surface laying cool in my hand. A myriad of cracks and crevices were beautifully molded together by a process I did not recognize. A true artisan must have created it. Instantly I knew this was a keepsake I would always treasure.

Next to the beautiful heart was a note. "Dear Mom," it read, "This is a 'fractured heart' created from recycled glass broken and molded into a heart shape, then fired in a kiln to become much stronger than any of the broken glass it came from. It reminds me of you…shattered, but re-shaped and formed to be stronger than ever before."

My tears flowed. What a unique insightful gift given by a precious daughter who strayed causing the dissolution of dreams, hopes, and joy. We were now well on the other side, the recovery side, of a difficult two year passage. Both of us had been crushed and bruised in the process. Although our hearts were mending it didn't take much to remember the sorrow of our journey.

How can the fractured human heart become beautiful? When it has been changed from a broken jumbled pile into a masterpiece, shaped and molded by the hand of the Master. This beautiful heart now intuitively understands the grief of another. Once so frightfully broken and destined for the trash, it is not only alive but calm and serene. Having experienced God's peace and comfort the "recycled" heart knows first-hand the depth of God's promises. "God causes everything to work together for good" is not just another empty platitude.

The molded reshaped heart is hopeful not buried in despair and self-absorption. It has moved beyond the questions of, "Why me God?" Instead this heart can ask, "Why NOT me?"

In retrospect I can clearly see the shaping of my character was (and is) hastened by crushing circumstances, by the sandpaper of difficult people and situations, and by the heat of the kiln called God's loving discipline. Although the grief of those two years is not something I want to re-visit I realize other times of grief and losses are still in front of me. My hope and prayer is my recycled heart can bless others with strength enough for the next wave of testing.

Has your heart been fractured? Don't be afraid to go back into the kiln. True, it's not comfortable but it's necessary. Seek comfort and healing from your Heavenly Father's hand. Nestle deeply into His palm allowing Him to bind the shattered pieces with His love restoring your heart to something more lovely and precious.

"…He will give beauty for ashes, joy instead of mourning, praise instead of despair." Isaiah 61:3 NLT

# Chapter 62

# BY STILL WATERS

By Lona Renee Fraser

By still waters I stand
And gaze over the landscape
Of my life
I see the hills and valleys
Peaks and the lowest of the low
I see dreams fulfilled
Dreams left behind
Dreams yet to come
I let the seasons of time
Wash over my soul
Like ageless whispers
Of paths walked and yet to be tread
I look towards the light of the horizon
And imagine sunsets and sunrises to come
I live and breathe in my destiny
Driven by a heart that longs to
Rest
By still waters

# Section Ten
## THIS TOO SHALL PASS
Photo by Lisa Rodgers

# Chapter 63

# THE FUTURE IS RISING

By Kayla Fioravanti

"Jesus said, 'Let the little children come to me, and do not hinder them, for the kingdom of heaven belongs to such as these'" Matthew 19:14

In a fragment of life, pregnant with pain, I caught a glimpse of unadulterated faith in the naïve prayer of my youngest child. Her prayer came out of a place of raw sorrow. I had already spent many hours face down in prayer on the floor sucking carpet fibers while blowing snot bubbles in between weeping gasps when I heard her prayer.

Her prayers were for her brother as the consequences of the world's ways pummeled through our family in waves. No one was immune to the desperation of this time. I walked through the park with my two daughters and I tried to explain issues above their age levels. In the end, I explained all they could do was pray for their brother and love on him.

My youngest stopped immediately and lead us in prayer. As she prayed my broken heart wept. I knew her prayer would literally take a miracle. God not only heard her prayer, but outside of the reach of our influence, He answered it. When we discovered her outrageous prayers had been answered, she squealed in delight, "I took part in a miracle!"

I caught a glimpse into the hope our future held when I witnessed my daughter pour out her expectant prayers. We're standing in the presence of our future. They are here, walking among us. They fill our classrooms wearing the evidence of snack time on their faces. Our future includes those yet unborn, however already planned by God. Our future is learning the song *Jesus Loves Me* for the very first time. They are singing, dancing, and praising Jesus. Our future includes those who have reached their awkward teenage years. They are being taught by the world what it means to be cool. They are learning to drive, taking their first college courses, working their first jobs, falling in love, and suffering broken hearts. They just got engaged, married, and are giving birth to the next generation. The future is young, hopeful, and impressionable. With every daybreak, our future sets and their future rises.

When grasping for glimpses of joy in the midst of raw sorrow, pray with the naiveté of a child. Squeeze in close to the children of our future and catch a whiff of their faith when yours is pregnant with pain.

# Chapter 64

# HE IS THE KING
*Even When He Doesn't Stop the Pain*

By Linda Reinhardt

When I was young I loved to play with dolls. My older cousins gave me some of their dolls when they were done with them. My mom passed down some of my own baby clothes to dress the dolls. One doll in particular was the perfect size. Although her hair was a bit more worn than the others, I loved to dress her and pretend she was my real baby.

When I got to the age where I was supposed to be too old to play with dolls, I would keep them in my closet. Sometimes when I had some time to myself I would take those dolls out and dress them in my pretty baby dresses or cuddly pajamas.

I hoped to have many babies when I was older to replace those dolls. Then I started babysitting. There were quite a few young mothers in the neighborhood with young children and babies. When the mothers left I would look at the pretty baby clothes in the closet. I actually hoped there would be a reason for me to put a fresh outfit on the baby. I enjoyed feeding the babies. I loved to play with the older children too. I enjoyed cleaning their homes. I loved the whole idea of being a mom.

I began to make one bad choice after another in my teenage years. The ultimate bad choice was to have an abortion. When I left the clinic I was completely different inside than when I entered the clinic. I had an empty hole inside of me. I was filled with confusion. The experience was so awful for me the day was a blur.

Years went by and I continued to make some really horrible decisions hurting myself deeply. I learned to emotionally hide behind a big wall I built around my heart. I no longer dreamed of having a family. Although, I was close to my nieces and nephews I closed my heart to the notion and desire of being a mom. I wanted nothing to do with the mom thing.

One day I asked Jesus for forgiveness of my sins and to be the Lord of my life. Not too long after, two incidences happened renewing my desire to be a mom.

First through listening to a radio program I received and believed Jesus had forgiven me for my poor choices, including choosing abortion.

Second, while out three-wheeling with my family I watched my two year old niece get a ride. She had such a good time. She hopped off the three-wheeler and toddled over to me with her arms out. I reached down and picked her up. Just as her fingers touched my neck the walls of my heart broke. I held her close with a rekindled desire to one day hold my own baby.

Having a child was out of the question because of the circumstance I was in at the time. With the desire renewed, though, I grieved daily for a child I didn't know. Then God brought the most incredible man into my life. This man loved God, loved to help others, and loved children. And most of all he grew to love me! Besides accepting Jesus as my Lord and Savior, marrying this man is the best decision I've made in my life.

We had a beautiful fairy-tale wedding. I stood next to a man who was perfect for me in front of a cross, pastor, family, and friends to commit our lives to each other. I wrote a love song my roommate and friend sang together. We even added our testimonies to the programs so people would have an opportunity to receive Jesus. After a fabulous honeymoon we came home to a really nice apartment. We both had jobs. Good cars. Life was amazing.

Then I got sick. I went to the doctor very concerned about how I was feeling. She had me take a test. I was PREGNANT!

I couldn't believe it! How on earth did my life become so incredibly good? Jesus was pouring incredible blessings into my life.

Right after I left the doctor's office I sat at a drive-thru in my car and I put my hand on my stomach. I was so excited there was a little person in there. Just as my hand touched my shirt the name Kevin went through my mind.

Well call it crazy if you will, but I truly believe God told me the name of my child. He named lots of babies in the Bible. And He is the same yesterday, today, and forever. Besides, Kevin was not a name I had ever considered if I had a boy. I had other names picked out, but I knew this baby was to be named Kevin.

I sent balloons to my husband at work to let him know. I found out later it wasn't the best idea. This news was too big to surprise him with in front of his co-workers. We got past it and back to *happy lana* being excited about having our first baby.

I couldn't keep the news to myself. I told the whole world. I was going to be a mom! My family and friends were ecstatic!

I told one of my co-workers and she replied, "Most people wait to tell for a couple of months in case they have a miscarriage." I was taken aback. *Miscarriage? Why would I be concerned about a miscarriage?* God gave me the desire to be a mom again and now He's given me a baby. Why would I be concerned? I snarled inside at her and shrugged it off. She could go ruin someone else's day. Not mine.

I couldn't wait to hold this little guy! I wanted to shop and shop to get ready for him. Nine months seemed so long to wait.

One morning I got up and went into the bathroom. When I stood to flush the toilet I noticed the water was all red. I assumed I was just having a period, like some people do when they are pregnant. I went back to bed, but my stomach didn't feel very well. When I showered a little later I noticed the bleeding was a little heavier. I convinced myself again sometimes girls did have a light period during pregnancy. I knew girls who had instances of bleeding during pregnancy.

We went out to dinner. I had a funny feeling in my stomach. When I went to the restroom I knew it was more than a period. Still, I didn't want to believe the worst.

We went to the doctor the next day. She compassionately delivered the bad news. I had lost my baby. They needed to do an ultrasound to be sure everything was passed and she wanted me to lie on my back for a few days.

My heart filled with a deep sadness. People wanted to come over and comfort me. I wanted to just curl up in a ball and not do another thing . . . EVER. I reached for my Bible for comfort. There had to be something that could speak to me in my pain. There just had to be. I turned to the Psalms because I draw comfort from them when I am down. Psalms 139 told me God writes the amount of our days before there was even one of them. I realized God had written short days for my baby. His plan for my baby's short life really hurt my feelings.

I wondered why. *Why did I have such a strong desire for a child? Why was I blessed with one only to have the baby be taken away before I even got to see his face? Why did I even know his name? How could I go to God who is my comforter, when He is the one who hurt me?* I didn't turn away from God. I just had to deal with so much pain while lacking understanding of His plan.

My husband had to go back to work. I lay in bed dreading each time I had to go to the restroom. I hated seeing evidence of my baby being gone. I hated it. Over and over again throughout the day I was reminded not only in my heart, but because of what I saw when I flushed the toilet.

Lying in bed I turned on my radio and heard a local pastor speaking on a talk show. He suffered with leukemia. He talked about how he got through some very tough days. He spoke about Philippians 4:13 saying we can do all things through Christ who strengthens us.

"That meant *all* things," the pastor said.

He said he could get through the day with leukemia through Christ who strengthens Him.

I decided to try to sit up and put my feet to the floor. I can sit up and put my feet on the floor through Christ who strengthens me. I can stand through Christ who strengthens me. I can walk across the room through Christ who strengthens me. I can do this . . . I can go to the restroom through Christ who strengthens me.

That is literally how I got through those first days. Some faithful friends insisted on coming over. They just sat with me. I didn't have to talk. I didn't have to do anything. They were just there. They were a clear representation of Jesus being there the entire time with me.

Still, even though I realized I could get through the day by His strength I struggled with how I could go to Him for comfort? Miscarriage is so hard to understand. Why does God give some people such short lives?

A friend at church the next week pulled me aside. She had also experienced a miscarriage and also hurt deeply. The only comfort she found was holding onto the children's song, "Jesus loves me, this I know, for the Bible tells me so." She would sing this song over and over holding onto the truth of those words.

I thanked her for telling me about her experience. Yes, Jesus loves me. I knew that. I thought about the type of person I had become before I gave my life to Him. Yet, He still allowed me to receive the precious gift of eternal life and forgiveness of all my sins despite my choices. I had no doubt in my mind He loved me.

It didn't happen overnight, but as I continued to hold on to Him, I got through each day as I continued to believe He loved me. I began to heal.

I had no answers for why He would allow this to happen. Only, it did. I had to decide and believe He was Lord of this situation. Lord of this painful part of my life.

*Could I bow down on my knees and, open my heart? Would I accept even though I didn't understand, He was my Lord of Lords and my King of Kings? If so, then could I also believe He was my comforter too?*

Even though it seemed weird to me I did go to Him for comfort. I prayed, I read scripture and I sang. I sat still in His presence. Healing after my miscarriage was a long, hard and painful road. It led me into the comforting arms of the one who loves with an everlasting love.

# Chapter 65

# NARRATE ME DOWN

By Kayla Fioravanti

A *deus ex machine means,* "god from the machine" is a plot device in which a person or thing appears "out of the blue" to help a character to overcome a seemingly insolvable difficulty.

I have a teenager. Enough said. End of sentence. No explanation needed. Everyone who has raised a teenager, everyone who is in the midst of raising a teenager and everyone who has ever been a teenager knows exactly what those words convey. There are moments of great pride and elation. Then there are days of despair, worry, and angst.

In *The Many Adventures of Winnie the Pooh* Tigger bouncing himself up into a tree perfectly describes how I feel as a parent.

> "**Narrator:** Well, Tigger, your bouncing really got you into trouble this time.
> **Tigger:** Say, who're you?
> **Narrator:** I'm the narrator.
> **Tigger:** Oh, well, please, for goodness sakes, narrate me down from here!
> **Narrator:** Very well. Hold on tight."

In reality my life goes on whether I am narrated out of the tree or I climb down myself. I can't live life clinging to the tree. To say I have spent hours *on my knees* doesn't quite express the gravity of my prayers for my son. In the depth of my grief it was hard to imagine a day when this experience would have strengthened me. It was difficult to see the brightness of the future. I wondered if perhaps God would use this crisis as an opportunity to change me. Or, maybe I would be granted a *deus ex machine* in which the ultimate Narrator will narrate us all down.

On the really hard days, I thought of what Christopher Robin said to Winnie the Pooh in *Pooh's Grand Adventure,* "If there's ever a tomorrow when we're not together, there's something you should remember: You're braver than you believe, and stronger than you seem, and smarter than you think. But the most important thing is, even if we're apart, I'll always be with you."

Jesus said in Matthew 11:28-30: "Come to me, all you who are weary and burdened, and I will give you rest. Take my yoke upon me and learn from me, for I am gentle and humble in heart, and you will find rest for your souls. For my yoke is easy and my burden is light." In Him we are complete. There will never be a day when we are apart. He invites us to come to Him with our burdens and He promises to give us rest. I have found as the mother of a teenager I must rest in His promises while finding my rest in Him.

# Chapter 66

# MY CHOICE WAS LIFE

By Deborah Petersen

All I ever wanted to be was a mom. When I was little I loved to play with my baby dolls. I would line them up and play mom. I talked about how I was going to have over a hundred kids and take care of them all, teach them school, clean the house, and be the best mom ever. Most girls dream of the day they get married and exactly how it would all go; how they would look and how everyone would be saying what a beautiful bride she was.

I dreamed of having a family to call my own. I dreamed of the day I could tell my husband I was pregnant. We would tell our friends and family. We would celebrate together with joy in our hearts and excitement on our faces. Every morning I would wake up with a big smile-and my husband would give me a kiss. We couldn't be more excited and we'd be inseparable. He would tell me how stunning I looked. We would get excited with every kick the baby made. He would be by my side at every doctor's appointment, hold my hair when I had morning sickness and bring me the most disgusting things I would probably crave. Most of all I dreamed of the day we would meet our baby and the way we would look at each other.

At sixteen, I wasn't the type of girl who slept around. Yet, I gave myself away long before I should have and I ended up pregnant. My idea of what it was supposed to be like and reality were so different. I will never forget the day when I told my boyfriend. The first thing he asked me was if I wanted an abortion. I didn't answer. The joy I'd dreamed of was stolen in that moment, replaced with disappointment and fear. Nothing could have prepared me for those words or how I was would hear them throughout my pregnancy. People felt they had a right to decide whether or not I deserved to keep my child or become a mom.

As I sat in the doctor's office waiting to hear a confirmation, most of me hoped it wasn't true. I would learn from my mistakes and still live life like my dream. Yet, a very small part of me had begun to love the child inside of me even though it was unplanned. I already loved the baby I was given, knowing full well I didn't deserve him or her.

When the doctor came in she confirmed I was pregnant and handed me some pamphlets. "You have some options," she said. "You can choose adoption, abortion or even keep the baby if you feel it is best." I will never forget the way I looked directly at her. With a straight face I handed one of the pamphlets back to her and said, "I won't need this one. I do not believe in abortion." I left the office even more confused, overwhelmed and afraid.

Shortly thereafter, my boyfriend and his mom asked if the pregnancy was confirmed and what I planned to do. Embarrassed I told them it was confirmed. I wasn't sure what I was going to do yet. I did know I would not abort the baby. My baby's father left me early in my pregnancy and didn't talk again during it.

Telling my parents was so hard. I grew up in a pastor's family. I was born and raised a Christian. I knew having pre-marital sex was one of the absolute most frowned-upon sins in the church. I anticipated being an outcast. People would see me as the least of them all. I hated the feeling I was about to break my family's heart.

My mother was out of town. I broke the news to her on the phone and asked her to come home. When I told her I was pregnant she just said, "I'm so sorry honey. This is going to be very hard." I didn't get to see the expression I dreamed would be on her face. I didn't get to experience her joy in expecting a grandchild. Instead, I had broken her trust. She was filled with heartache, disappointment and confusion.

I waited for my mom to get home before I told my father. Since my dad wasn't expecting to see her, he was happy and surprised at first. I told him I was pregnant. He didn't utter a word. His happy face changed to reveal frustration. He walked away. We didn't talk much for the next three days. I was so heartbroken. My dad had always been my number one fan and I broke his trust--and his heart.

Next, I had to tell my friends at church. Most of them were disappointed and confused, some even disgusted. With the exception of those who knew me best, they asked the same questions: *Was I going to have an abortion? Was I giving the baby up for adoption? What was my choice?*

Well, my choice was life. Even so, I expected this child to be taken from me because I knew babies were blessing. I never could have deserved this one. I woke up every morning expecting to lose my baby. I anxiously awaited each doctor's appointment so I could hear the heartbeat. At the same time the appointments were agonizing because I was embarrassed. I was embarrassed to sit in the waiting room around other moms. I wondered what the nurses were thinking and saying. I was even embarrassed to talk to the doctor. She would measure my belly, listen to the heartbeat and ask if I had any questions. I would say no, until my mom would remind me I did. I felt like I had no right to be there and no right to ask anything.

I had the cutest maternity clothes, but didn't enjoy any of them. The beautiful, pure, precious woman I dreamed of seeing in the mirror wasn't reflected back at me. I only saw an undeserved baby belly. When I walked throughout the grocery store I heard the whispers around the corner and felt the glares. I would lie in bed at night and the whispered words ran amuck in my head. I would lie there and think about my lost dream of rubbing my belly with joy. Instead, I cried.

People said the unkind words. "You don't deserve that child." "You should have just had an abortion." "I'd be willing to adopt the baby for you." Although the last one sounds nice, it was probably the most hurtful words of all. How could someone think they had any right to tell me they'd do me a favor by raising my child? Particularly since I had not indicated it was my desire?

Every Sunday I would put on my Sunday best, hold my head high and walk into my church with belly showing and tears flowing. I would try to ignore all the looks and the unwelcomed feelings. I went every Sunday to stand before God to worship and thank Him. I knew without Him, I couldn't have endured the pregnancy. I couldn't raise my child without Him.

I waited to take the birthing classes until the last weeks. I dreaded it so much. I could barely hold myself together seeing women with their excited, supportive spouses at the doctor's office. The thought of spending hours in a class for husbands to learn how to be a support of their wives sounded like the most miserable class I could experience. The night of my first class, I sat in the car for a good hour and cried. I walked into the class and saw the scene I expected. The moms were all beautiful and glowing. The husbands were kissing their wives' cheeks and rubbing their backs. I didn't have a husband. With my mom's help and support I survived each class.

As the months went by people started asking how I was doing and feeling. They began to support and love my baby and me. In turn I was more confident with becoming a mom, even though I continued to feel embarrassed. Fortunately, God gave me two very special friends during this time. Both women were older and already had kids of their own. They took me under their wings and helped me through all of my questions. They shared in the joys of my pregnancy. We went shopping and picked out the little outfits and fun toys. We talked about stretch marks, breastfeeding and everything in-between. They constantly texted me to see how I was feeling. They never once judged me.

As I look back, I also had two very special parents. The day I learned my baby was a girl my parent sat right beside me and cried with me. This time the tears were different. They were tears of joy and celebration.

My mother went to every doctor's appointment with me. She went to every birthing class and stayed up after a long day at work to hold me in my bed as I cried. She rubbed my back until I fell asleep. She selflessly loved and cared for me. She bought cute maternity clothes and food to satisfy my silly food cravings. She helped me complete my high school degree. She stayed up to read required assignments with me. It wasn't my mom's fault I got pregnant, but she sacrificed her life to take care of me.

My father was also strong. Even though he was disappointed at first, he quickly realized the role he needed to play for me. I didn't have the husband I'd dreamt of. My dad shared in the joy of having a child with me. He was the hand and feet of Jesus Christ. He selflessly loved me. I experienced terrible morning sickness. Every morning he would hold my hair as I got sick. He made me breakfast, lunch, dinner and even crazy snacks or dessert. He washed all my laundry, took me shopping and held my hand as we walked past the whisperers. He took me to pick out all the items for my baby registry. He took me out to lunch and kissed me goodnight. He set up the crib in the nursery. My dad was the man I needed to help bring me through this experience.

I had three baby showers. One was filled with laughter and given by friends from my previous church. My family threw a surprise shower full of the most wonderful memories and proof of true godly love and support. Then, over sixty people from my church attended a third shower blessing me with gifts beyond my imagination. I finally believed God had me in His hands and everything was going to be okay.

Yes, I made a mistake when I chose to have pre-marital sex. God had already forgiven me on the cross long before my days began. He brought people alongside me people who would accept and love me. He gave me the parents He knew I would need to make it through the trials. And He gave me the strength to keep going. Living through those nine months was the hardest experience I've had. It was also my best experience. I thank God every day for the people He put in my life and the life He has given me.

I graduated high school and am attending college. I have my own house and car. I have been promoted as a supervisor for the company I work for. I also enjoy volunteering and mentoring young girls. Most importantly, I have the happiest, smartest, and healthiest daughter, Annie Grace. If I had listened to people who said I should abort my baby I wouldn't be the woman I am today. I may not have gotten the life I dreamed as a child, but I wouldn't trade this life for the world. I live fulfilled because I chose God and I chose life.

# Chapter 67

# MISCARRYING NOAH

By Bethany Learn

I thought I had a guarantee. Things like miscarriage don't happen to good church ladies. Things like this don't happen to couples who start marriage with a pure courtship and have their first kiss at the altar. Things like this don't happen to healthy women who eat right and exercise. But, they do.

Miscarriage happens to one in every four women regardless of whether they are good, healthy or pure in the eyes of God. It happens and no one really knows why. I didn't know why.

When the cheerful obstetrician offered to do an early ultrasound so we could "see the cute little peanut," I happily climbed up on the table and held my husband's hand while the early-detection wand was inserted. But my soaring heart plummeted when the doctor's forehead wrinkled as he looked at the ultrasound. Then he asked me if I was certain about how far along I was.

I was sure.

He instructed me to go get blood work done.

I waited a week and had more blood work done.

And another ultrasound.

The results showed dropping hormone levels, dropping like my heart and the eyes of the ultrasound technician who couldn't meet my gaze. I clung just a bit longer to hope, until I received the call from the obstetrician who wasn't so blithe about my little peanut anymore. He told me over my cell phone I would be miscarrying.

The baby never had a heartbeat.

The ovum attached, but never developed.

"Sometimes this happens."

That is what he said while I stared across the Olive Garden® restaurant table at my husband. You see, we knew we'd be getting the call, but I had chosen to hope. Chosen to believe it would be good news. And I didn't even order wine because I believed I would still be pregnant, and the tests would just be part of a soon-over nightmare.

I wasn't even bleeding. Everything in me screamed LIFE. My swollen breasts had gone from barely "B" to pleasant "C" cups. My normally fit and trim waist filling out and my hormones . . . oh the hormones!

I hung up the phone. I ordered wine and began to cry. I ate, but I don't remember what. However, I could still take you to the exact table where we sat. *How was I numb, but also aware at the same time?*

The next thing I remember – as if I had amnesia and lost some time – was sobbing in my husband's arms on our couch at home.

I'm not a crier. I can count on one hand how many times I've cried so hard. Once when I didn't get a present on my sister's birthday (hello, I was just a kid!) Another time when my boyfriend of two years left me. And the time over a year after the miscarriage when I cried in the middle of the night because our second child woke me up for the third time and I realized I hadn't showered in four days.

When I lost my first baby, I simply broke down. *Why do people say "lost" as if you misplaced something? And why is it called miscarriage as if you missed the proper way to carry a baby? As if there is anything that could be done?*

All I could do was wait to begin bleeding. The obstetrician told me to call him if I didn't start miscarrying or if I developed a fever. As it turned out, I didn't start bleeding. I did develop a low-grade fever. They scheduled me for surgery. A dilation and curettage – or D and C as it's called. I balked because I knew the procedure was used for abortions. Although my baby never had a heartbeat--and some might say it never was a baby or just a blob of cells--regardless, I didn't want to have hope scraped out of me.

The nurse at my pre-op hugged me tight after I told her my fears. She gently promised me, "We don't do that here. We're the only place in Portland whose doctors don't moonlight as abortionists. Your baby is gone, and your body needs to be allowed to heal before you get sicker." Her words were spoken in truth and love over my shoulder as she embraced me. I felt peace from there on.

Peace as the surgeon's hand rested on my knee and the bright lights faded to black while he counted back from ten.

Peace when I woke up and my husband was there with my sister who took me home.

Peace as my little niece Betsy held my hand as I walked slowly and tenderly from the car to the couch.

Peace as she looked at me with wide, blue eyes and announced my baby had gone to heaven, but I would have more.

Peace from the mouth of a tiny girl who turned out to be right.

Peace yet grief.

I was told I could get pregnant again when I felt ready, but I felt the need to wait. My womb was tied to my aching heart which was connected to my legs that stay closed tight for several months. That was okay since both my husband and I needed time and space to grieve and move forward. We visited the Redwood Forest, camping and staying up late to talk by firelight. We went to Mexico where I wore a bikini for the first time in my life. I told myself it wouldn't be long before my athletic body would truly be gone for good.

I had also been told to see the doctor the moment I suspected I was pregnant again. All the blood tests from my failed pregnancy (there's another rough term to stomach) had revealed a progesterone problem. Getting pregnant would mean more waiting and tests. I would need to have more trust and hope and faith than ever…and I just didn't have it for a while.

Then suddenly I did. Suddenly I wanted a baby more than I wanted to keep hurting. A song had come out on the radio about blessing the name of the Lord who gives and takes away. I was found in the desert place, walking through a wilderness, blessing the name of my Creator and maker of the child taken away, and trusting The One Provider to make another.

I named my miscarried son Noah for the flood of tears and the rainbow promise of new beginnings. And for the GLORY revealed when I rushed in with my positive pregnancy test in December. Just six months after losing Noah, I was again ushered in for an ultrasound. This time I saw a beating heart.

*I'm here! I'm here! I'm here!*

She bounced to announce her presence with each pulse. The tech set her gestation at five weeks and three days, the exact day the heart starts beating. We didn't actually know she was a girl until she was born on her exact due date. I had to take synthetic progesterone through the first trimester to keep her inside me, and I had to do the same with my son who came three years later.

I pronounced her Petra Genevieve Grace, which means "little stone white wave of something I don't deserve but get anyway."

"Oh God, you're good. God, you're so good." Those were my first words after she emerged. "You're the one!" I said to her as I scooped her out of the obstetrician's hands, still bloody from the same womb in which Noah had resided, and held her to my breast, her suckling easing away the final remnants of pain.

Because God is good even when my world falls apart. He is still good when we get what we don't deserve. This world is ugly. Diseases, strife and torment happen. Rain will fall on the righteous and the unrighteous. God is still on His throne. He is good even when my circumstances are bloody messes, and His stone white wave of grace comes crashing over me when I least expect but ache for it. I just need to always watch for the rainbow in the rain.

# Chapter 68

# I CHOSE HOPE

By Sara Shay

"These things have I spoken unto you, that in me ye might have peace. In the world ye shall have tribulation: But be of good cheer; I have overcome the world." John 16:33

I cannot count how many funerals and memorials I have been to. I remember vividly how LOUD my grandfather's funeral was from the grieving. I was only seven years old at the time. After many more sad moments over my lifetime I believe I finally learned a godly and true perspective on what death should mean to a Christian.

*Where to begin my story for you?* There is so much involved in my story. A lifetime of preparation created by loss kept me from being bitter when I suffered my miscarriage. While, of course, I wish things had been different my faith has increased. I believe my walk with God has greatly transformed. I did a lot of healing through crying and praying in the tub. I wrote until the early morning hours.

The hardest part was probably explaining to our not yet five-year-old that I had suffered a miscarriage. We were truthful with her, yet protected her innocence and her future relationship with a loving and merciful God. Our missing child will always be a part of my story, of our marriage's journey, and the shaping of our children. It is one of life's large events that molded me into who I am.

In the months after I physically healed I sought out publishing a book about our family's journey through miscarriage. Quickly I found we were not in a financial place to self-publish. Six months later, on a night my husband was out working I launched into splitting up what I had written so far into blog posts. At least this could get it out there for God to use my pain and sorrow to help others.

My husband wondered why I would want to share my grief. It was mine – for me and God alone. My thoughts. My experience. My walk. But it wasn't. Miscarriage is one of those ultimately sad, but rarely talked about subjects. Blunt godly honesty is hard to find. Facebook® is full of fan pages of women sharing their grief, their disappointment of trying to conceive again and getting another "not pregnant" reading. Some of the sharing feeds our dwelling in sorrow, introspection, and self-focus. I am not saying we should not have these moments – but that is all they should be – moments. Not our life story.

I choose HOPE. I choose to be at PEACE. I choose to share and love, to help and grow. I choose to continue stepping forward.

Three months after our miscarriage we were surprised by another blessing, he is now almost two years old. I think constantly of our Hope. Some who have not lost a child think a new child makes up for the lost one. It doesn't. There is a hole. There will always be a hole, but it makes me cling dearer and hold closer to those here with us. Our youngest is almost a bonus, an extra blessing that we are not deserving of. A true gift! He would not be here without the loss.

# Chapter 69

# BABY JANE

By Shirley Logan

Oh baby Jane, I can't wait to see your face
Hold you closely, whisper love you's in your ear
You never looked me in the eye, to see the love that even I
Cannot explain, no one else could take your place
I know that you're alive, and I'll meet you in the sky

**CHORUS**
When I meet Jesus face to face
And I'll hold your hand and cry
Tears of joy that will replace the pain
I've been waiting
Sweet baby Jane

And oh baby John, you're my one and only son
I'm so proud of who you are, you wear my name
Oh I hope you know, I wanted more than I could show
To be your daddy, be your mentor, be your friend
I missed so much along the way, but I'll be there on the day

**CHORUS**
When you meet Jesus face to face
And I'll hold your hand and smile
I'll rejoice the time has come to tell you
I've been waiting
Sweet baby john

Oh little ones, don't you know I sent my son
To make a way for what I always meant to be
It's a mystery this love, you know you'll never get enough
I saved eternity to show you just how much
You know that I'm alive, and I'll meet you in the sky

**CHORUS**
And when I see you face to face
I will hold you for all time
I'll rejoice with angels singing
Holy, holy
I've been waiting
Sweet little ones

# Section Eleven
# AFTER "I DO"
Photo by Lisa Rodgers

Chapter 70

# TENDERNESS

By Zachary Fisher

"When Peter saw him, he asked, 'Lord, what about him?' Jesus answered, 'If I want him to remain alive until I return, what is that to you? You must follow me.'" John 21: 21-22 NIV

It took a while to find my wife in the parking lot after work. She was tearful and red when I finally found her. She found out today that another couple had become pregnant. Yet here we were, still not. This couple had been blessed with a life, though their addictions would suggest caring for life was not exactly high on their priorities. It was one more cruel punch in the gut. God was continuing to forget her.

I sat in stunned silence for several minutes praying for what to do; what not to do. I finally pulled the car away and held her hand. I could feel the Spirit telling me, "Don't speak." We were almost home before I finally felt the release to say something. All I could muster was, "I'm sorry this made you feel this way. I'm sorry situations like this put you in a state where you believe vicious lies about yourself, your value and your worth." I told her she should take a bath when we got home and I would get dinner.

When I returned with our Chinese food, she embraced me. She said she loved me and I was a good husband. She thanked me, apologized for "freaking out," and said if our lives never changed she would be happy with me.

Tonight, I understand a little better how Christ loves us. And how good it must feel for Him when we, His bride, tell Him He is good. When we thank Him, apologize for "freaking out," and confess if our lives never changed we would be happy with Him.

Amen.

# Chapter 71

# A MAN OF GOD, NOT REALLY

By Clay Crosse

The year was 1998. I was cruising along in extreme comfort mode. By most indicators my life was perfect. I had a wonderful and beautiful wife, Renee. We had two sweet daughters ages five and one. My career in Christian music was flying high. I was busy piling up number-one songs and multiple Dove Awards. Offers were streaming in for interview requests, cover stories, and concert bookings.

All this was my dream come true. I had imagined such a life for a long time. But growing up as an aspiring singer I had also known the odds of making it were slim at best. I'd been realistic, accepting I would probably never actually have the kind of life I dreamed of. I planned to work a normal job and music would simply be a side hobby, I thought. In the early nineties when it all started to really happen for me I loved every aspect of it. I was able to leave my day job as a driver for FedEx instead I was touring full time. I was living my dream. It felt great. It felt new. It felt right.

But something wasn't right. Specifically . . . me. I wasn't right. I was . . . off. Off from what I was supposed to be. Off from what God wanted me to be. Just off. I was so focused on me. So focused on my comfort, my fame, and my pleasure.

That year though, God reminded me He was still there and He still loved me. He really wanted my life to be different, even better. He wanted to be close to me. Sadly we just weren't very close. I was too busy with me. My life was too crammed with my desires to devote any time or energy to Jesus.

God has a variety of ways of getting our attention when He knows we need to be reminded to listen to Him. He got my attention through my singing voice. Sounds like a strange way to tap on my shoulder. I know it is what He was doing—and in retrospect it was probably the best possible way. I was on the Stained Glass tour with Jaci Velasquez. Stained Glass was my third CD release. To some observers it was my strongest project to date. We were all sure it would only propel me to a higher level of fame and success.

In the middle of the tour something interesting and terrible happened to my voice. I lost it. Maybe not entirely, but there's no doubt I lost much of my ability. It was so weird, so unreal. I couldn't do the little things vocally I had been able to do my whole life. I called Renee from the road saying, "Honey, something's just not right with my voice. I don't know what it is." She tried to encourage me by saying everything would work out or my voice would heal. Others said, "Don't worry, Clay. It will come back." I sure hoped they were right because I was having an extremely hard time trying to get through my concerts.

The weeks turned into months.

This situation upset me like nothing I ever faced before. I was scared to death I was going to lose the dream-life I had acquired. I put all my hope in my singing ability and was convinced if I lost it I would be worthless.

I looked for help at the Vanderbilt Voice Center in Nashville. It specialized in training, repairing, and maintaining the voices of singers. The doctors inserted a tiny camera down my throat. We looked at my vocal cords on the monitor. Truthfully, I was hoping they would look at them and say, "Ah-ha . . . there it is. You have nodules on your vocal cords. We found the problem. We'll have to do surgery, followed by months of rest. Then you'll be back to your old self."

Isn't it strange? I actually wanted the doctor to find a problem. Therefore I could make sense of what was going with my voice while on the road. But no, they didn't see a thing. My vocal cords looked perfectly fine. It should have been good news. However it left me even more confused and asking, what in the world is wrong with my voice? Why can't I sing like I used to? It was maddening.

As a result I made an appointment to see another vocal therapist--a specialist, a vocal coach. I went to Chris Beatty's office telling him all about what was going on with my voice. I had hopes he would put me on a schedule of vocal exercise and diet to fix the problem. He sat listening as I explained. I didn't mention anything about my personal life. I simply talked about my singing.

I'll never forget the first thing he asked, "Clay, what have you been reading . . . in the Bible?"

(Pause)

"How's your prayer life?"

(Pause)

"Are you serving anywhere? I mean, I know you're out doing concerts and I hear you on the radio and see you on TV and such. But are you plugged in anywhere really serving?"

(Pause)

"And how are you and Renee?"

(Pause)

"Clay . . . are . . . you . . . a . . . man . . . of . . . God?"

I sat stunned in silence, completely speechless. Like a deer frozen in the headlights. Grasping for something . . . anything to say. But I merely sat there. Nothing.

Next I felt the tears coming. You know the feeling when there's no stopping them. At first you think, *Okay, I'm getting kind of choked up here. I'll do it quietly. No one has to know. Maybe I'll just get a little misty-eyed.* Then you realize the feeling is deep. Something deep inside has been absolutely touched. The tears start flowing. And you can't do it quietly. There's no way. You just start sobbing.

That was me in Chris's office. I'd known this man for only fifteen minutes and I was crying my eyes out.

Talk about a wake-up call. Talk about a ground-zero moment. As it turns out the meltdown in Chris's office was great for me. The moment showed me something. Something I had been blind to. I saw I was far from God and my life was spiraling out of control. Chris asking me those questions (things I now categorize as Christianity 101 type questions) showed me where I was. And I didn't like it. I was far from God. I needed to get closer to Him. Being closer to Him is what I wanted most.

At the time of the meeting with Chris Beatty, Renee and I had been married for eight years after having dated the prior six years. We were close. Very close. We were the type of couple who thought alike, talked alike, and even looked alike. We finished each other's sentences all the time. We were tight.

Being this close also means you can't hide much from the other. Oh you can try. In the end your partner always knows something's up. It's nonverbal. She just knows.

I couldn't keep Renee in the dark about what I was feeling after my visit with Chris. She could see it in my eyes every day. Something was cooking in my head and heart. She knew it. Finally I blurted out, "Honey, we need to talk." We were at church of all places when I told her. I asked her to get a babysitter for the afternoon so we could talk. This alone told her I was serious. "Why do we need to be alone? Just what do we need to talk about?" she asked.

Once we were alone I unloaded everything. I let her know I needed to change my life. I informed her that our seemingly perfect life . . . was not. I had issues. I had a secret life.

She knew I had been agonizing about my singing difficulties. She knew how bad it was hurting me. Other than my voice she thought everything else was pretty much normal.

I told her, "Renee, I'm a mess. You know my singing has me very upset. I am feeling God telling me my whole life is a mess. And it is." She sat there looking at me wondering what on earth?

I had to tell her. It was time to take responsibility. It was time to own up.

"It's my thought life," I said. "It's wrong. It's sinful. Renee, I know you are aware of my seeing some porn before we got married. You must have thought, as I did, it was out of my life since then. Honey, I have to tell you . . . I have been seeing it again lately."

She stared at me. There was a deeply sad look on her face. There was anger and hurt. I continued, "Honey, please hear me. I have not committed adultery. There is no one else. It's just my thought life is driving me in that direction. I can feel it. And if I don't change things I know we will be destroyed."

It was the best day of my marriage. I'll admit it was tough. Actually, tough doesn't really sum it up. My admission wounded Renee and it was tough on me too. It hurt. We cried. We screamed. We cussed. We prayed. What? Wait a minute now.

Let's replay that . . .

They hurt.

They cried.

They screamed.

They cussed.

They prayed?

Yes, we prayed. It was one of those crying-out-to-God prayers. Yes we prayed with real tears. One of those "We-need-help!" prayers. Or more accurately it was one of those "I'm-so-messed-up, help-me-God!" prayers.

Here's why I refer to the day as the best day of our marriage. That afternoon marked the beginning moment of our rededication to Christ. Why do I call it our rededication to Christ? After all it was my problem with porn not Renee's. It was my failure not hers. Well, in the weeks and months to follow, we both started to realize the porn was a symptom of a much deeper problem. I was far from God. That was the problem. And Renee also came to the same realization about herself. As a Christian couple we were not where God wanted us to be. We saw clearly we had become flat-out in love with the world, with ourselves and with our comfort. We had managed to carve out a little life with only so much room for God.

God's Word was talking to us in a clear way. "Don't love the world's ways. Don't love the world's goods. Love of the world will squeeze out love for the Father. Practically everything going on in the world—wanting your own way, wanting everything for yourself, wanting to appear important—has nothing to do with the Father. It isolates you from Him. The world and all its wanting, wanting, wanting is on the way out. Whoever does what God wants is set for eternity." (1 John 2:15-17, MSG)

This passage and James 4:4 hit me hard. They held a huge mirror in front of me yelling, "This is you, Clay! This is you!" I could no longer deny I loved Planet Earth. Specifically, I loved our nice little existence in lovely Brentwood, Tennessee. I liked my house . . . too much. I liked my cars . . . too much. I liked my fame . . . too much. I was comfortable. Furthermore, I wasn't driven to pursue much more than my own happiness.

After my rededication God started showing me so much. Every area of my life began to change as I started looking for Him more and more. It was amazing. It was life changing. I felt like a different man. In fact I recorded a CD and titled it "A Different Man" for this very reason.

It felt great. It felt new. It felt right. Now, more than ever!

The following months were nothing short of amazing. There were times during this season of my life I remember praying, "God, I feel so close to You right now. It feels great! I see clearly what a clown I have been in the past. Now I see just how far Your love has extended to me. Thank You, Father!"

I would continue, "But Lord, I don't want to go back to where I was. I want to stay close to You. I want this fire to keep burning in me. I don't want to lose this. I don't want to get distracted with life and forget this."

I needed reminders.

I wanted something obvious placed in my line of vision. Somewhere I would be on a daily basis. My car! I decided to place a reminder on the dashboard of my car. At first I thought maybe a little scripture could be taped there. Not a bad idea. Then I thought maybe a picture of my family, another great idea. Eventually I wanted something even more obvious. I remembered having seen a little Jesus figurine somewhere. Thank goodness for the Internet because it made it possible to have a little Dashboard Jesus in my mailbox a few days later. I put it in my car and immediately knew I had done something strange. Something, well, abnormal. I kept it there anyway. (As a side note, it came as a bobblehead, but over time I couldn't stand the bobbling so I glued it down. Jesus doesn't bobble, does He?)

Yes, I simply put it in my car as an obvious reminder to myself. After all, how much more obvious can you get? The little statue was staring at me. As I said before, it was merely a plastic figurine. I didn't bow down to it. I didn't talk to it even as I did look at it. After all it was right in my line of sight. When I saw it, it reminded me of things. Important things.

Things like . . . Jesus is here. Jesus is always with me. The real Jesus, He is here. Don't shut Him out. Don't ignore Him. Don't forget Him, Clay. Don't ever forget Him because He certainly won't ever forget you. When you allow Him to be crowded out, when you are far from Him and when He's the last thing on your mind:  it is the very same time He is longing for you and the same time you are central in His mind.

I'm reminded to take Him with me everywhere I go. I'm reminded not to live a distracted life. I'm reminded to stay focused on Christ. Always.

Chapter 72

# WE NEED TO TALK

By Renee Crosse

It was the summer of 1998 when my husband was dealing with some ongoing vocal problems. He was a singer with a successful music career traveling all over the country performing concerts. Imagine if the one thing you do well, is suddenly reduced by half. He was beginning to freak out and so was I. It was a particularly stressful time in our marriage.

Clay's vocal problems led him to the office of a man who would ask Clay a handful of questions forever changing the course of my husband's life and our marriage. My husband went to him for vocal instruction. Instead, the man followed the lead of God asking my husband about the condition of his spiritual life.

The following Sunday morning we were in church. Picture this: The music is playing. Everyone is shaking hands. There is a good feeling in the room. Well, Clay ruined it for me when he whispered four words into my ear. "We Need To Talk." What is it about those four little words? You know from the moment you hear them it is not going to be an enjoyable conversation. I knew Clay was well beyond concerned about his voice, but I also recognized my husband was really struggling. To be honest I wasn't sure if I wanted to find out what we needed to talk about. I was terrified of the outcome. Several scenarios played out in my head as I sat through church services. I felt numb walking to the car to go home with him.

As we entered our home Clay, immediately went to the family room and sat on our sofa. He waited patiently for me. I joined him and he began to confess an issue he had struggled with for a long time. He assured me he loved our daughters and me. He wanted to be better for us. He wanted to be the spiritual leader of our home. He knew right from wrong and he knew God was getting his attention about this one particular area in his life.

I managed to blurt out, "What is it, Clay?"

My husband admitted he struggled with pornography and how lust began when he was a little boy. The first exposure to a magazine had such a negative impact on his life. The image stayed with him fueling his desire to see more. It was something he managed to hide from me. God was instructing him that this had to be revealed before it destroyed him. It wasn't something he did all the time. A few movies, a magazine . . . however the lust factor in his life raged. He confessed while he had not physically committed adultery, in his mind he had many times. He knew what God's Word said about this. As a Christian man he knew this was something he had to confess and receive forgiveness both from God and from me.

The grief washing over our home this day was palpable. On one end of the sofa sat a man completely broken, asking for forgiveness. On the other end sat a wife who felt betrayed by her husband's thought-life. I wept as I asked questions about why he needed to see this type of material. *Was it my fault? Did I not satisfy him sexually?* I thought we had a great intimate life. *Why? How could he hurt me like this?* Clay answered my questions honestly and humbly. Assuring me it was not my fault. It was completely *his* problem and struggle bringing all of this pain upon us.

There were so many tears. We cried out to God asking for Him to heal our hearts and heal our marriage. A fracture occurred. I never once thought about giving up on Clay or our marriage. Was I grieved? Absolutely. I don't recall ever crying out to God as passionately and intently as we did that Sunday. What started out as a confession on the sofa ended in both of us on our knees crying out to our God for help. I don't know if you have ever experienced such a moment. I'm talking about crying out loud, tears flowing, snot bubbles blowing out of your nose crying. There was something about the release of this through prayer and tears that was a balm over our hearts and minds.

We both knew there was a long road of rebuilding trust ahead of us, establishing accountability and seeking counsel. We both felt grief leave us as quickly as it came upon us. The grief we experienced was self-inflicted. Foolishness in the sight of God will not go unnoticed. As we lifted up our heads, the sun was streaming through our family room window. The slice of sunlight illuminated the area where we knelt. God will always bring light to what needs dealt with in the lives of His children. Our faith led the way to heal our grief. We are thankful for the healing and growth we have experienced in our individual lives and in our marriage. Grateful for the fact He continues to allow us to share our story to help other people struggling with the same issue. God heals. God restores.

# Chapter 73

# I WANT THOSE DAYS BACK AGAIN

By Paul Dengler & Gary Forsythe

**VERSE**

I look back and remember
The moment is so clear to see
We promised forever
I'd be there for you, you'd be there for me

**CHORUS**

A whole lifetime together
Side by side, holding hands
I want those days back again

**VERSE**

Our love was easy
Never a need to pretend
There were no secrets
No wounded hearts to defend

**CHORUS**

A Lifetime before us
Side by side holding your hand
I want those days back again

**BRIDGE**

Lost in forever, the nights would slip by like the wind
Closer together than any two lovers have been
I want that again

**VERSE**

Sun through the window
Touches the tears on your face
Where did our love go
How did I lose your embrace

**CHORUS**

I'll never leave you
For better or worse, I'm still your man
Baby, I want those days back again
I want those days back again

# Section Twelve
# THE AFTERMATH OF DIVORCE
Photo by Lisa Rodgers

# Chapter 74

# BILLBOARDS, GOSSIP AND AWAY

By Lynn McLeod

Only a couple of the heads up calls from "well-wishers" warning about the billboard came from people trying to soften the blow for when she would inevitably see it. The others were from gossipers trolling for reactions to fuel their appetites. She recognized the difference and hugged her privacy as a new best friend. But now just as she expected, when she rounded the corner from her neighborhood street lined with pretty homes, onto the main thoroughfare with six lanes decorated by a multitude of signs touting a brand . . . was the billboard.

The traffic light turned red, resulting in a full two minutes of idling to ponder the details missing from the "well-wishers" calls. Under the headline, "New name . . . same old service." were the professional headshots of her husband, the attorney, and the realtor wife who had taken her place by his side. The new couple formed an alliance giving way for a marketing scheme, but failed to estimate the voyeuristic nature it would create. Nonetheless, there it was.

The photos they chose were dated, and she knew at least for his, over fifteen years passed since it had been taken. They both looked smart, professional and successful, yet hardly identifiable as themselves in this day or time. She wondered if five hundred dollars would be enough to entice someone into climbing up and painting "Wife stealing service" below the headline. As tantalizing as it may have sounded, it was a fleeting thought shifting into awareness--it wasn't anger she felt, but a profound sadness.

She delicately placed the image of the billboard into the "this too shall pass" category as the light turned green and she traveled to her destination, even as she lost track of where she was going. What appeared to be wandering in the wrong direction by way of a daydream was instead a practice she'd become far too familiar with. It bought her the extra few minutes she needed to adjust from the tragedy of her situation to the harsh reality of putting one foot in front of the other. Some would call it "rebuilding" her life, but she was at a loss as to how to begin. So she circled around the same familiar patterns searching for an opening to lead her where she would go. The vague fog blanketing her journey was a shelter from the unbearable jagged edges of sharpness heartbreak couldn't avoid.

On the sidelines were many who with the intention of being helpful weighed in with specific instructions as to how she should be, what she should do, and how she should move on. None of the advice seemed familiar. Still she followed some of it simply to be in motion. It wasn't the misstep frightening her as much as becoming stuck. Stuck in a place where her situation was befitting and the opening never came. It was by way of the encouragement where she accepted an invitation for a dinner date with a friend of a friend. It went well, awkward and distracting. He seemed to be a nice man. The second date came with plans to meet at a quiet neighborhood restaurant. He arrived before she did. When approaching the table and sitting across from him she noticed an uneasiness that hadn't accompanied their previous meeting. He ordered two glasses of wine, saying he had some things he wanted to ask her about before they decided on dinner.

In his enthusiasm from their first meeting, he explained, he asked some other friends about her. What he learned troubled him into compiling a list of sorts. A list of rumors and gossip he now wanted verification or explanations for, including some she had heard before. A couple of them were new, striking in places far more intimate than was acceptable table talk between two people who recently met. She could feel the muscles in her face become tighter, her smile change from genuine to rigid and her eyes grew heated. Hidden below the tabletop resting on a black linen napkin her fingers twisted around her hands in a clenched format of controlled displeasure. It wasn't simply in his asking, but in his confrontational manner of distrust that struck such a visceral chord within her. He had given an audience to the one thing she despised. Lies.

Knowing there was nothing to be said to erase his suspicion, she listened. When he came to the point where questions solicited answers, her only response was if she refused to gossip about anyone else, she would not begin by gossiping about herself. Placing the black linen napkin on the table she excused herself and quietly left.

She hadn't considered hers as a high profile divorce. It appeared to be growing into such within the borders of the small town where she tried to live. Before she could uncross her eyes from the highly calculated sucker punch her husband delivered, she was navigating the public perception that seemed to strike when least expected. For in her naivety there was no room for anticipating an opponent quite as adept at unpredictability. The roller coaster ride was unavoidable when she ventured beyond her own doorstep. She found her natural pace in life interrupted as her comings and goings changed from being spontaneous, to being designed with precision. Her energy was low and her spirit was lower. She hardly recognized herself.

Somewhere out there lingered the woman she knew, trusted and loved. She simply couldn't find her through the maze of wandering or the abruptness of her circumstances. Almost with regularity she woke in the morning making promises to herself. Today, she wouldn't cry. Today, she would keep moving. Today, she wouldn't listen to the voices trampling in her head. Today, she would ignore the beast chasing her into the darkest places of her soul. Today she would pray.

And almost with regularity, she failed.

In her failure came the fruitful details of life to distract her. She sometimes remembered to take the garbage to the curb on Sunday evenings; to unload the dishwasher; to set the thermostat when weather changed; to fetch the mail and from time to time to buy groceries. And sometimes she forgot. Her meals became a necessary evil as she ate standing up or walking, always avoiding the table. On her bed lay an array of decorative pillows fashioned for the perfect picture of contentment. The secret arranged neatly among them hid how when she slipped in between the covers rather than remove the pillows she gently pushed them to his side to fill the void she could not sleep with. She was lost.

The promise she kept to herself one arbitrary morning was to actually attend a cocktail party where friends were gathering to celebrate a birthday. To guarantee her resolve, the day was spent in distracted preparation. Nails, hair, clothes all practiced and designed for the precision she feared was necessary. Far from being relaxed, once at the party she met a woman who projected a warmth and confidence she envied. As they chatted about random subjects, each with a combination of significance and irrelevance, she was drawn to the idea of making a friendship with the woman. It seemed to rest in a natural place for her to have a girlfriend who hadn't known her during her previous life. One who apparently didn't associate her with the rumors. And perhaps she could make an unfettered first impression. The woman was a curator for a museum in town, single with grown children, bright, funny and kind.

No sooner than when the woman stepped away to refill her glass of wine, one of the familiar "well-wishers" took the woman's place asking if she knew whom she had been speaking with. Unbeknownst to her, the "well-wisher" was adamant to explain, the woman was the ex-wife of a prominent businessman in town. Despite having changed her last name and being divorced for over ten years, the woman remained concreted to her past. She remembered vaguely hearing about their scandal. As in keeping with her values, she rarely paid attention to the gossip. Now ten years later, the woman she envied stood in the shadow of her own former life. Forget the time, the accomplishments or the circumstances that should have passed. Focus landed like a thud on the one tragedy of the woman's life she knew was not who the woman chose to be. Nevertheless the whispering "well-wishers" did not relent in feeding their appetite.

As she watched the woman from across the room filling her glass, crystals fell from their exchange as clarity sliced through the fog. It was unmistakable. She too would forever stand in the shadow of her former life, if she stayed. There was no escaping the past until one flung open the path toward the future. She could change her name, profession or appearance and let time take its toll. None of it would rebuke the shadow. Not even her denial. Perhaps the woman found a comfortable place to settle within the captivity. She knew she wouldn't.

She found the opening to where she would go. Away.

The "well-wishers" considered it rash, unstable or peculiar when they found the realtor's "For Sale" sign staked in her front yard. Like a feeding frenzy over the last tidbit of morsels left for prey, the chatter rose and the vividness of the lies increased in color. She rested in a peace knowing her category of "this too shall pass" did not come from endurance any longer, but from the freedom of hope.

It wasn't simply a hope for where she would go. It certainly would be the first step. More importantly, it was for the woman she knew, trusted and loved to step out from a future in the shadow of her previous life. The world was wide open. The possibilities were abundant. And her wandering became an intentional journey where anonymity from "well-wishers" was a practiced safe haven.

As unintentionally as when she first heard the rumors, she ended them with one intentional step. She looked around, but not much. She considered her options, but not carefully. She compared the pros and cons, but not specifically. No really, she didn't. She looked north and it seemed colder. East and west looked like more of the same old-same old. So she headed south. There was nothing significant about the step apart from it being intentional to move her away and out from her previous life.

If you've ever felt the weight of a shadow, you know it is enormously elusive while you're carrying it. It bears down like the heavy woolen winter coat draped across shoulders at first for warmth and then begins to feel as if it can't be shed. Ahhhh . . . until the first warm sunny day when benign signs of spring fade in and out dancing for attention you are so eager to give. The flowers aren't quite in bloom as they press toward the surface. The grass isn't quite green as the browns begin to turn brighter. The hours aren't quite long enough as they stretch a subtle bit longer before the sunset calls for an ending. And the smell isn't quite so chilly as you inhale a full, deep breath. Thus was precisely how she went away.

# Chapter 75

# EMPTY NEST OF THE BARREN WOMAN

By Rebecca Marmolejo

The Barren Woman awakens - -
        a room full of light, but there remains an empty bed.
Her lover chose--
        a room empty of light where there remains full beds.
                        Tears fall.
By God's grace she's forgiven him, causing love to increase the more.
She thinks to herself, "What cruel rapids of love that have nowhere to pour."
She struggles still to forgive herself for who she chose to love.
Tears stream down her face with unseen blessings from above.
Though emptiness tries to swallow her, she breathes in gratitude still,
At least her heart can feel again –life signs showing, it's not ill.
The Barren Woman starts her day like this time - and - time again.
        "When did grief become a lifestyle? Oh God, when will it end?"
There is a pain much greater, than your love tossed out like trash,
The pain that comes from a love filled heart – spilling over, where can it splash?
She wipes away the tears and calls on the name of the Lord.
Then cries out again, "Dear God, what's all this for?"
        Her nest is empty, her pantry is empty,
        The silence is loudest of all;
        Not even a babe's cry, no less laughter to fill the walls.
She remembers her child who never saw light, at least not on earth.
God rescued her child stealthily, before she could give her birth.
What a grace; what a tragedy,
That a vacant womb could be a gain.
This child went from life to life, though no one knows she came.
The Barren Woman thanks God again for saving her daughter's life
Her one request over her womb was that her child would know Jesus is Light.


Sovereign God births life from death, God did it in the Barren Woman's womb
He even did so in a covenant's death, When He emptied His own tomb.
God is faithful and more faithful still even when you aren't
He loves you so very, very much and you will not be forgot.


He did not forget Hannah, nor can He forget you.
No respecter of persons, He can make your womb brand new.
Like our mother Sarah, who was far too old to birth
He speaks life into being just as He did the earth.
Sing oh Barren Woman, wail if you must
Your Father is the comforter who makes life out of dust!
You may find your nest empty; yes, He's made you for love it's true.

You may find empty photo frames with nothing yet to do.
You may find the woman in the mirror a stranger to your eyes.
But rejoice oh Barren Woman that's only grief's disguise.

Father will not forsake you. This He cannot do.
He's always true to Himself and forever true to you.
Only He is more than able to give and give and give
To give you what you can't give yourself. So you may fully live.

What you could not do for yourself, your child or for your love
He will do within you, not just somewhere up above.
He is love that is Right and True, His love is everything
So sing oh Barren Woman, Sing, sing, sing!
Sing oh Barren woman, wail if you must!
Go ahead, let it out – go ahead – just bust!

Trust Him with your heart again and He will give it wings
Let His heart fill up yours and watch just what this means.
If you find your nest still empty it will not be the same.
Do not forget dear love, why it is He came?

Barrenness is NOT your portion; it was taken at the cross
Lift your heart, lift your head, give thanks for what's not lost.
You're in His heart and thoughts, you are in His care
See the life signs of fruitfulness every- everywhere
It may not look like what you thought, but your heart is still alive
God is giving you new life, for this reason Christ did die.
Let your heart overflow, Let your heart run free
You were made for fullness of love, emptiness is past you see.
Sing oh Barren Woman as the Word of God declares,
        "More are your children, than of the woman with a man."
Arise oh beautiful daughter. Tears, rejoicing and all
Life is a mixed bag of events and sometimes we do fall.
Get up - get up – arise.
Run your race now.
No one else can run like you.
It's only you who will know how!

# Chapter 76

# SITTING IN THE PEW ALONE

By Dana Lyne

No matter who left whom, divorce feels like rejection. It's a fog surrounding your very being with every step you take away from the life-altering decision.

One of the altered aspects of your life might be your church experience. Now when you attend, it's with a gaping hole in your heart. Maybe you attended church with your spouse. Perhaps, you were invested in taking your children too. Once divorced, the weekend parent has the privilege of taking the children to church. Maybe you were involved in several ministries you don't fit in anymore.

When my daddy died, the church sent a gift and I received a phone call. When I got divorced no one sent a card or called.

As you look around you notice the married couples with shining eyes. As a divorced woman now, the married men act differently towards you. The brave ones still speak to you only in a guarded way. They're afraid to get too close because you may be lonely and cling to them. The rest won't even make eye contact leaving you to feel as if you don't exist at all. The women are worse somehow. If they know you, they hug you saying things that make you feel so pitiful. If they don't know you they ask, "Where is your husband, your child?" Every time you repeat your little memorized story the knife cuts into your gut again and the fog thickens. It isn't her fault when she looks at you with her sad eyes you feel ashamed.

Sitting in the pew you listen to the pastor tell a joke to lead into his sermon. Of course, he's talking about family again. He speaks of the roles of each family member. You notice a wife nudge her husband and smile as he puts his arm around her. Somehow it feels like they mock you. No one touches you anymore. You are alone in the pew and alone afterwards. Happy families dart off into their busy worlds and leave you behind. You go home to eat alone and to nap alone.

And the adventure of discovering a small group where you fit begins. Why do I feel like a leper? Like I have a dreaded disease no one wants to catch. Sometimes you're in a room filled with married couples when they mention someone getting divorced. "Why didn't they try harder? The Bible says it's wrong. How could they just give up? Didn't they make vows to one another? Didn't it mean anything? How could they do it to their children?" And the wound deepens; the fog thickens. You sit alone in the pew reliving the pain of your own divorce. Somehow you wander into the single parents' class only to sit through an hour of people commiserating and putting down their "ex." Wow, that was uplifting.

Suddenly there are a million more things to do. Everything needs repair. The toilet leaks. The car makes weird noises. Maybe you have to figure out laundry, cooking, bathing the baby. *How in the world will you fix your daughter's hair? Pay the bills? Feed your children?* You feel so inadequate and overwhelmed. The weight of making decisions alone is enormous. You don't feel like there's anyone to lean on. *If I mess it all up, who can I ask for help?*

I experienced all of this loneliness. I felt the rejection. I lived in a fog. God placed some people who did not attend my church in my life. They were angels, true friends. They offered a place to stay when I had nowhere to go. They gave food, clothes, and hugs. They held my hand. A friend said, "Let me help you think this through. Let's get your child into counseling." These friends were like a rest area on a road trip. They gave me a safe place to rest and get refreshed for the drive ahead.

I also encountered a group of Christian men in one of my circles. They were kind men who weren't afraid to speak to me, look me in the eye or even touch me. They were bold, wise, and intuitive. They gave safe, warm hugs. Those interactions were very healing. Each time I received a safe hug the big red "D" etched into my forehead got fainter and the fog faded. It helped make it okay to smile again.

# Section Thirteen
# GRIEF OF AN EMPTY NEST

Photo by Lisa Rodgers

# Chapter 77

# FLY AWAY BIRDIES

By Cathy Koch

Unless you have experienced childbirth, a colicky baby, an unruly adolescent or a truant teen you have only just heard about parenthood. You can't really know about it. The same is true of the *empty nest* period of life. We were going to be *cool*. After all, we're baby boomers and nothing takes us off guard. We're self-sufficient. We won't make the mistake of being clingy!

We read up on the *empty nest season* and worked hard at having a good marriage so we would still be in love when the kids left. We anticipated having unlimited funds to spend when it would be *just the two of us* again. We laughed at cartoons such as: "You know all the kids have moved out when you can find a clean towel" and thought, "Won't it be fun when we can … without …"

*Nothing could be as difficult as the turbulent teen years we had just weathered, right?* Our goal of parenting had been to guide our children to become spiritually sound, well adjusted, financially responsible, and yes . . . independent! We have given our children roots *and* wings! *Then why does it hurt so much? Why didn't our parents warn us?*

The situations are as varied as the family, and each individual child. The timing of a child's leaving may be fully expected, it may come as a sudden shock, or it may be delayed way beyond what a parent would have ever envisioned. As hard as it is for young people in our society to *make it on their own*, some parents may feel they will never enjoy the *good fortune* of an empty nest. Or maybe they had an empty nest for a while and now are wondering how to squeeze one more box into the attic. Each family nest has its own timetable for evacuation. When the birdies fly away it affects the whole family.

A father goes to the room of his college-aged son each morning and turns the page on the daily calendar on the desk. Even though his son is two thousand miles away, he tells his wife that is his way of saying, "Good morning son." A younger brother leaves the bedside radio volume on low every night to divert his thoughts from how much he misses his older brother. The family pet loses its appetite and looks mournfully at the front door. A mother goes into her daughter's room to feel close to her, seeking comfort from the stuffed animals and little trinkets left behind.

One family was in a mourning state for several weeks when their oldest daughter left for college. The mother said, "It was as though the light had gone out! We would find ourselves aimless, wondering what to do next. Then one day at breakfast we seemed to sort of wake up, look at each other, and come to the unspoken realization that we had to get on with the business of living."

A father is surprised to find that he misses his daughter's parade of friends coming and going. A mother never thought she would actually be wishing for a weekend back in bed and breakfast mode of operation. *Who will tell Dad how to improve his golf swing? Who will tell Mom not to buy anything made of acetate and rayon?* Maybe we'll just become helpless old fuddy-duddies drifting aimlessly on a sea of forgetfulness and polyester. Now that we've gotten to be good friends, we're *left alone*!! I guess it could be worse.

Parents also grieve over their children's shattered dreams, mistakes and poor choices. A mother will see the premature lines of sorrow under the eyes of the daughter who is barely twenty-five and wishes she could somehow turn back the clock. She wishes she could rock her thirty-year old six-foot tall son in the rocking chair when he gets turned down for his dream job. Ironically, a shred of silver lining appears when we realize that we're spared certain information because they are no longer in the house. Yes, it is best.

It has been said that a mother is only as happy as her unhappiest child. Just because a son or daughter leaves home after declaring, "I can't wait until I'm on my own!" The grieving is no less painful. If anything, your heart is not just bleeding, it's completely turned into mincemeat! We wonder, remorsefully, if we could have been a better mom or dad. *Could we have averted some of the hard lessons if we'd been paying better attention? Did we do anything right? How do we cope?* The logical side of our brain tells us to *get a life* while the emotional side still wants our kids to need us. And so we make adjustments.

As these well-intentioned parents told their children so often, you can't live your life waiting for certain events to happen. *But wait, who's doing that now?* The calendar is marked in anticipation of when the kids are here or when we are visiting the kids. These events are planned frequently and as far in advance as possible. Other priorities play second fiddle to spending time with a son or daughter who has become our best friends. We have learned new ways to reach out via e-mail, text messages, and Facebook®. *We are hip, after all!* Those memorable holiday traditions we worked so hard to establish are set aside for new ones. We commiserate with other parents whose suffering matches ours. We feel almost angry when someone tells us how good it is that our married children live in another state when their children live in the same town!

We invent new names for those empty bedrooms--den, office, media room. Take your pick. We find excuses to interact with the twenty-something group, even to the extent of casually *adopting* one or two. We're amazed to realize that the thought of being a grandparent is quite enticing although we *will* be *cool* at all costs and not pressure our children by dropping hints! Above all, our Heavenly Father gently reminds us that we're not really alone. In His sight we are still acceptable, valuable, lovable, forgivable, and capable!

# Chapter 78

# THE SWITCH

By Lona Renee Fraser

I was in the middle of the cracker aisle and lost it. Not because I received a call someone was hurt or dying. It was a simple moment, an everyday moment as I looked at the box of Cheez-It® crackers realizing I no longer needed to buy them for my daughter. She was now away at college. Yep, you never know when something is going to hit you like that until it does. The switch. It is an internal timer going off when you least expect it. Your day-to-day is now so different, so quiet, so lonely and purposeless. At least it is at first. *What are you supposed to do now?* You had the list for so long of all the things you wanted to do. You are stuck in between the moment of who you were and who you are yet to become.

A mother's journey is such a complex tapestry of endless threads of activity, events, emotion, coordination, encouragement, disappointment, sweet memories, laughter, prayer, and tears. You pour your heart, mind and soul into your children from the womb into eternity without applause, vacation time, sleep or pay. And you do it without blinking. Then you make the mistake and blink.

I am not naïve to the fact my job was to bring them up to spread their own wings and fly away. Yet when the moment happens, you just never know how you will truly feel or react. You have loved, listened, celebrated, disciplined, guided, taught, fought, provided, protected, persevered, and prayed for so many years. *How can you be expected to let go so abruptly? How do I become part of the audience rather than a team player? Or move on the sidelines instead of being in the game?* And you know when you are used to playing in the game; the sidelines are never where you want to be.

I believe the weaning process begins somewhere in the tweens when little by little co-dependency turns into independency. You are no longer needed twenty four hours a day, seven days a week. And as they work their way through the teens, more and more you see you may not be the strongest influence in their life. Then the day you drop them off at college you ask yourself, *"Ok, what just happened?"* You are more "on call." You feel in a daze, stunned, shocked…in a twilight zone of sorts. You don't know what to do or how to do it anymore. It is like having training wheels on again or being a toddler who wobbles and falls repeatedly. All you have known, all that was expected has come to a screeching halt like at the end of a rollercoaster ride you want to end. Yet really you don't. You were made to train up your child in the way they should go. Go. That's the part ripping your heart out.

Mondays are the hardest for me. They are a reminder I am not a mom in the same way anymore. Whether the kids, I mean *young adults,* are able to come home on the weekend or there is some other activity of distraction, at least for a little while, the universe is functioning as it should. Then Monday comes. I remember sitting at my kitchen table in the silence. All I could hear was the clock ticking so loudly like a nagging bully shouting in my face, "They're gone remember! They're gone. They're gone." No more lunches to make, last minute runs to the store for poster board, meetings or field trips. The hustle and bustle of friends, laughter and oh mom…guess what?

The silence was more than I could bear. I turned on the radio, TV, went to my computer to distract myself with anything, even chores. Oh yeah, the kids used to help me with those too. I would try to think of any reason to get out of the house. It was a constant reminder what a huge chapter of my life has ended. Whatever regrets I had about what I wanted to do, should've done or could've done different cannot be changed. I had my time to play and the game is over. I have to accept it, move on. *But how do I that? How do I fill this void in my heart?*

The switch.

I will never forget when my son just finished a grueling orthodontist appointment and could not take the pain. The dentist went on her lunch break after the appointment. When I asked the receptionist to speak with her regarding what pain meds I could give, the dentist would not talk to me. She simply told the receptionist to tell me all the information I needed was given to my son. *Really? Are you kidding me?* I thought to myself. She actually believed it was responsible to give a teenager in pain the vital information he was supposed to not only hear, but also actually understand and apply. She knew full well he was only thinking of his pain. Even when my husband had shoulder surgery the doctor gave me all the post-surgery care instructions. When I got home I called and spoke with her over the phone. She simply kept stating it was the law and she was abiding by it when she gave my eighteen year old son his information. Her attitude was the sort that made me feel like a clingy helicopter mom who simply needed to let go. *Really?* It should clearly be within my rights as a mom paying for a procedure to receive basic information.

I learned quickly what has been expected of me for the past eighteen years no longer applies. I live in a new world of having an *adult* as my child. There should at least be a warning before they drop the bomb on you. I felt like I was the mayor in Looney Tune® town! Surely there was a candid camera somewhere and this would all be a big joke.

I remember while preparing for my son's high school graduation, thinking back to when he was a newborn looking up at me with wonder. I thought, "How can this be?" You are all mine. I have no idea what to do! Then you do it for years. Even though you know you are still not done pouring your heart, mind, and soul into him. It is graduation time, not only for him but for you as well. You are releasing him into the unknown on his own. Thinking, "What if he doesn't know what to do?" And time is not the enemy, even though it feels that way sometimes. This is all part of life and our story. It is the beginning without me by his side, but forever in his heart.

I remember my mother told me, "Honey, this is all a part of life. Be happy and enjoy it. It's hard at first, but it will get easier. You and Jim will have time for each other again. It will be wonderful." My best friend also encouraged me by changing the term "empty nesting" which signifies loss to "open nesting" which signifies new opportunities now open to all of us. She quoted Isaiah 43:19 "See, I am doing a new thing. Now it springs up, do you not see it? I am making a way in the wilderness and streams in the wasteland."

I am thankful. Both my kids are great kids. They are kind, funny, lighthearted, fun, forgiving, gracious, hardworking, intelligent, and gifted in many ways. They each have Jim and me in them. Now I see them coming into their own. Mondays are getting easier. Instead of Cheez-It® crackers, I buy the Brie that was not in the budget before. I can go out with my girlfriends anytime. I am involved in several ministries. The house stays a little cleaner for longer. Jim and I are free to go about our days like newlyweds again. We have more date nights and snuggling on the couch after dinner watching Star Trek®, Next Generation just as we did twenty years ago.

We may be a little older, but we are a little wiser too. We have loved our children well. They will always be our pumpkin pooh and diddly doo. And they will always need us. Our job as parents is never over. The landscape is different, but we never stop being parents. We now welcome the silence. Yet the noise will always be missed.

I may need to put training wheels on again from time to time. That's ok. There are many seasons of life. One epic chapter just ended. Another has just begun. The rollercoaster has stopped. We jump on another one and a new adventure begins. I wonder where the twists and turns will take us this time. I am thankful for the journey that once was. And for the journey that will be. I will always love my children. They will always love me. Most of all I am truly blessed...a mom I will forever be.

# Chapter 79

# SPREAD YOUR WINGS & FLY . . . BUT EMPTY NEST?

By Maria Gelnett

Whoa! I didn't see that one coming. It doesn't matter that I raised just one child or how old he was when he left home to start his own life. The separation from the sacred connection with him affected me. It didn't matter if I was super busy with tons of plans for this time of life. I knew I had to cut the apron strings to spread his wings and fly. Plus I wanted him to have a better more enriched life than me.

But whoa! Not only did it stop me in my tracks to look at myself. It also made me ask and wonder, "What now, God?" Wasn't raising my child my main purpose in life? What do you want me to do now? Yes, work and a part time business kept me busy. Why did I feel so lost? I was told over time I would get used to him being gone. That didn't seem to be the case with me.

At the same time I was blessed with caring for my aging mother, my son was spreading his wings. I say blessed because of the beautiful person she was coupled with my need to fill the transition from an empty nest. I realized the need to fill it after she had passed. The empty nest contributed to me taking her passing so hard. It didn't matter how old my mother was or what the relationship may have been. When she left, the separation from the sacred connection with her affected me.

When I love so deeply as with my child and mother, I carry them inside me no matter where I go. But this feeling of loss put a hole in my stomach. I couldn't focus. I was asking again, "What now God?" Also, I realized Mom's passing became a renewed bonding with my son. I was just taking it a day at a time, putting one foot in front of the other, doing the best at daily activities and thinking: so this is it? Holidays were horrible, birthdays unbearable and meaningless.

Contact with my son was minimal in large part because of the different time zones and how he worked so hard to achieve a successful life of his own. In an effort to find employment in a challenged economy, my son mirrored his ancestors with a brave move of over twenty-five hundred miles away from home. Driving across the country safely was a responsibility he held for himself, his girlfriend and their dogs. Of course, they had to find a place to live and secure jobs. Accomplished in three weeks! Oh, I was on my knees for that move.

Mom's Last Will and Testament gave her wedding rings to us. It was time. My son proposed to the love of his life using mom's diamonds which were reset in a ring especially designed for her. A bald eagle showed up to watch and confirm their experience. Ah, my heart was full again with those I thought I was separated from. Their wedding day was magical. To say mom was there was an understatement. Her body had aged and gone, but her spirit was profoundly present.

My son has grown into a fine man. I didn't lose a loved one. I gained a new family member--a beautiful daughter-in-law who is honored to wear mom's diamonds.

An empty nest can mean taking it all a day at a time or seeing what's next, like it did for me. If you hold on, it doesn't have to be a meaningless, empty, or sad time. Every day does have meaning. It is exciting to wait to see what God has planned for us. Yes, the nest is empty, but they are always with me in spirit. I carry them inside every moment of every day.

# Chapter 80

# FLY

By Gary Forsythe

You're running, you're plunging
Into blue skies of faith
Into a story written just for you
You're launching
Now all we can do is trust the lord
To keep you safe and make your journey true
Oh to fly is a dangerous thing
But it's time it's time to find your wings
Fly

Exciting, inviting
This sense of purpose in the air
Your future reaching out for you
Your past days now give way
To brand new visions and dreams
And all that you've been made to do
Oh to fly is a dangerous thing
But it's time; it's time to spread your wings

Fly, baby fly
Into the great unknown
Fly, oh now fly
Above the earth and stone
Fly come on and fly
It's good to see you've grown
Fly, baby fly
Until you make it home

## BRIDGE

Rise to the sun and rain
And thunder clouds
And wonders found
In questioning and working out
The hope that you're possessing
Go now, with my blessing

God knows
Letting go
Can be the hardest thing to do
But it's how it's meant to be

# Section Fourteen
# LIES & BRUISES

Photo by Lisa Rodgers

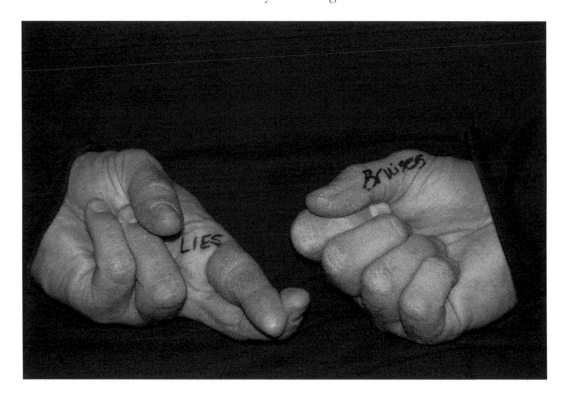

Chapter 81

# THE MURDER OF MY DAUGHTER

By Emily Joy

On Friday night, June 28, 2013, I texted my daughters Emily-Anna and Amanda to inform them I was having surgery on my neck. A few minutes later I received a call from Emily-Anna.

"Hey Mama, when is your surgery?"

I replied, "July."

She said, "Mom, I'm going to take a few days off and come stay with you and take care of you."

I replied, "Emily-Anna I know you need to work. I'll be fine."

Her response was, "No Mom, I will be there for you. You have always been there for me and Amanda and I love you."

Emily-Anna was finishing up her first year of Greenville Tech College in Greenville SC. She was doing great as an A/B student. Her only problem was she had been in an off-and-on relationship with someone I did not approve at all of her dating.

The conversation continued, "I love you too EA. More than you'll ever know. I know we have been through a lot in your lifetime. I'm sorry."

You see, her dad and I had gone through a nasty divorce ten years earlier.

Emily-Anna replied, "Mom our family has been through a lot. There are many who have made us angry. Then again, we have made many angry as well. No one is perfect and everyone makes mistakes. It's up to us to forgive. I don't think you've failed as a mother, a friend or a hairstylist. I think all of these jobs have made you a strong-headed woman. I look up to you for it. I think Psalm 59 reminds you not to hold grudges. Remember the Lord is always with us. He will take care of us and our enemies. You haven't failed, nor will you ever as long as you believe. You're my Hero! I love you."

Tears were streaming down my face when I replied, "Thank you for sharing that with me. I love you and Amanda more than anything in the world! Please have a good evening. I love you."

Emily-Anna replied, "I love you too Mom. I'll see ya soon."

I told my best friend about the conversation telling her what Emily-Anna said to me was so sweet.

The following Saturday night my firefighter and first responder boyfriend, Brad, and I were watching the 11:00 o'clock news. His pager went off at 11:22 p.m. with the dispatcher saying, "Station 12 report to 502 Calvert Ave. Clinton, unconscious patient!"

I jumped to the middle of the floor and said, "Let's go. That's Henry and Cynthia's house. It's going to be Emily-Anna."

He looked at me and said, "I don't think it's their address?"

I looked in the phone book. It was.

We jumped in his truck and took off. I was praying the whole ride. As we turned on Calvert Avenue, Emily-Anna was on a stretcher on the sidewalk. Ambulance lights were flashing. EMT workers were administrating CPR.

I jumped out of the truck while it was still moving running toward Emily-Anna screaming, "What's wrong?!"

Josh, a Public Safety Officer on the scene, grabbed me saying, "Ms. Emily, they are working with her. Please stay back!"

I screamed, "No, if she can hear my voice she'll be fine!"

The stepfather of Emily-Anna's boyfriend pushed me and said, "Stay back."

Josh told Brad, "Take Ms. Emily to the emergency room. They'll be right behind you."

With lights from the fire truck and police car blaring, I stood by a tree looking across the yard when I heard Michael say, "Emily-Anna come back to life twice!"

I turned to Brad and said, "Did you hear him?"

Brad answered, "No."

On the way to the hospital I called family and friends to give them instructions on getting to the emergency room fast.

After we waited for what seemed like forever, the doctor came to tell me Emily-Anna had passed. He wanted to know what happened.

I said, "I don't know. You tell me."

The doctor walked out of the room.

By the time support arrived from our church and family, we were able to see Emily-Anna. She was lying with her beautiful long hair pulled to the side and had a tube down her throat.

I pleaded, "Emily-Anna, get up. Mama's here to take you home and take care of you. Please get up."

Our coroner, Nick, and deputy coroner, both good friends of our family, walked over to me. Nick said, "We will find out who did this to her."

I asked, "What?"

He said, "Emily, she has been murdered!"

I just stood crying.

Emily-Anna was pronounced dead at 12:02 a.m. Sunday, June 30, 2013.

Our town of ten thousand people was blown away. The police arrested Emily-Anna's boyfriend Michael for murder and his friend William, for accessory after the fact.

On July 2, 2013 I buried my precious Emily-Anna. I had her grieving sister Amanda by my side with more than seven hundred fifty five people at her funeral. It was a beautiful service. I realize why God allowed the last conversation between Emily-Anna and me.

A few weeks went by.

I had my surgery. The morning after I was looking out the hospital window crying, "Emily-Anna you were supposed to be here with me."

Suddenly clouds formed into an image of her beautiful face with a smile and her long hair flowing behind her. I knew she was with me.

Another setback struck when my counselor admitted me into a mental hospital for a nervous breakdown. On the fourth day in the hospital, laying in my bed I started praying, "God, please help me! Emily-Anna wouldn't want me to be like this!"

I was released six days later and began attending church again. October was Domestic Violence Awareness Month. My friends and I made over fifteen-hundred purple ribbons to hand out for people to wear. I attended the Silent Witness program in Columbia, S.C. for victims of families who lost loved ones the previous year.

I was able to speak with our Attorney General who invited me to his office. It gave me an opportunity to meet with dignitaries about Domestic Violence Laws in South Carolina.

Shortly after the headlines read, "Another tragedy strikes in S.C. Greenwood County!" Ten people were killed within a sixteen day period due to Domestic Violence.

I watched the news on TV sitting in tears. I cried out, "My GOD, what is going on?" I wanted so badly to reach out to these families.

A cousin of mine posted on my Facebook® page how a man in Greenwood had written a song called, *Lies and Bruises*. Prevo Rodgers and Dwayne Moore put the song together. Josh Owens, a friend of mine, was going to sing it.

I was able to contact Dwayne via Facebook®. We talked for an hour and a half. I sent him a picture of Emily-Anna's headstone.

Dwayne said this made the song so real. I met with Dwayne the following day and traveled to 308 Productions Studio, where Lisa and Prevo Rodgers lived. I listened to the song. The lyrics struck me as so realistic. From the meeting our *No More Lies and Bruises* team was established. We now have over sixteen people on the committee. We are working hard planning an event to raise funds for Meg's House, a home for battered women and children. We are praying God will lead us in the right direction to take the *No More Lies and Bruises* message state and nationwide.

God made the tragedy of losing my Emily-Anna into something good. Emily-Anna would want me to be involved in *No More Lies and Bruises*. She was always helping people. I will continue to help people, as God's will.

I praise Him for the strength He is giving me. I will continue to fight this fight!

"But understand this, that in the last days there will come times of difficulty. For people will be lovers of self, lovers of money, proud, arrogant, abusive, disobedient to their parents, ungrateful, unholy, heartless, unappeasable, slanderous, without self-control, brutal, not loving good, treacherous, reckless, swollen with conceit, lovers of pleasure rather that of God, having the appearance of godliness, but denying its power. Avoid such people." 2 Timothy 3:1-8 ESV

As I continue to grieve, I know my Emily-Anna is resting with our Heavenly Father.

As of this writing, we are still awaiting the murder trial.

# Chapter 82

# LIES & BRUISES

D.W. Moore, Prevo Rodgers, Jr. & Josh Owens

Dang girl I can't believe you're really gone
And I'm standing here looking at your name in stone
You don't know how bad I wish that it was true
When you smiled and said he'd never hurt you
Your mama called me on my job and I hit my knees
And I cried oh God I can't take this please
So why can't we see how everybody loses
When someone confuses love... for lies and bruises

## CHORUS

And I dang sure do anything to have you back here today
It's so hard to believe how he lied and took your life away
And he's left us all here to live . . . with nothing more
Than just these memories and tears . . .

Girl you just gotta know that something ain't right
When a man tries to control you both day and night
So girl don't let him play tricks with your mind
If he's hit you once it sure won't be his last time
Now girl I beg you, you gotta run and please don't stay
There's some people strong enough to help you get away
So girl I pray that you can see how everybody loses
When someone confuses love for... lies and bruises

## CHORUS

And I dang sure do anything to have you back here today
It's so hard to believe how he lied and took your life away
And he's left us all here to live...with nothing more
Than just these memories and tears . . .

## BRIDGE

So I just stand here and pray...that another girl will hear your song....and she might
run the other way...before her name too is written in stone...

## CHORUS

And I dang sure do anything to have you back here today
It's so hard to believe how he lied and took your life away
And he's left us all here to live...with nothing more
Than just these memories, and tears....

# Chapter 83

# ESCAPED WITH MY LIFE

By Karyn Pugh

"You have *got* to go underground – go as far away as you can, go into hiding – do whatever it takes to get away. Change your name, change your life, *and change everything you can*. He continues to make threats against you even while in jail, and we both know how willing and able he is to follow through on those threats."

I sat in disbelief listening to my court liaison's voice on the other end of the phone. She had a unique role serving as my advocate while also communicating with my jailed ex-boyfriend's caseworker. From hundreds of miles away she then relayed important information to me. Despite him being in jail for repeatedly violating a restraining order, stalking and harassment, he was sharing details of plans to hunt me down. His intentions were to make me pay for this supposed hell of being incarcerated. He felt I was responsible for putting him through.

I thought fleeing the oppressive abusive environment to a new location a few states away would be enough. I thought the distance would be enough to keep me safe. But his blind rage was all the more determined to "seek high and low, leaving no stone unturned" to hunt for me. It truly made me feel he was still the predator and I was his prey.

I took her advice because I was willing to take any suggestions to be safe and get him out of my life once and for all. I legally changed my name and cut off all communication with everyone except my immediate family and four close friends who I'd known prior to moving. Although I felt isolated and lonely while in the relationship with him, moving took it to an entirely new level. At twenty-seven I was in a new state with no friends. I was unsure of my next steps. Constantly looking over my shoulder I believed I could not trust anyone while struggling with the trauma of my new existence.

The hardest part wasn't hearing his threats or disparaging remarks over and over in my head. Or finally admitting how dysfunctional the relationship was and the guilt for not knowing better. I had an Advanced Counseling degree for goodness' sake. We went through the classic cycle of abuse. After once ending it, I'd allowed myself to get sucked back in. Something now in hindsight was one of the worst decisions of my life. The hardest part wasn't the flashbacks or the constant fear of wondering if he'd just appear from nowhere. Nor was it the frustration, guilt, shame, or the grieving. Actually, the hardest part was giving up my name and selecting another one.

*After all, what's in a name?* On one hand, it could be perceived as fairly inconsequential. I know many who are known only by their nicknames and never referred to by their birth name. This phenomenon never seemed to bother them. On the other hand, I didn't grasp how much of one's identity was tied up in a name. It was carefully selected at birth when my parents finally discovered I was a girl. My first and middle names were both French, (which I think greatly contributed to my excitement for most things French) and spelled untraditionally. My last name was very common. As I daydreamed about marrying Prince Charming, he always had an exotic, *and of course French*, last name.

I didn't consider any of these things in the heated rush to select a new name. I was told to choose something I liked. A name easily misspelled and a common last name. It may make it more difficult for him to find me in the future. Since my last name at birth was extremely common I couldn't keep it.

As I settled into the new community introducing myself to others, my new name didn't roll off my tongue easily. I'm sure people thought it odd I'd stumble over my own name when introducing myself. I had to be deliberate about saying it as Karyn wasn't an easy adjustment. For twenty-five years I'd referred to myself and was known by a different name. We say "Hi, I'm _____" so often it's a natural reflex. It took a lot of work to ensure I didn't slip up.

As I said my new name out loud, I'd often hear an internal voice saying "no, that's not who you are." When alone, I'd say my full name trying to convince myself the true essence of me wasn't gone. She was simply hiding, literally and figuratively. Still I felt I was playing a part in a movie. One in which I always felt a step behind, moving disjointedly. I put up barriers not letting anyone get too close. I didn't share many details about the past and certainly didn't tell anyone my birth name.

Looking back, now I understand it was Satan's attempts to shame me into feeling this new life was a lie. He certainly didn't want me to experience any redemption and transformation through Christ.

I felt guilt for quickly abandoning the name my parents carefully selected for me. Along with it were the silly songs, rhymes, and nicknames inside family jokes. I didn't think it fair to ask them to call me by the name I'd selected on my own. I also knew this was how it needed to be. It was hard for them to adjust. At first they'd slip into the familiar habit of calling me by my birth name. Sometimes I didn't have the heart to correct them and didn't want to. It was such a comfort to hear the name and know I still had a connection to my past with all the good memories.

After I selected a new name I thought I needed to also distance myself from the memories of the past—all of them, not just the painful ones. I switched into a "those things happened to someone else mode." I thought I needed to focus on the present and future concerns. I stowed the gift of my beautiful memories and experiences into a memory vault away from the forefront of my mind. I experienced significant healing when I merged my old life with the current life into a beautiful tapestry in my mind.

During my healing process I renewed my relationship with Jesus putting faith and a relationship with Him at the forefront of my life. Through counseling, prayer and support from family and friends I was able to work through the many layers of grief and loss. I processed the fallout of ending the relationship including losing my birth name. I forgave myself for taking him back and the mistakes made while in the relationship. Most importantly, I even forgave him

He tracked me down years later and started harassing me again with attempts to smear my name and businesses online. Forgiving him didn't mean I condoned his behavior. Instead I let go of my own anger and bitterness trusting God to deal with him. I couldn't have moved forward with my life until I had let go. I pray he surrenders to Christ and releases the desire to continue to harm me.

Scripture has been a critical component in helping me accept my new life and name. Psalm 139 is very important to me, especially verses 13-14: "For you created my inmost being; you knit me together in my mother's womb. I praise you because I am fearfully and wonderfully made; your works are wonderful, I know that full well."

Upon first reading these words I dropped to my knees with an outpouring of grateful tears. I realized He knew me all along – ME – the true essence of me. He created my inmost being even before I was given a name on this Earth. It didn't matter to Him what my parents wrote on the birth certificate. I am a child of the One True King. He has known me all along. He knew even at birth my legal name would change, but it never affected Him. He's known me, seen me and loved me at my best and at my worst--far before anyone on earth could have ever thought of me. No matter what name I may call myself; I am still His.

I've also been encouraged by reading the story of Paul in the New Testament. Prior to his conversion his name was Saul. He was a despicable and feared man, ruthless in his persecution of Christians. After his conversion he was given a new name, a new identity and a new calling on his life. Paul spent the remainder of his days praising the Lord, rejoicing in his transformation and sharing it with anyone who would listen. I'd like to think of this as an opportunity to share my beautifully messy and imperfect transformed life with others.

Another verse comforting me is 2 Corinthians 5:17 "Therefore, if anyone is in Christ, he is a new creation; the old has gone, the new has come!"

I'm thankful no matter what I've suffered in the past, no matter the mistakes of my past, my previous life is now gone. My new life is completely different. Like Paul, I have the opportunity to encourage others by sharing the hope of Christ.

# Chapter 84

# SECRET

By Shirley Logan

Maryanne was just a girl she was barely five
She found comfort in imaginary friends
Mama knew the secret well
She told her not to tell
But she cried whenever he came in (mama take me with you)

Maryanne took the long road home
She took her time to escape her Daddy's hand
When Aunt Virginia came to call
She could see it in her eyes
Mama died, she was only ten

**CHORUS**
Take me with you
Take me with you
Take me with you

Maryanne went off to school
The demons wouldn't die
Daddy never even said goodbye
Jack Daniels was her only friend
She dreamed of angels every night she cried

**CHORUS**
Take me with you
Take me with you
Take me with you

**BRIDGE**
We all have them
Secrets, in the closet
Wanting, waiting, crying

**CHORUS**
Take me with you
Take me with you
Take me with you
(I have a secret)

# Section Fifteen
# THE BROKEN STATE OF LIFE
Photo by Lisa Rodgers

Chapter 85

# CHANGING LANES

By Lane Reed

Romans 8:28 says "And we know that in all things God works for the good of those who love him, who have been called according to his purpose." NIV

My mother enrolled me in dance lessons when I was four years old because she was concerned that like my father, I wouldn't have any rhythm. I proved her wrong. I became an avid dance student throughout my childhood years.

In the eighth grade, my parents moved me to a private school. There I was asked to be the prop manager for my high school dance/drill team. Our school mascot was the Huntington Hounds so our dance team proudly held the title of *"Canine Cuties."* I officially become a "Cutie" my freshman year of high school. I was an officer on the dance team from the tenth grade until my senior year when I became co-captain. I also attended at least two dance team camps every summer. Dancing was my passion. I graduated from high school at the wise age of seventeen. Without taking a summer break I attended Louisiana State University studying what else? *DANCE!* I had four dance classes each day. Two days a week, I took scholastic classes like math and English. I did very well scholastically, but my heart was in my dance classes.

I also worked a variety of jobs including being a bill collector, office manager, fitness instructor, and aerobics-choreographer. The day my life changed forever I was working for an oil company as an office manager/paralegal.

On that day, I suffered a severe closed head injury from a near-fatal single car accident. I was in a coma for nearly four months. All of the doctors said, "If by some miracle she does wake up she'll be a vegetable for the rest of her life."

I proved them wrong. I began my awakening process sometime in August just before my twenty-fourth birthday. The person who was supposed to be a vegetable went back to college and earned a Bachelor's of Science degree and a minor in Business Law. It wasn't always easy. But what is?

When I began to awaken from my coma, it wasn't sudden. I didn't wake up all at once like people in movies. Sometimes, I think I'm not fully *awake* yet. I am and I will have to live with the results. Due to my head injury I totally lost my balance. I have come to realize: *balance* is used for a lot more than just walking. I had to re-learn every major body function. I had to fight to regain my memory.

Before my accident I had what the world considers everything. I had a well-paying job, a fully furnished three bedroom house, a new sports car and I had attended my dream school Louisiana State University where I was able to focus on dance. Truly, I was dancing through life to my own beat.

My feet may have been knocked out from under me, but somehow my accident became a blessing. I would never be where I am today. All of the abilities that I lost have been replaced with an unstoppable determination. I was motivated to fully live and to earn my degree. Most wonderfully, though, I began to attend a great church where I've gotten to know God. Growing up I only knew *about* God. Now, He is my personal God of endless mercy and grace. Now, I dance with Jesus through life. He's my passion and together we will dance into eternity.

# Chapter 86

# COLLAPSED TO MY KNEES

By Cherie Funderburg

My son is a homeless drug addict. An alcoholic. He lives in the woods of western Washington, in a moldy tent along with a few other addicts. He has no job. He has no money. He has no car, belongings, phone--nothing that most Americans would equate with necessities of life. Worst of all, he has abandoned his faith in God and denies the existence of Christ as Savior.

I thought I knew what grief was. I had experienced grief from death of a loved one, losing a job and from the end of my dream of a large family. I had witnessed the life-threatening injuries and agonizing road to recovery that my newlywed sister and her husband endured. But nothing could have prepared me for the day my only child, my precious son, the blessing that we were so thankful to have been gifted by a gracious Heavenly Father, informed us that he was "no longer that good Christian boy we thought he was." He had been drinking, using drugs, and carrying on in such a way that we had to issue a devastating ultimatum--change or leave our house. He chose the latter.

At eighteen years old, he was out on his own. Living it up with his wild friends. Partying, drinking and doing things that made me collapse to my knees in anguish. I thought I'd hit my emotional rock bottom at that time. I definitely couldn't see past each agonizing moment, nor could I imagine how bad things would get. Oh, to be back in that easier moment again. The moment that seems so out-of-reach. My grief has brought me to depths I never thought possible. And yet, through this, I can see God's great love for his children. I see His mercy allowed me to slowly acclimate to each terrible new thing. I recognize His Grace brought people to support me when the thought of facing another day seemed overwhelming. I have sensed His protective hand held over my wayward son, keeping him safe when it seemed he would surely perish.

I've cried more in the past three and a half years than in all the years of my life leading up the point when my son decided to lead such a foolish, dangerous life. If I could have seen where we'd be now, back when this nightmare began, I don't think I could have withstood the shock and horror, the utter depths of despair and sorrow. I thought the drinking was bad, and then came the marijuana. Followed by the loss of one job after another. Then the car was gone, his room rental and then most of his belongings. Just when I thought he must have surely hit bottom came the meth. I thought my heart would never beat again. I thought it was not possible for anything to get worse . . . until it did. When the word came that he had fallen in with a gang of white supremacists, it felt like a knife plunged into my back. He was deceived into the belief that his "brothers" were watching out for him and he didn't need God, us, or anyone else.

I wept for my son as though he had died. *Why would God only give us one child when we yearned for so many more? Why would God allow our one and only child to fall to such depths?* In reality, he is dead. This empty shell of him that walks around in the woods is not my son. It's filled with poison and reeks of evil. It hates God with a passion that is shocking and disgusting. No, this is definitely not my son. This is definitely not the life I dreamed for him or our family.

I certainly didn't dream of dealing with late night phone calls from the police. I had never imagined talking with my husband about meth, alcoholism and street bums, especially in reference to our son! I never imagined, and still have a hard time grasping, that this is happening. This is our life now. I feel as though I'm living a real-life episode of the Jerry Springer® show. It's embarrassing, disgusting, shameful, and about as far from what we'd imagined life would be like for our son as possible. When our friends share of their joy as their children graduate, get into college, or receive job promotions--we have only silence to offer in return. *What would be the other option?* One cannot beam with pride when their child is living like a wild animal in the woods.

When we first were set upon this path I barely slept. The grief and fear was overwhelming. The thoughts of what could happen to him consumed me. It was all-encompassing. *Our precious son! What had he done!* The horror of discovering his drug and alcohol use, the fear of getting a phone call stating he'd been arrested for a crime committed while high or drunk.

At that time, if I could have seen the level to which I'd sink three years later it would have been unbearable. Because now my fear has taken on an even scarier turn: his death. On his current path, death is sure to come, and quickly. *Where will he spend eternity? Forget what he's done and where he's at--where will he BE?* The very thought of my only child perishing in Hell for all eternity is a grief I simply cannot come to terms with. Without the support of my patient and enduring husband and my own personal faith, this fear would be my undoing.

It is during my darkest moments that I find such solace and peace in Scriptures like Psalm 18:2: "The LORD is my rock, my fortress, and my savior; my God is my rock, in whom I find protection. He is my shield, the power that saves me, and my place of safety."

I cry for the time that has been lost. I cry for the children I cannot have. I cry for the grandchildren and great-grandchildren we will never have the joy of experiencing. I cry because what I imagined my life would be has not come to fruition.

But I also can smile. I can smile because of my beloved husband who has been like a pillar of strength, a rock on which to grasp hold of when the waves of grief and sorrow threaten to engulf me. I can smile because of the peace that comes with knowing that God loves me. While I cannot know where my son will spend eternity, I am so grateful to know where I will be, alongside my husband and with God. I smile because I'm a mother who continues to pray for her son and hope for a day when God will be his Rock for eternity, too.

# Chapter 87

# TRANSPARENT JOURNEY THROUGH CANCER

Collected Stories by Drenda Howatt

### You Are Going to Die

Everyone wants to relate. They want to help, reassure, and even encourage me. So many people have told me about someone they know who has battled breast cancer. Very often, as the conversation progresses, the message that is relayed loud and clear is: "You are going to die."

That is the message. I don't believe it is what they intended, but it is the message delivered. I have heard just as many cancer stories that did not end well, as those that did. It seems that people want to tell me about all their close relatives and friends who are dying of cancer. Not so helpful.

So far, I've managed to get through these conversations graciously--saving my terror and tears for the dark of night. *That won't be me, not me. I am done with cancer. Not me. I am done with cancer.*

*Right, God? I am done, right, right? Oh, God! Tell me, please, that I am done!*

Sometimes, the storytellers are oblivious of my discomfort. Other times, I see on their faces the moment when they realize their stories have gone in the wrong direction, but they have no idea how to salvage the conversation and end on a positive note.

I know that death is the end result of life. I know that I will not live forever. I do not like to hear that cancer may be my end.

### Invited

I had a wonderful conversation with one of my sisters recently. It was good to really talk. I asked her if she thought that our family was different after going through cancer with me. I wondered if we now knew how to help others in the midst of their cancer battles.

She said, "Yes. Since you invited people in as you went through cancer, our reactions are different now. Our family knew what you needed because you were so open and willing to answer our questions."

Her words made me stop in my tracks. *Invited?* No, not really. I hadn't thought of what I had shared as an invitation into my cancer experience. It felt more like I was throwing out a lifeline, asking – begging – for people to grab the rope to pull me in.

I was drowning and needed to be lifted out of the quicksand that was engulfing me. I didn't share my pain, terror, the drained energy, and sadness for pity. I didn't show the photographs from the overwhelming tide of chemo, surgeries, radiation, nausea, and hair loss to invite people into what I was enduring.

I shared those things because I didn't know what else to do as I lay in bed. I shared because the choice for me was often between more tears or more typing. I wrote because to speak the words out loud was more than I could bear and to keep them inside would have killed me. There really was not a conscious invitation. But I am thankful for all whom RSVP'd.

## Priceless Presence

So many people have been by my side as I have stared cancer in the face. Some people had gone before me to fight their own cancer battles. They took my hand as I walked into the darkness of cancer. They held their light onto my path. Their presence made the darkness on my path less scary. Strangers came to my side even, people who read my blog, or heard my story from someone close to me, and then they reached out to let me know I am in their prayers.

Others were so frightened of breast cancer that they needed to hear my story so they could find the differences between us. They felt they were probably safe if our stories were different. Once they felt safe, some stayed connected, but still others stayed away.

But some people were completely absent. Those who chose to be absent made me wonder: *Are they afraid of me now? Are they scared to say anything for fear of saying the wrong thing? Afraid that cancer may be contagious? Are they afraid of being a bother?* Perhaps they just didn't understand that any effort to reach out would make a difference to me. I don't know the answer, but experiencing their absence made me realize that I have also been absent when others needed me before. That made me sad, because now I now realize how important it is to be present during each other's personal battles.

The difference of being present for a loved one when they need you most-- priceless.

## Pride

In the first weeks after my breast cancer diagnosis, I told myself that I wouldn't ask, "Why me, God?" Instead, I asked, "Why shouldn't it be me?" I inquired, "How did this happen?"

Oh, those words sounded so noble, mature, and, perhaps, even strong and courageous. I wasn't going to be the Christian who questioned God. No. Not me.

I don't know how cancer happened to me. It doesn't matter, really, because it did happen. There was no alternative, but to walk through it.

In reality I was asking God, "Why me?" and I was asking in a very prideful way. My question wasn't the problem; it was my pride.

I had my life planned out, and my outline did not include breast cancer. My outline did not include suffering, pain, emotional turmoil, or anything difficult or negative. Cancer has taught me that it is time to scrap my outline. It's time to live by God's outline. He has my hand, so it's time to let Him lead.

Funny that I have never asked God "Why me?" when I receive good news, or something I consider a blessing. Perhaps I expect and even think I deserved good things?

I am starting to see suffering can be a blessing, too. God even tells in James 1:2: "Consider it pure joy, my brothers and sisters, whenever you face trials of many kinds."

God knows my questions. He knows my fears and my sins, such as pride. He loves me anyway. At the cross, He covered my sins. He won't remember them.

It is time to push pride away and live out God's outline.

## It's not all about Me

I've realized everything is not all about me. Not breast cancer, not the treatment, not life. I've wanted to know the purpose of this trial called cancer. I thought I knew it is ultimately for God's glory. That *is* true, but I wanted cancer to clearly produce good results in me. I wanted only great things that would come from this. It is quite possible that the outcome of my cancer may not actually feel good in my estimation or for my family.

In fact my definition of good may not be the same as God's. I am hopeful to see the purpose God has for us in short-term. But what if I can't see the good? What if the outcome is different than I want it to be? Will God not be glorified if I don't like the outcome? No.

I know that good will come from this journey. What it is may be a mystery to me for a long period of time, perhaps forever in our earthly timeline.

Good will come. I know this, because Romans 8:28 promises, "And we know that in all things God works for the good of those who love him, who have been called according to his purpose."

I want the outcome to be complete healing, a return to my normal routine and life back in place. My hope is for health, happiness, and the American Dream. These are my ideas – my definition of a good outcome.

I am slowly understanding, in my heart, that *my good* and *true good* may not be the same. I am praying that my definition and understanding of good will be redefined to align with true good.

I struggle with what I am willing to deal with and what I am unwilling to go through. But, again, everything is not all about me. All of this led me to wonder: *What is God's will (or plan) for my life? What does God have for me to do?* I believe the real question is how do I fit into God's plan? It is all about Him.

He tells us in Micah 6:8 what He has for us, "He has shown you, O mortal, what is good. And what does the LORD require of you? To act justly and to love mercy and to walk humbly with your God."

## Strength in Numbers

I am a strong person. I can and do take care of things. On Saturday, I met a fellow breast cancer survivor. She is eight years cancer free. I have been ruminating on something she said.

She told me that she wanted to go alone during her chemo treatments. She wanted to prove to herself that she could do it. To prove to herself that she was strong.

I was amazed and in awe. Really, she wanted to go by herself? I have only been brave enough to go see my oncologist without my husband accompanying me for the past few months.

Her mother kept asking to go with her, to take her to her treatments. Finally, she realized that her mother needed to go for both of them. She realized that by allowing her mother to be a part of the treatment she was letting her help out.

My strength in cancer may have actually been my extreme and overwhelming weakness. My strength allowed others to comfort me in my terror.

My strength was when my tears allowed others to cry with me. The strength of my vulnerability when sharing my innermost thoughts publicly helps others understand. Maybe my loved ones needed to help me almost as much as I needed to be helped.

I don't know, but I do know together we are strong. Together, we are strong like the links of a chain.

## As for Me

There are fears that come with cancer. Utter terror. I have never felt anything like it. Never. Ever. I never heard anyone admit to having a fear of dying. I felt alone in my fear. Ever since my mom died twenty years ago, I have wondered if she was scared of death. It was a physical relief for her, but was she scared? I don't know.

My heart is conflicted about my terror of death. I know the one true Christ. I am assured in His salvation. Terror of death conflicts with this, I know. *How can I be a Christian and be so scared of death?* Surely, my relationship with Christ, if true, would shield me from that terror, right? And if I am not shielded, if I feel this terror, what does that mean?

I've gone back to the Lord and asked many times. His answer came and continues to come. *I am not alone.*

His answer was spoken by my friend Sue. I shared with her about my terror. As I spilled my upset over my conflict, her words were reassuring, "Drenda, you are not alone." His answer came again from my friend Joyce as she spoke the same words, "You are not alone."

I am encouraged that David wrote about his own terror of death in Psalm 55: 4-5 by saying, "My heart is in anguish within me; the terrors of death have fallen on me. Fear and trembling have beset me; horror has overwhelmed me."

Even though David honestly expressed his fear, he also expressed his trust in his God. David ends Psalm 55 in verse 23 by writing, "But as for me, I trust in you."

My heart has been in anguish within me. The terrors of death have fallen upon me. *As for me, I will trust in Him.*

## Prognosis

I have been asked about my cancer prognosis a number of times. I don't like the question, because I must face my mortality each time it is asked.

I know what I hope my prognosis will be. I hope that cancer is gone from my body, never to return. I hope that I will never have to be as terrified, ever again, as I have been these last months. I hope that my dear husband will not have to be so strong for me again. In many ways, my cancer has been harder on him than it has been on me. I hope I can return to being a wife and mother, who takes care of her family instead of her family taking care of her. I hope my precious children will not have to be scared of breast cancer again. I hope they will not be scarred from the trauma.

All these *hopes* are not my eternal prognosis.

My eternal prognosis is the assurance I have in Christ. My eternal prognosis is the peace that comes amidst the terror. My eternal prognosis is the strength and courage that come from the fountain of life.

My eternal prognosis comes from whom I cling to, because any other prognosis is uncertain.

## Change the Past

Would I, if I could, change the last year of my life? Would I blot out the pain and awfulness of breast cancer? Take away the surgeries and chemo? Reclaim the time spent on so many doctor visits? Call back the millions of tears? Erase the sudden and terrific fears that gripped me? Take away the pain my daughters experienced?

These are interesting questions to ponder. Honestly, other questions answer them for me. Would I return the courage and strength that God has granted me? Take back the boldness of sharing my faith in the one true God? Would I go back to being a stranger to my family? Would I be willing to release the ties of reconnection I've made with so many friends during the battle? Am I willing to live, again, with no thought of my own mortality? Give back the renewed understanding of what a solid, strong, and wonderful man I married? Take away the joy my daughters felt when they heard the words cancer free?

It doesn't take me much time to ponder, now that I've reached the other side, because I know the answers. The difficulties that came with this cancer also brought tremendous blessings.

I wouldn't change my life. I am thankful for the difficulties, because I am thrilled with the blessings.

# Chapter 88

# LIVING AS GOD'S INSTRUMENT

By Lisa LaCross Wethey

"May our Lord Jesus Christ himself and God our Father, who loved us and by his grace gave us eternal encouragement and good hope, encourage your hearts and strengthen you in every good deed and word." 2 Thessalonians 2:16-17 NIV

God has been orchestrating my life long before I could sense His loving presence. When I was in fourth grade my father bought me a five-dollar flute as a gift. Band classes didn't start until the fifth grade so I started playing my flute along with the radio music. By the time it came to start band I decided to play the clarinet since I had already learned the flute.

On the first day my friend asked me to play a little something on the flute. I played *Have You Never Been Mellow* by Olivia Newton John. The band director turned toward me when he heard me playing and declared, "You will play the flute!" I was crushed and started to cry. So began my journey as a flutist. It would lead me through high school, to the University of Michigan for music and by the age of twenty all the way to the first chair flutist at Carnegie Hall. All of it was empty. I was living as a lost soul.

During high school as I was getting ready to play as a soloist with an orchestra, I heard Billy Graham speak right to me through my black and white TV. I surrendered by accepting Christ. I called the phone number on the screen. They sent me a Bible. I didn't know where to go to church or how to get plugged in. Later a boyfriend made me cry when he threw my Bible away. I found myself unplugged and lost. As a young flutist, audiences applauded me. I came forward, accepted my praise, bowed, and went back to a life of empty sin.

After experiencing the hard reality of life in New York City, I moved to Miami where I became an adjunct professor of flute for Florida International University. At the time, my daughter was two years old. I was a faraway lost soul. One day I had to squint to see as I played in the orchestra. I wondered what was wrong with my vision, as I needed to see. The doctors thought I had eye problems. Suddenly I couldn't see at all.

The doctor discovered the biggest brain tumor she had ever seen. She said I would never be able to see or play the flute again. They planned to cut into the top part of my lip and go through my nose to access the tumor. The tumor was not cancerous.

I was whisked off to the hospital after only fifteen minutes alone. I used the time to pray to God, "I have known you all my life. I know my walk has been far from you. I have known you . . . if I cannot see and if I cannot play the flute again it is okay. I am going to change my life. If I'm going to actually be alive then I am going to do it all for you."

When I woke up, at first I couldn't see. There was blood inside of my nose. I woke after a six hour surgery to people asking me if I could see or if I was okay. I opened up my eyes and began saying random numbers. I was reading from an eye chart with perfect vision. It was a miracle.

The tumors kept growing. Two years later I had the same surgery for another tumor. My husband Bruce and I decided God was bigger than we could imagine. Lots of people at the church began praying for me. The pastor and the children's minister sat with my husband through the six hours of surgery. The pastor prayed and asked the Lord to "wash away my tumor." After the surgery the doctor told Bruce, "Something strange happened. I cut into her nose and all of a sudden it felt like something just washed away the tumor. I've never seen anything like that before." God answered prayers in such a specific and unheard of way.

We became strong Christians and were baptized together. I had surgery for a third time to remove another tumor. We decided to do use our gifts for God and moved to Tennessee. Bruce was to play violin and I was to play the flute in a music ministry instead of for an orchestra. We were on fire for the Lord. We were playing concerts all over the United States from Chuck Swindoll, David Jeremiah, even at the Pentagon at the time.

Four months after arriving in Tennessee I had my fourth brain tumor. The doctor advised us to have radiation after the surgery. For six weeks I went through radiation five days per week. The tumors were shrinking. For about a year I was feeling fine. Then I started to fall asleep. The doctor gave me medication to help keep me awake.

During a nine and a half hour drive home from seeing my parents I began feeling funky and tremendously stressed. I was exhausted and wanted to go to sleep. At four a.m. I woke up my husband telling him I had a really bad headache. He took me to the hospital where they found I had one of the worst strokes they had seen at Baptist Hospital in Nashville.

The doctor told Bruce he was sorry, but I was going to die. He also told him if by any chance I survived, it would mean I would be wheelchair bound for the rest of my life. The doctor said I was a real fighter and close to God. He said to Bruce, "I'm so sorry, she's going to die." My husband began to cry. Suddenly he stopped and asked for a moment alone. He started texting people all over the world asking them to pray for me. A Caring Bridge® page was started. People all over the world then learned about me and began praying.

I didn't know where I was when I woke up that night. I was looking around the hospital room. I could see my husband asleep in an uncomfortable bed, a door open to the left and hear a doctor walking past. I couldn't swallow at all and was trying to say, "I need water. I can't breathe." All of a sudden I was in a place I had never known before. It was full of pure joy and happiness. It was as if I had died. It felt like I was dancing. My hands and my arms were not like my own. My eyes were completely closed. I could see brightness all around my face. My feet were dancing. It was pure joy. And it was as if I was there dancing for thousands of years.

I heard the Lord speak. His voice sounded like an enormous amount of breath as He spoke, "I love you." I kept dancing unlike anything in me. Then He said, "You will be blessed." And while dancing I was instantly transformed back to my bed at the hospital.

I started looking around. I couldn't believe I was back in the hospital again. I saw my husband and I started shrieking, "Honey, wake up! Tell me I am here." Bruce rolled out of the uncomfortable bed gasping. I looked at him making a breathy scream with no breath to speak. He started rubbing my arm to comfort me. I fell asleep.

The next thing I knew it was another day. I woke up to someone squeezing on the left side of me. Even though I couldn't open my eyes I knew it was bright and sunny in my room. In a loud and exaggerated voice the woman squeezing on my hand said, "EVERYTHING. IS. OK." I still couldn't open my eyes. She kept squeezing my arm and speaking as she said, "The doctor wants to talk to you."

A very serious doctor with curly brown hair and little glasses was standing by my bed looking at me. He grabbed his tie, shook it and while looking at me with serious eyes deliberately said, "TIE. Do you hear me?" I could hear him, but couldn't say anything. It felt like there was a hole in my brain preventing me from speaking. I stared at him wondering what was wrong with him. Wordlessly I took the rail off my bed, pulled the IV pole and started walking towards the bathroom. Surprisingly I said, "I'm sorry doctor, please forgive me, I really have to use the bathroom." He jumped in an enormous way. He was shocked I could not only talk, but I could get up on my own and walk.

Even though I closed the bathroom door behind me, I heard him outside the door sounding just like the teacher from Charlie Brown® saying, "Blah, blah, blahblahblah, blah, Lisa, blah, blahblah Lisa!" When I was finished, he was standing outside the door with his mouth wide-open and enormous eyes explaining "Wow!" Instead of communicating with me he immediately started giving me heavy medicine. He was certain I was having a before death burst of energy and not a miraculous healing.

The medication made me asleep. People kept saying I didn't seem like I had a stroke. When the medicine kicked in I would be out of it. When I was awake I kept trying to say, "I understand everything. Please just let me be normal." They wanted to tie me down. I just wanted people to know I was okay and didn't need the medicine. At one point I begged a Christian nurse, "Please don't do this. I heard the Lord speak to me." She believed me and had the medication stopped. The next thing I knew I felt better and was able to leave the hospital to go home.

Bruce left me alone to go get my medicine. I pulled my flute out. I raised it up and said to the Lord, "This is my flute. You have given me this gift throughout my life. If I can't use it again, it is okay. I am still here to walk with Christ. What I am going to do for you is different than anything I have ever done. My life has changed because I know you love me."

I started perfectly playing, *I Can Only Imagine* by Mercy Me. I cried. I stopped. I slid my flute under the bed and didn't tell Bruce I could actually play. The next Friday, our ninety-four year old mentor died. Bruce was going to play his violin at the funeral. I took my flute with me. While he was warming up, I walked in and told him I could play. We played the hymn *Fairest Lord Jesus* together at her funeral.

My miracle is the most incredible blessing I would never have even imagined. God has His hands on me. He loves me. He puts his heart towards me. I am not someone who is special. In fact, I am not someone who is glorious or perfect. I am a regular Jane who has walked in the darkness of many years. Now I want to be more like Christ.

Every morning I ask in prayer, "Lord show me what you want me to do." I lie down on the floor all the time and plead to God, asking what I can do for Him. He has given me a gift where I have become somebody different by dying to myself and living through Him.

Christ is my heart. God is my strength. The Lord is every part of who I am. Jesus holds my hand every moment of my life. My love for Christ is unbelievable. To know who He is and to hear his voice is enormous. He is my world. He is my Father. He is my everything. He is my Alpha. My Omega.

"It does not, therefore, depend on human desire or effort, but on God's mercy. For Scripture says to Pharaoh: 'I raised you up for this very purpose, that I might display my power in you and that my name might be proclaimed in all the earth.' Therefore God has mercy on whom he wants to have mercy, and he hardens whom he wants to harden." Romans 9:16-18

Chapter 89

# WHY DID WE GRIEVE? A FATHER'S STORY

By Ric Minch

Jesus said, "A woman giving birth to a child has pain because her time has come; but when her baby is born she forgets the anguish because of her joy that a child is born into the world." John 16:21

And thus had been the case for our first two sons. Our first child was born in an Army hospital at Ft. Meade, Maryland. His birth occurred within an hour of the start of labor. The second childbirth in South Jersey was a grueling eight hours of labor. Both were completely uncomplicated with the exception of mild cases of jaundice.

Less than a year after the second birth, our family was involved in a major traffic accident. No fatalities, but my wife's jaw was broken in multiple places requiring her mouth to be wired shut for nearly three months. She lost weight as a result of the three-month liquid diet. During this ordeal she became pregnant, miscarrying in the first trimester. A mere two weeks later in the spring of 1974, our east coast family unit moved to Portland, Oregon. We left every extended family member nearly three thousand miles away.

Within a few months, we felt comfortable in our new environment establishing friends, succeeding in business as a young mid-level manager for a national contractor, and enjoying God's natural glory revealed in the Pacific Northwest. Life was good, full of promise. A portion of the promise was my wife's current pregnancy, with an anticipated arrival in late April. Seeking and finding an obstetrician was nothing new since we first had military doctors and then a hospital with osteopathic doctors. Our house was in the outer suburbs near the country. Therefore, the obstetrician and hospital were chosen for geographical convenience. Typical of a peripheral hospital of the mid-seventies, it served the common and mundane ailments of suburbia. The obstetrician practice included a pair of brothers who had served the medical community for three decades. A routine birthing event was well planned. What could go wrong?

The pregnancy went past the expected birth date; the first week passed, then the second, and finally into the third. Calculating the date, as well as doctor visits became a daily routine with an equal number of assurances that all was normal. Early in the morning, as labor often begins, we began the trip to the hospital. Pre-packed suitcases were secured for not only my wife, but also for our sons. They were to be taken to predetermined households for the day. Everything was going as planned. What on earth could go wrong?

Arrival at the hospital was the first indication something could go wrong. The nurses were on strike over a wage issue. Driving through the pickets, we arrived at the admissions desk to find a skeleton staff of young, temporary replacements. Who were doing their best at the tasks in hand. The preadmission forms were found and the questionnaire reviewed. One of the queries particularly stood alone. What was the duration of your last labor? I wanted to record the history of both of her previous pregnancies, because they were different and not normal. They insisted I only record the information for her last labor. My protests to record her full history were unheeded. We were led to the preparation room to wait. This was the first of my wife's pregnancies when my presence was acceptable in the delivery room. It was now time to wait.

Very shortly, the water broke. There was a problem. The liquid was brownish; an indication the fetus was in the breach position. The doctor was notified. Upon reading the chart, he turned with assurance to us not to worry. The baby would be born by Caesarian section. We had time. He hurried on to schedule a room and to gather a surgical team. We remained in the hands of novices. Shortly, our baby began to enter the birth canal. Unaware of the urgency, it was necessary to immediately convince the neophyte medical staff to find the physician to begin a standard birth procedure. He rushed back when he was found, gathering whoever was available. There was no comfort found by us when he commented, "You have forced me into this."

Five adults were inside the delivery room; my wife, the doctor, a young girl to assist him, a woman to provide the oxygen, and me. Oxygen was administered to my wife, stirrups were placed and the hasty delivery began. "Forceps," yelled the doctor. The assistant fumbled leaving the doctor to proceed himself. Another instrument was requested without success. The oxygen administrator looked at me and said, "You should take this over. Simply watch this gauge and make sure it stays in this field." I accepted the responsibility as she moved to relieve the young untested assistant.

Moments passed like hours. Yet, every second counted. Someone exclaimed, "It's a girl!" a fact only verified from her breach position. Our daughter was lodged in the birth canal, arms above her head, umbilical cord pinched, starving for oxygen. Eventually, in what seemed to be an eternity, she was traumatically extracted from the womb. Barely alive in her first moments of life, oxygen was forced into her lungs. Suddenly an ambulance crew arrived. They were there to deliver her approximately ten miles away to the neonatal intensive care unit at Oregon Health and Sciences University.

Life would never be the same. At the time, the Lord's word in Jeremiah 1:5 was not comforting to me, "Before I formed you in the womb I knew you, before you were born I set you apart. . ." I was encompassed at once with anger, fear, confusion, responsibility, and grief. Today we understand the comfort is in his Word and what it now means to all of us.

What to do next? Where to go? My wife had experienced a harrowing body experience while watching her daughter rushed out of the room in critical condition. Our two young sons, expecting a baby brother or sister, needed a parent to comfort them at a time of fear and uncertainty. Then there was our newborn daughter with her life very much in jeopardy. Could our recovery be achieved if she spent the only day of her life without her father? All three were justifiable demands, with only one of me. My five initial negative feelings grew stronger, especially grief, as the adrenaline of the first hours wore off. The decision was made to stabilize my wife for about an hour letting the sedatives take effect; call the boys explaining to them what was not understood by me; and then depart to spend as long as possible with my daughter. As for my grief, that process would be resolved later.

Tears swelled up in my eyes when meeting my daughter for the very first time at Oregon Health Sciences University. After scrubbing, gowning, capping, gloving, and masking it was time to visit her newborn, plastic, environmentally-controlled bassinette. Access to her was obtainable only through the side portals where a mere latex membrane separated father from daughter. The seizures embodying her caused her to shiver. I touched her side gently using my hand. For that night, as well as many nights to follow, the only communication between us was the pulse in my finger letting her know there was someone who loved her by her side. By her pulse she answered likewise.

Our daughter's mother was hospitalized or bedridden for nearly a week. Once home, she was able to give comfort to our two boys. Later, she comforted our daughter with visits to the hospital. In the meantime, for the first week a father's touch was my daughter's only family contact. During the visits, staff members would come to me offering support and were willing to answer any questions. The support was greatly appreciated, but the ultimate questions could not be answered. What is going to happen to my daughter? Will she live? If she lives, what consequence have these seizures had on her quality of life? Will there even be a quality of life? On the third night a female physician who was in charge of the neonatal intensive care unit sat down at her bassinette with me. Observing my grief and sorrow she simply said this, "We do not understand the extent of a parent's touch to a baby of this age. Please take faith in the fact your presence has a very positive impact on her recovery. We are doing everything we can; just don't you give up or stop loving her." Tears flowed!

It has been said one only needs three things in life: something to do, someone to love, and a reason to hope. One hour in the delivery room and our daughter fulfilled all three needs. I had been removed from our sanctuary of comfort and safety where some life goals had been achieved and many more were left to accomplish. For me it was the solitude of the two of us that allowed the pouring of tears from grief in these unclear reasons. *Was the grief from retracing steps of preparation if done over could we have prevented this event? Was the grief from the unknown of a baby girl's life, perhaps ruined and caused by human error alone?* For the first time in my life my selfish goals and desires were set far behind. My grief was first; my daughter's wellbeing began and ended my prayers.

I spent days differently for that week. Once the family's needs were addressed, my profession took center stage for a few hours. The day would start with assuring both my wife and two sons everything was going to be fine. Every day, whether real or perceived, a glimmer of hope was relayed from our daughter's actions. Her breathing improved and seizures weakened. At work my actions were less benevolent with a view everyone else was more fortunate than my daughter, my family, or me. From early afternoon and into the remainder of the day, came the prospect of joining my daughter's fight while processing my grief.

After the first week passed, my wife was able to double our parental time at our daughter's side with her hospital visits. Improvement was observed in the form of both less frequent and violent seizures. I must speak candidly with my wife as to how we were going to deal with our lives herein. It was also time to speak to the boys honestly. How their lives would change, especially our family unit, maybe for the rest of their lives. How difficult was this? None of us had ever experienced this event. Our extended family unit was across country. None of us knew the severity of our daughter's condition.

It became apparent the time had come to leave grief behind and look forward to hope, perhaps even faith. If grief continued to grip us it would control us. It was time to accept our circumstances, begin to do everything possible to assist our little girl, healing all our lives in the process. For the Lord has said, "Come to me all who labor and are heavy laden, I will give you rest. Take my yoke upon you and learn from me, for I am gentle and lowly in heart, and you will find rest in your souls. For my yoke is easy and my burden is light," Matthew 11:28-33. Grief was now to be set aside.

Over thirty-eight years have passed since that significant day in May. Our daughter has grown into a beautiful young woman, loving and well loved. Very early in her life she was diagnosed with cerebral palsy. Daily medication for a lifetime has kept the seizures in check. The palsy causes muscle tension. As she grew, many surgeries were required to prevent limb withering. Only one side of her brain was affected, the logical and analytical. Therefore the intuitive, thoughtful and subjective side is dominant. As a family we worked as a team with a balance between protecting without being overly protective. As parents, activity choices were always considered in light of potential physical limitations and always striving for main stream; bicycling, sledding, swimming, etc.

As children, our three boys would go to therapy sessions, hospital visiting rooms, family support groups, and the sort. Subconsciously they learned patience, compassion and accord. This is especially true for her younger brother who for his first eighteen years stood as her protector, confidant, and mentor. As a result, every year he matured beyond his years. Between mother and daughter a bond developed like no other, the mother of an exceptional child. Mom became an activist for special education specifically for our girl, of course. Collateral educational improvements followed. In addition, she developed into an advocate for parents who were newly facing similar experiences. As for me, twenty-one years were spent coaching basketball for Special Olympics with many of them being with my daughter. One year, Coach of the Year was awarded to me. It was accepted knowing the true reward came from the joy of sharing and caring with all the very "Special Olympians," including my daughter.

Many times growing up it appeared our daughter was the happiest and most well-adjusted of our four children. Our daughter is now blissfully married with a wonderful husband, who treats her as if the world rotates around her. The hypothetical question has never been raised to her. If your life could be rewritten, would you change it? Probably not! Why then did we grieve when the Lord gave us a blessing?

# Chapter 90

# Dead or Alive

*Losing a Brother to Schizophrenia*

By Valerie Geer

I don't know the day of his death. I can't go visit his grave—he doesn't have one. There was no funeral for us to reminisce about the good ol' times we had together. We had no memorial service to talk about his marvelous sense of humor, athleticism and bright intellect. We had none of that.

If I want to see him, though, I can just hop in the car, drive to his town and find him wandering the streets muttering to himself. Oh, sure, *technically* he's alive. He is one of the walking dead. The little brother I grew up with is dead and gone. It wasn't until his late teens or early twenties when schizophrenia came and took him from us.

The little brother I once built forts with is dead and gone. The kid, who reset the pop cans up on the fence post while I got into my BB gun stance, is dead and gone. The compassionate boy who befriended the new Latino kid in town, despite a language barrier, is dead and gone. The teenager, who was on the soccer team, basketball team, football team, earning honor roll grades, is dead and gone. The young man, who looked like Brad Pitt, is dead and gone.

*I don't know how* to grieve this kind of living death. An actual, literal death would be so much more bearable. Then we'd know the boy who gave his life to Jesus and lived for Him, was in Heaven, in perfect peace, even if it was sooner than any of us would have wanted. We would have cherished his memory. Instead, my brother's living death has been dragged out. If my brother is the hostage, schizophrenia is the twisted terrorist who makes the family members watch his torment.

I know without a doubt my brother is dead and gone. Yet when I see his living face and take in his flesh, I don't know what to think. Is he dead or alive? He bears in his physical body his deteriorated mental condition. There are stories in his scars, his gait, his bone structure and everything telling me schizophrenia is alive and well. But my brother is dead and gone.

My brother reminds me of the demoniac in the tombs (Luke 8:26-35) who was unclothed, out of his right mind. Jesus crossed over to his region, delivered him, clothed him, and put him in his right mind. I regularly pray Jesus would do this for my brother. He has not done it yet. Maybe this kind of healing will only be realized in Heaven. If so, then God speed the day for my brother. But, will he be in Heaven? I have no clear soteriology for the mentally ill.

Secretly, I am terrified my brother will be lost for eternity. He accepted Christ as a child and continued to affirm his faith as a teenager. At some point, seemingly before the schizophrenia, he started bearing bad fruit—drugs, alcohol, cohabitation—so how could I be sure he was in the true vine? He was not living like someone who placed his faith in Jesus. He started using methamphetamine. Was that a catalyst to his schizophrenia? Was schizophrenia already starting to take over and the substances were just a poor attempt at self-medication? Was schizophrenia unrelated to all of this behavior and merely a result of genetics? When he comes before the Lord, how will he be judged?

I don't know the answers to these questions. I wish I could clearly and confidently say I know my brother will be in Heaven someday, free from the torment of schizophrenia. I'm not sure, though. I hope, I beg, and I pray for mercy. I somewhat guiltily admit I look forward to seeing my brother in Heaven more than I do Jesus Himself. *What a day that will be when my brother I shall see!* May it be so, Jesus.

# Chapter 91

# ME, HIS SHADOW AND THE LOST SOUL

By Michelle Titus

"Sweetheart, your addiction is showing," I whisper softly, but he doesn't hear me.

His shadow, on the other hand, is seemingly pleased with itself. It grimaces in my direction while tightening itself around him. I suspect it is already stage four addiction, but he won't go get it checked out. He is too proud to ask for help even if it's killing him. *Insidious little beast--addiction—stealing bits of a once dazzling individual.* One who was wise and excepting; hopeful but contented with himself; funny and who believed truly he was enough. At least that was him twenty-five years ago.

At some point things shifted from the pursuit of self-discovery and one's own divinity to the pursuit of worldly acquisition. A great dark shadow of discontentment came along with it. At first I thought it was strife, but I see otherwise now.

I remember those beginning years--beach sunsets, flea market shopping and a night out was a three-dollar vegetarian burrito. *How much free pizza did we eat from your work?* We were growing a partnership while learning those beginning life lessons together. I never wanted to *be* anything, ever content with just *being*. Being alive, being full, being housed, being educated, and being with you.

We photographed the first time you cooked; you were so silly, deciding to put on my apron. I wish I could remember the meal or what you cooked. But so much of our time together has been lost.

Bus rides, mid-terms, writing papers and work is how we spent our days. Holding hands through the aisles of the grocery store was our quality time, and it was. The games we played: sweet and sour, grossest item in the store, next person we see is your new partner.

The laughter.

I see you occasionally through your wounds, your soul shining. But then the shadow is never far behind, covering any light you may shine. I miss it--the "we" that we used to be. I miss the laughing; "the way" only we held hands, the once feeling of safety, your musk-yes, your musk the way you would smell after shaving and how sweetly soft your skin was when I kissed it.

Those feelings, what he had. The love will always exist, but only there in *that* time. It can't be seen here in the now; the shadow is too thick and engulfing.

I don't see you much anymore. Only traces of the best of you left in our children. *How she looks like you, more and more every day.* I tell her when she does, so she knows it is okay to love you and that part of herself. Our other child with your intellect and wit. How often I say "you remind me of your dad." The term, "Dad-Abba-Father-Poppa" still holds much honor in our household.

Strange how the once seemingly so real, can turn into the surreal. How it can be good until it isn't. It seems another lifetime ago, a distant echo of an "us" existing elsewhere.

"Wake up, beloved, wake up!" I call but to no avail. I pray your slumber is sweet but I know. I know what it does to you. How it cuts you so with whispers. Of course you want to run from it, drown it out, and medicate it until it goes away. How frustrated you are when it greets you from your slumber. I know.

If it hadn't been for my name sake I am not sure I would have looked so deeply into the matter as we are called to do. Titus 2:11-12, "For the grace of God that brings salvation has appeared to all men, teaching us that, denying ungodliness and worldly lusts, we should live soberly, righteously and godly in this present age." And Titus 3:10-11, "Reject a divisive man after the first and second admonition, knowing that such a person is warped and sinning, being self-condemned."

I can't. I won't. Not to them or myself, not anymore. I am too tired to fight with your shadow. I so badly want it not to be true, not to be real, and not to be present. But it is. I have to put you down now, Sweetheart. Sadly, I cannot help. I have discovered I am part of the problem and therefore will never be part of your solution. Addiction has turned you into a dangerously sick liability. We can't risk it anymore. It could kill us too.

Why? Why do you insist on treating yourself so poorly? Self-condemned not by the Father but by the self. It is a gift from God, this salvation, poured out on us through Our Lord and Savior, Jesus Christ. You need only to raise your glass. You are safe, beloved. God has you. Step out from behind the shadow into his light. It is beautiful here. Don't listen to what it is telling you. It is lying to you. I wish you could tell addiction to get behind you and to stay there, that you could do it for yourself. That you believed enough, that you believed you deserved to live.

Live, Beloved, live. Choose life.

# Section Sixteen
# OUT OF THE DORMANCY OF GRIEF
Photo by Lisa Rodgers

Chapter 92

# HE WON'T LET GO

By Deborah Petersen

"Every person the Father gives me eventually comes running to me. And once that person is with me, I hold on and don't let go." John 6:27

Have you ever experienced a day when God puts a verse right in front of your face? One day, I felt like He was sitting with me and turning the pages of my Bible to this verse in John. He spoke into my heart, "Look child. I am here. I love you. I have never left you."

I have suffered with depression since I was a small child. When I'm depressed I feel like I'm in a pitch black room screaming for help, but no one hears me. Logically, I know those close to me care about what I'm experiencing. When I am depressed, a million people could tell me they love me and I'd still be deceived. I go to this place in my head and my heart where the only thing I hear is lies. *I am worthless. I am unloved. I am broken and used. I am a mistake. I don't belong anywhere.* I know I am loved. It's like I fall into a trap so deep I can't climb out. I hate it when I fall there because it feels impossible to escape.

I am embarrassed to tell people I suffer with depression. The world has made it seem like there is something wrong with people who struggle. When I was sixteen I planned to commit suicide. I turned the lights off in my bedroom, sat on my floor and planned to tie an electrical cord around my neck. I sat there with the cord right next to me, crying out. I felt worthless and ashamed of my sins. At that moment I heard God say, "Debbie, I love you!" As I sat in God's presence, I told Him I was sorry. He saved my life. Truthfully, though, it wasn't just a onetime rescue. It's a daily battle with daily commitment to trust in His love for me.

Months later, still imperfect and still struggling, I found out I was pregnant. After being a single mom for three years I was working full time, going to college, maintaining a home with my sister, loving my family, maintaining friendships, and of course, being a great mom. I felt like I couldn't do it all anymore. Again, I felt like I had failed.

I decided one night to go home, where I knew no one would be at the time. I would end my life. I had allowed the negative thoughts to go so deep in my head and my heart, again. I felt like I was unwanted. Again the voice called out to me, but this time was different. God asked, "What are you thinking Debbie?" He said, "You have lives to change for me. You have a purpose on this earth. I need you here. I need you to be honest with people. I need you to share your struggles, your suffering, and your joys." I felt His complete love overflowing in my heart. I understood His guarantee.

He wasn't going to let me go. He wasn't going to allow me to walk this journey alone.

He has kept that promise. Not once have I walked alone. In my deepest, darkest moments, in my lowest points, in my sins and failures, He has walked beside me and held my hand. If I didn't know God I wouldn't be here today. God is alive and powerful. God does miracles and I believe He is at work protecting me, carrying me and talking me through the pains and joys of this life.

I'm not ever going to let go.

# Chapter 93

# FRAIL NERVES AND SOLITUDE

By Kayla Fioravanti

After fulfilling my daily work obligations I exited the gray outdoors of Portland, Oregon to seal myself into the solitude of my apartment. The cool dampness of a late winter caused a long-term chill to seep deep into my bones. I would sit with a remote control firmly planted in my hand with my body nearly engulfed in an overstuffed garage sale couch. The mounting responsibilities of growing up and the pressure of supporting myself paralyzed me. I was felt terrorized after being stalked for years by a former boyfriend. I responded to the constant fear like a potato bug pulling into myself. I chose to roll up on my couch waiting for the fear to vanish.

Even the little stressors of life and the cheery voices of well-meaning friends threatened to push me over the edge. The walls of my residence gave me the feeling of a temporary sanctuary. Shutting the door each day behind me was comforting as the stagnant air of my apartment coated my frail nerves with familiarity. The solitude both did and didn't bother me since, even in a crowd I felt alone.

While sitting in a dimly lit living room my promising future appeared muted. I wrestled with what I wanted to be when I grew up. Barely out of college, I was already burned out from my high-stress outside sales job. Despite my depressed mood my job tenaciously clung to me because it required me to be personable with strangers. My own expectations my own expectation that I would further my education competed with my obligation to pay bills each month. I felt numb and overwhelmed at the same time. The added anxiety of looking over my shoulder to see if the stalker located my current residence was the final excuse needed to throw a gala-sized pity party.

Just months earlier, I considered myself too busy for TV. Watching it was an activity I considered mundane. When life overwhelmed me, my relationship with TV changed. During this span of time, I craved the break I found in the electronic lives of strangers. As much as possible I ignored ringing phones or invitations to spend time with real friends. I pretended to be gone even when the doorbell rang. I didn't feel safe giving me a reason to cocoon myself into my apartment.

On the first day of my great reality escape I sat immobilized on the couch after arriving home from work. I found the silence deafening. The next day I covered the quiet with the sounds of TV. I spent hours watching the alternative world of scripted lives of other. Their fictitious lives were appealing as they offered an escape from my own truths. I sat stationary with little energy for anything healthy or productive. My hours slurped up into one-sided relationships with TV characters.

I spent at least a half dozen sunless Portland months curled up on the couch. During every free moment I lived as if I were electronically handcuffed to the couch.

Any ambition I had drained from me seeping into the cushions of the couch. The TV literally sucked the will to move out of my body. I had no energy. My desire to exercise vanished with willpower to eat healthy following suit. As the months passed the results of apathy began to show on my body. I had gone from athlete to couch potato and from health food nut to junk food junkie. Self-loathing set in. Not liking myself pushed the tail-spinned pity party into hyper drive.

I wondered each night when the eleven o'clock news started, "Where did the day go?" In the stagnation of my apartment I accomplished little. My to-do list accumulated undone tasks. Depression oozed into all my empty spaces as solitude sucked me deeper into self-imposed prison. I was successfully escaping reality as I vanished into a dark and lonely world.

I only left the couch when I had to and would rush back to its safety as soon as the obligation of my job was finished. I left the TV on while I slept because I was afraid to be completely alone with the deafening silence. TV noise covered all the outside noises igniting my fears of being found, by my stalker again. Rather than cope, I allowed the racket of the TV to occupy my mind in order not to hear my own thoughts. I avoided as much human contact as possible playing hooky from the previously active social life.

Despite my withdrawal from social life I was drawn each week to church for Sunday service. My pastor was preaching a series on the idols we set up in our lives. I felt confident I overcame those obstacles until his sermon addressed electronic idols. I squirmed in my seat, vowed to cast off my idol and then promptly went home to watch TV. My habits were deeper than I realized. Back in the solitude of my apartment I mentally beat myself up for feeling out of control and powerless.

One day I sat watching a slow-moving police chase on TV when I suddenly realized the absurdity of my habit. Right in the middle of the O.J. Simpson car chase I unplugged my TV, threw it into the closet, and walked away. While the world sat riveted by one of the most famous police car chases in history, I cleaned my apartment, organized my to-do list and picked up my neglected life. In the span of someone else's attempt to evade authority, I finally submitted to the ultimate Authority of my life. Leaning on His power I broke the locks on my self-imposed electronic prison cell.

Today, if I sit in front of the TV for more than an hour, I feel restless and fearful sitting still for long will steal momentum in my life.

# Chapter 94

# GOD OPENS A NEW DOOR

By Mary Humphrey

One day, after reading several submissions as an editor for *360 Degrees of Grief*, I sensed a feeling of heaviness in myself. I knew the process of editing had not brought me into a depression. Instead, I recognized it as a personal weight of sadness I had not yet released.

Most of us know how grieving works. One day we do not feel the hurt, the next day it seems to pop into our bloodstream. It surges through our entire being in one short heartbeat and thoroughly consumes us with excruciating throbbing pain.

I clearly remember the day I released the heavy sorrow laden yoke I carried around my neck. I tried to take a reviving nap. Instead, I ended up sobbing into my pillow. My normal day consists of silent prayer and serene steps with God. This day was no exception, except to my surprise, I cried out in sheer agony, "I cannot let go!"

I became acutely aware of my reasoning pattern at that very moment. If I let go, I'll lose the love I had for them, right? I'll lose my memories. They'll be totally gone, erased…they will vanish. I did not want to say goodbye. They really were gone and I needed to move on. It was not my fight to fight. I was the obedient one. The anguish began to float away, replaced with a sense of peace. I was not surprised. He was present, He always is. I needed to still myself, to listen.

As if I heard his soothing fatherly voice, He reminded me to open my bible, to study, something which I had not done that week. I began to read a devotional about grief when scripture on the other side of the page caught my eye: *Though you have not seen him, you love him, and even though you do not see him now, you believe in him and are filled with an inexpressible joy.* (1 Peter 1:8 NIV)

Joy – it is not the childlike delight of jumping up and down on the bed type of joy. Instead, it is a peaceful sense of tranquility and trust.

My answer came rapidly, sharply clear; nothing less, nothing more…faith.

Reality filled my head. He could not close the door needing to be shut as long as I blocked His will with one foot in the way. I could not grow in my new life; free myself to step into my new role or step through the door He had opened. He could not close the door He wanted shut if I was still forcibly holding it open.

It really was my choice.

I removed my foot from the door.

Thank you, dear Father. Thank you.

Thank you writers, as well, for your beautiful stories. As painful as the thoughts may have been to form into words, your submissions help others recognize and reveal the strength and ability each of us have to heal.

# Chapter 95

# WHEN SILENCE GETS LOUD

By Gary Forsythe

There's a whisper in the wind and I am listening
With a quiet desperation in my soul
There's an echo in the stars
Of a gentle voice so far away and yet so close
So very close
Yet the fear of the unknown begins to rise
As my troubles all seem hidden from the Father's eyes

**CHORUS**
When silence gets loud
My heart reaches out
And clings to the faithfulness of God
When the heavens won't speak
I'll choose to believe
His arms will carry me through loneliness and doubt
Oh, when silence gets loud

There are moments in the night when I am dreaming
Of a time when I will know as I am known
Then I wake up in the dark
To a cold and trembling heart
And sadness found in being far from home
So I pray with all my heart to feel your touch
For an angel visitation, or a burning bush

**BRIDGE**
I am listening, I am listening
For an answer in the wind
I am wrestling with the questions
And my need to understand
I am waiting, I am waiting
For my joy to come again
I am trusting and believing
I am held within his hands

# Chapter 96

# FIND ME HERE

By Gary Forsythe

**VERSE**
Where doubting and faith collide
Where hope and despair reside
Where judgment and hate and pride
Wound me deeply

Where foolishness comes to life
Where failure and shame survive
Deep in my mind of minds
I need healing
This is the broken place I'm in

**CHORUS**
Find me, find me, here
Jesus, find me find me here

**VERSE**
I'm searching for sacred ground
But feeling more lost than found
Listening to hear the sound
Of your voice speaking
This is the desperate place I'm in

**CHORUS**
Find me, find me, here
Jesus, find me find me here

**BRIDGE**
No alibis
No more pretending anymore
This is where I'm breathing
Nothing to hide
Into your light I fall
Find me

Come to this broken place I live
Find me, find me, here
Jesus, find me find me here
Find me, find me, here
Jesus, find me find me here.

# DELIVERANCE

# Chapter 97

By Tammy Lovell Stone

I want to speak.
But, the words won't come.
They are lodged in my throat,
And they linger there.

Afraid that someone might see,
The depths of me.
The inner most parts,
I'm unwilling to share.

God must be close.
I can't feel Him at all.
But, I know He sees my plight,
Whether great or small.

Weary and worn,
Sleep is hard to find.
As times gone by,
Wander through my mind.

The prison of regret,
Waits at my back door,
Saying, "It's too late, forevermore."

But, regret is a word,
I can't afford.
It's a jail cell, a way to hoard.

God's promises are true.
His statutes stand firm.
Even in my grief,
There is something to learn.

I'm reminded of Christ's sufferings too.
What are mine compared to His?
If I focus on me,
I can't focus on Him.

I see the ray of hope,
In the dark cloud above.
He alone can save me,
Deliver me with His Love.

# Chapter 98

# A NEW ME

By Lona Renee Fraser

The beauty of a sunrise
Warms me from the inside out
And kindles the fire of the day
Bringing new hope
New possibilities of wonder
A freshness of new beginnings
A second chance
To make the wrong right again

As I rest under the sun
It blinds the darkness
As I listen to the breeze
It whispers hope
Of who I once was
To who I will become
Not knowing what may transpire
Who I will meet
Where I will go
How I will feel
The adventure of just the thought
Of a fresh start
A new me
A clean slate
Under the rainbow of forgiveness
I can see color again
The light at the end of a tunnel
As this chapter ends
I turn the page
Of one unwritten
I have the power to choose
To turn to the left or the right
To begin again in the light
And all of a sudden
I feel giddy with anticipation
Like falling in love
I love myself again
And shatter the sadness of my soul
As the sunrise ascends
A new me is awakening
And I will…

# Chapter 99

# FIRE RUNS THROUGH ME

By Shirley Logan

Fire runs through me
Cold that's too deep
I can't face the wind
Anger fills me
Memories haunting me
I am at my end

**CHORUS**
I don't want you to judge me or condemn the way I feel
And I don't want you to run
Won't you help me to open up my heart and let you in
Oh my soul

Fear runs through me
I can hardly breathe
I can't face this truth
Hope holds loosely
Wanting, waiting
Anchored deep within

**CHORUS**
I know you're there in every moment that I feel alone
And I don't want you to run
I know you know all the secrets of my longing, oh
Oh, my soul

**REPRISE**
Hope is burning
Fire that's so deep
I will face my soul
I will face my soul

# Chapter 100

# THE LETTING GO

By Paul Dengler and Charles Garrett

**VERSE 1**
Leaves they drift to the ground
What was before comes back around
Seasons come and seasons go
As life arrives, it's letting go

**CHORUS**
Letting Go
Letting Go

**VERSE 2**
The old, they bear a debt to time
The young, they spend and pay no mind
But death will have the price it's owed
It leaves no choice, but letting go

**CHORUS**
Letting Go
Letting Go

**VERSE 3**
Up from the dust that we become
A seed will burst when breath is done
Far beyond the grave below
He's holding on we're letting go

**CHORUS**
Letting Go
Letting Go

**VERSE 4**
Leaves they fall to the ground
Spinning world turning around
Seasons come and seasons go
New life arrives in the letting go

# Chapter 101

# AWAKEN

By Lona Renee Fraser

Whistling willows
Torrent streams
Flowing in the aftermath
Of a tumultuous storm
Stirred from slumber
First dusting, then drenching
As if remembering
Something had offended it
But be not weary, for it comes to bring
New life, new growth, new blossoms
As the affect of the sun
Awakens the earth
And germinates its members
Beckoning the rivers to flow
Out from the streams and babbling brooks
Into the seas allowing us to breathe new life
As well, as we are then
Revived, refreshed, renewed
As our own roots multiply
And show forth
A revolution of
Our mind, soul, body
As transformation becomes
Revelation and we are
Awakened

# Chapter 102

# IN THE ARMS OF THE SHEPHERD

By Kayla Fioravanti

When I was very young, straggling behind the others,
out of my youthfulness I was stolen in the night
By the enemy of all.

I became disoriented and confused, lost.
I wandered deeper and deeper
Into the vast wilderness around me.
I could hear the Shepherd calling,
Feel His footsteps near me, but
I could not find my way to Him.
It seemed as though the darkness
Would separate us for all of eternity.

I wandered farther into the wilderness, and
In the darkness I became blinded.
The depth of my emptiness consumed and paralyzed me.
I was drowning in my own total despair.
I became cast, totally helpless,
Weighed down by my own hurt, anger and filth.

When my body could move no further
The Shepherd called again. He was near.
I could run no further away, go no deeper into myself.
Body and soul, I laid down helpless at His feet.
Exhausted, empty and consumed with guilt.
I could feel the Shepherd reaching out to heal me.
I turned into His support and surrendered completely.

He restored me, healed my soul, cleansed my body.
He lifted me tenderly into His loving embrace
And covered me with His amazing grace.
He healed me, renewed me.

My overgrown coat had been laden
with guilt, dirt and shame.
Yet as He took His place at the throne of my heart,
And I released myself into Him,
It all fell away and scattered as far as East is from West.

I was free - In His arms
I became white as snow.

The all-consuming emptiness
Was all at once filled with His presence,
And I was totally satisfied, finally longed for nothing else.
I had found my way home, the Shepherd, my Savior
Was the remedy I had sought in the darkest of days.

He restores my soul in every present day.
When I am burdened I lay my worries at His feet and
Crawl up into His mighty lap and rest.
I surrender each day to His will, and am comforted
By His very presence. My Shepherd,
My Savior whispers in my ear,
And I can hear Him now. I know where He is.
He is here, always here.
He lives in me.

# EPILOGUE

By Managing Editor, Kayla Fioravanti

Many of the authors of *360 Degrees of Grief* have written about their relationship with Jesus Christ. They have credited Him with carrying them through the aftermath of crisis. This may have raised a few questions for some readers. *What does all this mean? How do I have a relationship with Jesus? How do I find the Comforter?* I often wondered the same things. As I struggled through life I asked people and got no answer. I searched a variety of religions in search of the God people referred to as the Comforter, Healer, and Redeemer.

My life story is in *360 Degrees of Grief* in the final poem of *In the Arms of the Shepherd* on the previous page. I don't often speak of the moments in my life filling me with shame and misdirecting me. However, at eight years old while frolicking through life, I very suddenly experienced a hurt and shame so deep it changed the course of my life. A babysitter abused me. I overheard him blame me. I took the blame to heart, and the "Enemy of all" used it to confuse and disorient me. I believe Satan is the Enemy of all and the great deceiver.

From that period of my life onward, I could feel and sense a darkness I had never known before. From within the darkness, I changed directions in life onto a path leading me deeper and deeper into the wilderness. As early as I can remember, I was always seeking God. A veil of darkness blurred my vision. I listened to the world around me and found myself running. I grew further from God despite an echo of His voice making me desire to seek Him.

As the years passed, I entered my teen years seeking to fill a void I felt ever present in my life. I filled it with alcohol and parties. I put myself in dangerous positions fueled by mind-altering and inhibition-numbing drunkenness. I ended up being used and taken advantage of, leaving me feeling paralyzed by guilt and shame.

The party abruptly ended when I was twenty-five years old. One morning, with no memory of the night before, I awoke feeling life inside of me. The feeling of life was foreign and altogether consuming as I had been so dead and so numb for so very long. I knew with certainty I was pregnant. Just as suddenly, I also knew life began at conception and I had to protect this new life with all of my being.

I was only hours pregnant when I chose to stop drinking for the good of my child. I had studied fetal alcohol syndrome in college and couldn't bear to injure this baby. I was instantly converted from being pro-choice to being ready to sacrifice everything to protect life, especially this life. My future plans to obtain my Ph.D. were quickly abandoned. They now become meaningless in the face of this new life.

I went to the store a week later to buy a pregnancy test and bottle of wine. I decided one or the other would be my future. The test came up positive, so I gave the bottle of wine to my neighbors. The next day I went to confirm the test at a women's clinic. I stood beside the nurse waiting for the test results. It came up negative.

I insisted I was indeed pregnant. She administered another more accurate test. This one came up with a very faint positive sign. The nurse turned to me and said, "Don't worry. It is early enough we can get this taken care of before you even know you're pregnant." I suddenly realized the women's clinic I had gone to for help was, in reality, an abortion clinic. I flew out of there never looking back.

Later that day in downtown Portland, I told the biological father I was pregnant. We had been friends for a lifetime, so I felt safe as I told him. He turned to me and said, "Don't worry, I will be there…for the abortion." My resolve to protect my child grew. I settled in for a battle as pressure to abort my child continued to come from every direction.

Those around pressured me daily with arguments like, "I never chose to be a father" and "Having this baby will ruin your life." For the first time, I realized I had been playing Russian roulette with my life making choices that caused the creation of children. I also knew this new choice would save my life. I didn't know how, but I knew this child was a life preserver. Another argument proposed to me was, "It would be better to have an abortion than to live with this mistake forever. At the very least consider adoption and get on with your life."

And at twenty-five, with a college degree - world travels accomplished already - I knew for me, adoption wasn't the best option. I was willing and able to let go of the future I had planned to grasp hold of the hope of a new future. I never wrestled with the decision to abort my baby because I knew I would never recover from it. I did take the time to wrestle with the decision of adoption.

Someone close to me said, "But you don't even like children." To this I answered, "But I love this one."

I realized everything about my life was wrong. I went out searching in earnest for God. I searched church after church and denomination after denomination. I wanted to either prove the Bible as true or the whole Bible as false. In my mind there could no longer be any half-truths.

Jesus either was the "way, the truth and the light," or He wasn't. Growing up, Priests taught me the Bible was full of myths God used to teach us lessons. This spun me further into confusion. In the midst of my search, I quite clearly heard the message, "For all have sinned and fall short of the glory of God." Romans 3:23

All my running, all my blaming and all my confusion ended with the realization I am a sinner. We are all sinners. We all fall short of His glory. And with this I surrendered my life and gained a whole new life. "But when the kindness and love of God our Savior appeared, He saved us, not because of righteous things we had done, but because of His mercy. He saved us through the washing of rebirth and renewal by the Holy Spirit, whom He poured out on us generously through Jesus Christ our Savior, so that, having been justified by His grace, we might become heirs having the hope of eternal life." Titus 3: 4-7

I was pregnant, single and "heavy laden." I hit bottom and was cast. However, instead of leaving me to suffer the consequences of my life, Jesus found me in the wilderness and tenderly rescued me. "Suppose one of you has a hundred sheep and loses one of them. Doesn't he leave the ninety-nine in the open country and go after the lost sheep until he finds it? And when he finds it, he joyfully puts it on his shoulders and goes home. Then he calls his friends and neighbors together and says, 'Rejoice with me; I have found my lost sheep.'" Luke 15: 4-6

I was free - In His arms

I became white as snow. "'Come now, let us reason together,' says the LORD. 'Though your sins are like scarlet, they shall be as white as snow; though they are red as crimson, they shall be like wool.'" Isaiah 1:18

God restored my broken life. It would be a mistake to infer my life became painless and carefree. In reality, challenges could have buried me alive, especially in the early years as a Christian. God gave me enough faith for each step forward. When the burdens of being responsible to answer to God for my actions alone were lifted from me, I was suddenly stronger than ever. I was fortified by the promises of God and the sureness of Jesus standing before me when I come face to face with judgment covered in the perfect blood of Jesus. "God made him who had no sin to be sin for us, so that in him we might become the righteousness of God." 2 Corinthians 5:21

Education, partying, people, and travel never quenched my thirst for a purpose bigger than myself. Nothing satisfies the soul like surrender to Christ. I do not deserve His grace and love, but He gives it freely to anyone who asks. The problem God solved, through Jesus Christ, is my separation from God. He is perfect and I am sinful.

Becoming a Christian simply meant I recognized myself as flawed, sinful and broken. I came to the solid realization God's way is best for me. I stopped resisting Him. God created us. Our souls exist for the singular purpose of being filled by Christ. The unique act of Christianity is to surrender, handing our lives fully to God. It is to die to ourselves--to worldly desires—and trust God's perfect plan. When I surrendered, He filled me with indescribable joy, unquenchable hope, and meaningful purpose as I express His love through my life.

All of us have a God-shaped vacuum in the center of who we are. Our souls are meant to be filled by Christ. The truth is we are all sinners separated from God. The truth is Jesus bridges the separation. He is our salvation.

We only need to surrender. Why do I tell you this? Because over the years I asked a million unanswered questions to Christians while seeking to understand what was so different about their faith. What was so special about their relationship with

Jesus Christ? No one had the courage to answer my questions. If you have questions and you want the answer continue reading.

*Are you surrendered?* Will you stop right where you are and give the Lord everything, all of it, even the parts you are hanging onto in the deep recesses of your mind? The steps of surrender are quite simple.

Recognize you are a sinner. "All have sinned and fall short of the glory of God." Romans 3:23 and "Salvation is found in no one else, for there is no other name under heaven given to mankind by which we must be saved." Acts 4:12

1. Realize human works cannot make us holy before God. "The wages of sin is death, but the gift of God is eternal life in Christ Jesus our Lord." Romans 6:23 Salvation is a free gift. "For all have sinned and fall short of the glory of God, and all are justified freely by his grace through the redemption that came by Christ Jesus." Romans 3:24

2. Rely totally on Jesus Christ alone for your salvation. "For God so loved the world that he gave his one and only Son, that whoever believes in him shall not perish but have eternal life." John 3:16 and "All those the Father gives me will come to me, and whoever comes to me I will never drive away." John 6:37

3. Pray the prayer below or cry out in your own words to God. "But what does it say? "The word is near you; it is in your mouth and in your heart," that is, the message concerning faith that we proclaim: If you declare with your mouth, "Jesus is Lord," and believe in your heart that God raised him from the dead, you will be saved. For it is with your heart that you believe and are justified, and it is with your mouth that you profess your faith and are saved. As Scripture says, "Anyone who believes in him will never be put to shame." For there is no difference between Jew and Gentile—the same Lord is Lord of all and richly blesses all who call on him, for, "Everyone who calls on the name of the Lord will be saved." Romans 10: 8-13

If this message resonates with you, and your desire is to commit your life to Jesus, you can pray the suggested prayer below. If you still have questions, you can pray and ask God to show you He's real. You might also want to read the book of John in the Bible. This book will give you more insight about Jesus.

Prayer: Dear God, I come to you in the name of Jesus. I admit to You that I am a sinner. I am sorry for my sins and the life I have lived. I need your forgiveness. I believe Jesus Christ died for my sins, was resurrected and lives at the right hand of the Father. Please wash me clean from all my sin, shame, and guilt. Take up residence in my life, as my Lord, King and Savior. Thank you for giving me the gift of eternal life and the assurance that You will never leave me. Amen.

Next Step: Find a church where you can celebrate your new relationship with God and where you can grow in faith. It's important the church teaches directly from the Bible. It's also important you start reading the Bible on your own, too. This is how you'll nurture your personal relationship with Jesus and it'll give you discernment. It's important to always verify what you hear being taught by others with your own study of the scriptures. You can pray God will help you grow and He will help you find the best church for you.

I would suggest you start with these three books of the Bible in this order: Gospel of John, Romans, and Philippians. Then you should talk to the pastor in the church you find. Ask to be baptized, which is something the Lord told His followers to do as an act of obedience and a public profession of the faith you now claim as your own.

This is just the beginning of a life-long journey. There are tons of resources to help you grow in your faith. I've listed a few resources in the back of this book. Talk to your pastor, get plugged into a small group Bible study and know your eternal salvation has just been ensured.

# ABOUT THE AUTHORS

**Kayla Fioravanti, Managing Editor and Author**
Kayla Fioravanti is a wife, mother, author and speaker. Kayla is happily married to her serial entrepreneur husband Dennis. They are the blessed parents of Keegan, Selah and Caiden. Kayla and her family live in Franklin, Tennessee. Kayla is the Managing Editor of *360 Degrees of Grief* and *CCA Magazine*. Kayla's blogs are **KaylaFioravanti.com, Selah-Press.com** and **GogoNaughtyPaws.com**. Books by Kayla include: *How to Self-Publish: The Author-preneur's Guide to Publishing*; *How to Make Melt & Pour Soap Base from Scratch*; *The Art, Science & Business of Aromatherapy*; *DIY Kitchen Chemistry* and poetry *When I was Young I Flew the Sun Like a Kite*.

**T.G. Barnes** is a Life and Wellness Coach and Natural Health Enthusiast. With a background in Clinical Counseling and Nutrition she is drawn to help people experience genuine healing and transformation in their lives. Having gone through a fair amount of struggle, the way that she faces and overcomes struggle is a direct input into what makes her services unique and valuable to others. Outside of business she is a wife, homeschooling mom of two ambitious superheroes (boys seven and four) and their Terrier sidekick Alice, an actress, lover of reading and studying the Bible and Children's Health Advocate. Originally from New Orleans, L.A., she calls Hampton Roads, Virginia home.

**Duane Bigoni** spent thirteen years as a paramedic in the Portland Metro, followed by thirty-two years of service at the Multnomah County Medical Examiner's Office. During ten years of his career he was the Team Commander of Disaster Mortuary Operations Response Team. For the past five years Duane has worked for Operations with Health & Human Services Incident Response Coordination Team. His vast experiences have given him a unique perspective as an author.

**Heather Blair's** world changed forever in 2008 with the sudden loss of her fourteen year old son. Therapy, and often survival, came in the form of writing, beginning at a memorial blog remembering Austin. Along the way, she realized the pouring out of their story was also helping others. With a gentle nudging, Heather chose to take another path, challenging herself to find the JOY in every day, despite the sadness she still felt. She loves and misses Austin daily, but she is living her life to honor him - and celebrating every moment it brings. Heather shares her journey at **joyfulchallenge.com**. She is a monthly contributor at *Still Standing Magazine*, as well as being featured on *BlogHer*, *Exhale* literary magazine, and as a guest blogger for beloved moms she has met on her journey.

**Jacquelyn Bodeutsch** (a.k.a. Gwen) is originally from Portland Oregon. She now resides in Olympia, Washington with her husband Justin and two children, Dahlia and Valen. She absolutely loves it there. Her favorite parts of the city are where the land meets the water. She lives within one mile of the Capitol of Washington and the Puget Sound. She is an artist, writer, mother, cancer survivor and lover of Jesus. Jacquelyn's blog is **Gwen.bodeutsch.com**.

**Joyce Bone** is an accomplished entrepreneur, author, speaker and nationally recognized authority in business start-ups. She has been featured on CNBC's *The Squawk Box*, and in *Money, Forbes, Kiplinger's, Woman's Day* and *CEO* magazines for her business expertise. As co-founder of EarthCare, an environmental service company, Joyce went from stay-at-home mom to building a $125 million NASDAQ traded business. She is the founder of **MillionaireMoms.com**; a community and a book for entrepreneur-focused women helping them master the art of raising a business and a family at the same time.

While maintaining her standing within the environmental sector, she is also a partner in BLAMtastic®, a family focused consumer products company based in Atlanta. BLAMtastic is nationally and internationally in mass retailers like Walmart®. Joyce holds a Bachelor of Science and a MBA from Kennesaw State University and lives in Atlanta with her husband and three sons.

**Beverly G. Brainard's** passion is to bring the Hebrew Scriptures to life one book at a time through meticulous research and excursions to the Middle East and Egypt. She is the author of two works of historical fiction set within the ancient Near East: *Esther's Song: A Novel* about the biblical Esther, and *Babylon: Center of the World* about the prophet Daniel. She has graduate degrees from Vanguard University of Southern California and Portland State University, which fueled her life-long passion to make sense of the intricacies of the Hebrew Bible, Mesopotamian archaeology, and ancient Near East history. She lives in Oregon with her husband, five hundred orchids, and a little red barn. To learn more about the author and upcoming books, please visit her website at **bgbrainard.com**.

**Tom Burgess** has been a pastor for fifty years with two churches--eight years in Mooresville, Indiana and forty-two years in Portland, Oregon. Tom was raised in Los Angeles, California and received his Bachelor of Theology degree from Northwest College of the Bible and his Masters of Ministry degree from Kentucky Christian College. His is executive director of Global Missions International and has traveled to Africa, Central America and fifteen times to India on mission trips. He taught theology and practical ministry classes at Northwest College of the Bible for ten years and was host of a Television program in Oregon for ten years. He also began Crossroads Christian School and served as principal for nine years. He has written articles for numerous publications and has authored the book, *Documents on Instrumental Music* published by College Press. He and his wife Esther were married for forty-seven years before her death. They have two children and four grandchildren and one great-grandchild.

**Sharon Steffke Caldwell** is a Christian wife, mother of three wonderful sons, grandmother of five boys and one girl, author, lover of music, art, and travel. A native of Michigan, she and her husband, Bill, retired to Florida where they enjoy time with family (especially their grandchildren), golfing, gardening, and friends. The tragic loss of their son, Brian at age twenty-nine, inspired Sharon to write *Kiss An Angel Good Morning: The Brian Caldwell Story*. Sharon founded a Compassionate Friends Chapter before moving from Michigan and continues her journey toward joy, hope and healing. You may contact Sharon at **smc@caldwellfamily.com**.

**Elin Criswell** is a Jesus follower, wife, mom, soapmaker and author who gains great encouragement simply by encouraging others. She lives in Central Texas with her husband, Danny, and family. Elin's blog is **ElinCriswell.com**. Books by Elin Criswell include: Bubbles to Bucks: *How to Make Money Selling Soap* and *Creative Soap Making*.

**K.A. Croasmun** was born and raised in Ohio. She obtained her Laboratory Science Degree in 2001 and has been testing things that gross people out ever since. She lives with her husband, children, cats and one crazy dog. When she isn't writing, she's busy collecting books and odd antiquities. She can be found on Twitter at **@KCroasmun**.

**Clay and Renee Crosse** were married in 1990 and have four children: Shelby, Savannah, Sophie (adopted from China in 2005), and Garrett (adopted from China in 2007). Clay is a four-time Dove Award winner, including the 1994 New Artist of the Year. He has nine number-one songs, including *I Surrender All*, *He Walked a Mile*, *I Will Follow Christ*, and *Saving the World*. Clay continues to maintain an extensive singing, speaking, and worship leading/pastoral schedule.

Clay speaks at men's events, and he and Renee speak at various churches, seminars, and marriage conferences nationwide. Founded by Clay and Renee after they went through a life-changing recommitment to Christ in 1998, Holy Homes Ministries challenges those in Christian homes to be less like the world and more like Christ. In 2012 Clay Crosse releases his new album reDedication. Clay is the Worship Pastor at First Baptist Church in Bentonville, Arkansas. Follow **ClayCrosse.com**.

Books by Clay and Renee Crosse include: *Dashboard Jesus: Distinctive Reminders for Distracted Men; Rare Girl: Plain Talk to Lead Your Tweens and Teens in a World that Screams "Go Wild!";* and *I Surrender All: Rebuilding a Marriage Broken by Pornography and Reclaiming Stolen Intimacy*.

**Kimberly Crumby** is a wife, momma, daughter, and public school educator. Most importantly, she is a child of God. She has witnessed both the best and worst that this life can bring; she has a permanent scar on her heart that will never be completely healed this side of heaven. Kimberly considers one of her life's callings to be a grief educator oddly enough; she enjoys talking about loss when many people avoid it like the plague. She is southern with a little bit of sass, and you can find her at Sonic happy hour pretty much any day she can get there. She reads as much as her sleepy eyes allow, and is an admitted recovering perfectionist. Kimberly strives to live with joy. Her website is **kimberlycrumby.com**.

**Paul Dengler** is an artist (starving artist), poet, singer-songwriter, "philosopher" and Forrest Gump impersonator. Paul's music can be found on ReverbNation at **Reverbnation.com/pauldengler**

**Kolinda King Duer** is a Wife, Mother, Singer, Writer, Natural Health Coach

**Wendi Fincher** is a high school mathematics teacher. Her *modus operandi* is to create a plan. Wendi learned the fine art of surrendering when God turned her plan A into His ultimate plan. Today she is a teacher, mother and author following God's direction day by day.

**Zachary Fisher** is the son of a United Methodist pastor and wife. He works with computer software, plays music, and generally tries to avoid the sun. He lives in Nashville, TN with his beautiful wife Rachel.

**Bruce Fong** is a husband, father, ordained minister and Dean at Dallas Theological Seminary. He has a B.S from Western Baptist College, Masters of Theology from Dallas Theological Seminary and Doctorate of Philosophy from University of Aberdeen. Bruce has been President of Michigan Theological Seminary; Professor of Bible Exposition, Homiletics, and Pastoral Theology, Multnomah Biblical Seminary; Missionary with Student Ministries, Inc. to Scotland. He has held a variety positions as Pastor, High School Pastor, Assistant Pastor, Lead Pastor and Interim Pastor over the years.

Bruce's publications include: *Always Hope Life is Rough. Never Give Up. Believe; Hunting for Life; Messy Church: Living 1 & 2 Corinthians; Real Life: Determined to discover that each new day is worth living; Shepherd Strong: Living 1 & 2 Timothy; The Wall: Jesus Destroyed the wall of hostility; His church must never rebuild it. Ephesians 2.14; and Racial Equality in the*

*Church.* His articles can be found in Evangelical Quarterly, Journal of Evangelical Theological Society, Berry's Bible College and Seminary Handbook, Decision Magazine, Moody Magazine, PK's *Stand in the Gap* New Testament. **Brucefong.wordpress.com**.

**Gary Forsythe** is a songwriter/musician living in Franklin, TN. Originally from North Texas, Gary moved to the Nashville area in 2004 to pursue his dream of songwriting, producing and performing. Over the years, he has had various songs published and recorded by Brentwood Music, Brentwood Kids and New Spring Publishing. In 2005, his song *Crucify* was recorded as part of the Dove award nominated musical *My Savior My God*. Recently, Gary founded Collision-Point Publishing which is committed to intersecting art and real life experiences with the hope of the Gospel. Once a Christian radio station manager and worship pastor, Gary now works at Thomas Nelson Publishing and resides in Franklin with his wife Pam and two sons Joshua and Cory. His music can be found at **Reverbnation.com/garyforsythe**.

**Lona Renee Fraser** is a sassy Italian freelance writer, warrior poet and motivational speaker. Her heart for writing utilizes a dash of nature, foundations in faith, a hint of humor and waterfalls of love. She encourages and inspires others to always hope no matter what the circumstances. She believes that as you inspire others you will in turn inspire yourself. Originally from Upstate New York, Lona now resides in Franklin, TN with her husband Jim and two children, Brendan and Kayla, their dog Ellie and Z.J., Pretty Boy and Trey, their three cats. Her blog can be found at **inspireothersinspireyourself.wordpress.com**.

**Cherie Funderburg** is the oldest of six girls, wife of twenty-two years to her husband Dennis, and mother of one. She and her husband have lived a nomadic life for a number of years, moving all over the continental US, and are currently enjoying life in the tropical paradise of the Hawaiian Islands. Her website is Cherie.net.

**Charles Garrett** is a Nashville Area based songwriter, producer and guitarist. He has worked with artists such as Charlie Peacock, Rebecca St. James, Steve Green and David Phelps. His songwriting has been featured on the albums of Rebecca St. James, Margaret Becker, Code of Ethics and several other Christian artists.

**Maria Gelnett** is an Instructor at **Soapstudiobrookside.com**, Certified Soapmaker and Handcrafted Soapmakers Guild Board Past Director. Maria Gelnett founded AngelicGlow in 2001. Maria offers beginner, advanced and master soapmaking classes at Soap Studio Brookside and at various locations throughout the upstate NY area.

**Steve Green** is the son of missionary parents. Steve celebrates twenty-nine years in the Christian music industry. Steve Green Ministries was established in 1984. Steve had spent two years with the group TRUTH and four years with the Gaithers when the door opened for Steve to make his first recording with Sparrow Records. Following a significant spiritual awakening, Steve and Marijean began responding to invitations from churches all over America.

Throughout Steve's years of ministry, his music has been honored with four Grammy nominations, eighteen number one songs, and seven Dove Awards, Christian music's highest honor. Steve has thirty-seven recordings to his credit, including children's projects and Spanish-language albums; Green has sold over three million albums worldwide. Steve is a regular contributor to CCA Magazine.

Steve has been married to Marijean for thirty-five years. Their daughter, Summer, and son-in-law Mark Schulz, along with their two granddaughters, live in Atlanta. Their son, Josiah, and his wife Jamie-Lee live in St. Louis where they are attending seminary

Steve has shared the gospel in almost fifty countries around the world. According to Steve, "In the end it will be clear that He alone is the hero of not only my story, but of all our stories." More about Steve at **SteveGreenMinistries.org**.

**Valerie Geer** earned her Bachelor of Arts degree from Northwest University (Kirkland, WA) in 1999. She double majored in Church Ministries: Missions, and Biblical Studies, and earned a certificate in Teaching English as a Second Language. Valerie continued her education at Wheaton College (Illinois, WA), earning a Master of Arts degree (2004) in Intercultural Studies and Teaching English to Speakers of Other Languages. Valerie has been working in higher education for thirteen years, including two years at Northwest University, two years at Beijing Institute of Technology (Beijing, China), and seven years at Huntington University (Huntington, IN). Valerie is currently at Corban University (Salem, OR), where she teaches courses in Intercultural Communication and Teaching, and works with the chapel ministries.

Valerie has been married for thirteen years to Nathan Geer, Dean of Students at Corban University. They have four sons, ages eight, seven, and four (twins). The Geers love outdoor adventure, reading, and traveling.

**Chuck Hagele** knows firsthand how much God loves His children and how He relentlessly pursues their hearts. Chuck has witnessed many miracles of the heart in working with youth and with youthful adults, which he has enjoyed doing since working at his first summer camp in 1988. From that time until now, he has been involved in serving youth in both paid and volunteer positions. Since 2003, Chuck has served a vital role at Project Patch in various positions including Chaplain, Youth Ranch Administrator, Operations Officer, and his current role as Executive Director. His background in pastoral work, his studies in psychology, and his MBA from Boise State University have all contributed a great deal to his success in leading Project Patch through several key transitions.

Chuck has been married to Kelly for nineteen years and is the very proud dad of two adorable and energetic young girls. When not focused on Patch or on being a dad, he most enjoys participating in triathlons, fly-fishing, and pursuing other adventures.

**Drenda Lane Howatt** is the author of *Strong & Courageous: A Survivor's Facebook Journey through Breast Cancer.* Active in her local church and area ministries, she also works as a Policy Coordinator for local government in Clackamas County, Oregon. Drenda has been married to Don for twenty-nine years, and they are the proud parents of three daughters.
Her blog is **iamstrongandcourageous.blogspot.com**.

**Mary Humphrey** is a Christian author with two books published and several others currently being written through her business His Pasture Press. Mary's mission is to help others realize their God-given talents and to follow their resulting passions, with her motto being: Share, Encourage and Grow. Mary maintains blogs at **Anniesgoathill.com** and **Hispasturepress.com.** Mary's books include: *Advanced Soap Making: Removing the Mystery* and *Essential Soapmaking.*

**Emily Joy** was a single mom for the two daughters to whom she was fully devoted for twenty-three years. Emily has been a cosmetologist for thirty years and an instructor for the past four years. On June 30, 2013 her life was changed forever, when her youngest daughter Emily-Anna Asbill was murdered. Her daughter Amanda is who she stays strong for now. Amanda is a student at the College of Charleston, SC. Now Emily's life mission is now to help others in a domestic violence situation. This is what Emily-Anna would want her to do. She is closer to God now more than she has ever been in her life. He is working through Emily.

**Cathy Koch** (pronounced like "Cook") has ministered to women for more than twenty-five years as a small group leader, Bible teacher, event coordinator and Women's Ministries Director. She has assisted several churches in developing and/or expanding their ministries to women. Cathy, along with her husband Earl, served as Ministers of Involvement at Crossroads Church in Portland, Oregon. Cathy's passion is to encourage Christian women to become all they can be by discovering and developing the purpose and calling for which God created them. When teaching and writing, she enjoys transforming the "dailies of life" into practical, easily-understood illustrations with heavenly meanings.

Cathy has been happily explaining the odd spelling of her married name for forty-five years of what has been a rather mobile married journey. At the beginning of 2014, Cathy and Earl moved to Troutdale, Oregon, where Earl is on staff at Mountainview Christian Church in Gresham. They have three married children who serve in ministry in their home churches. Six grandsons and six granddaughters round out the family circle. Her website is **Alakate.wordpress.com**.

**Kyle Koch** lives in Sheridan, Wyoming on a small ranch where he raises a few head of cattle and horses. He has worked as a Ferrier in high demand for many years in the Wyoming and Colorado area. His specialty is restoring horses thought to be hopelessly lame back to health. Kyle, who is an accomplished vocal soloist, has written hundreds of cowboy poems, many of which were published in a book in the 1980's. These days, he considers his writing to be the best possible therapy to help him deal with grief. He and Julianne (Juli) were married for forty-five years until her death in April of 2013 after a short but very intense illness. He has five children and nine grandchildren.

**Shila Laing** is a redeemed writer, foodie, artist and artisan redeemed by grace who lives in metro San Antonio, TX with her two special needs kids, sweet nerdy husband, a precious Great Pyrenees dog and geriatric cranky calico kitty. She can be found at **facebook.com/shila.n.laing**.

**Bethany Learn** is the CEO and founder of Fit2B Studio, an online fitness portal at **fit2b.com** with members worldwide that provides unlimited access to almost one hundred wholesome workouts for the whole family. Her family-friendly focus keeps things modest, safe and fun for all ages. She is passionate about standing in the gap for those who have been led to believe that they will always look pregnant or will always leak when exercising. Bethany is happiest when she is proving to people that they don't have to injure themselves to get into the best shape of their lives, or when she's just talking about birth and fitness. Bethany lives in the Pacific Northwest on seven acres with her husband, two children, three goats, ten chickens, a Chihuahua, and a horse.

**Shirley Logan** grew up on Wrightsville Beach, NC, where she has returned from Nashville a little over a year ago with her children, barefooted and guitar in hand. A realtor by day, Shirley lives the life of mother and singer/songwriter in every space in between, "I am pushing. Pressing against the odds, and I am thankful for a bullish determination to do what I love—music!" Her 2008 CD release *So Much to Say* continues to receive rave reviews and heartfelt response from around the world. "I am a storyteller. I love music—GOOD music. I have been influenced by many different styles and don't exactly fit into one box. My desire is to write excellent music that will be appreciated by many, crossing over the lines that separate style. Songs that are an expression of myself, my experiences, my struggles and issues that are universal to the human soul. I want to write music that identifies with people at their core—honestly!" Her music can be found at **Shirleyloganmusic.com**.

**Dana Lyne** is a single mom engaged to a handsome prince. Her blog is a platform to share her thoughts and have an expressive outlet through words and visuals and colors. Dana's blog is **Danalyne.wordpress.com**.

**Rebecca Marmolejo** has a career background in Wellness Industries such as Nutrition & Weight Loss, Skin Care, and Anti-Aging. As a new author, Rebecca is currently writing to the heart of women, celebrating their unique beauty in a new way. This book is an invitation to celebration. God and his daughters unite in the true liberty of beauty, extending more freedom through each woman into the world around her. Rebecca's passion is for the vibrant heart of women at the core of femininity, identity and personal beauty. Find Rebecca at **Linkedin.com/in/rebeccam2**.

**Lynn McLeod** has been described as a "Noticer" who writes then shares. Although an avid lifelong storyteller, she is relatively young as a fiction author. Her interpretation of the world betrays this newness as if it is comfortably aged. Being raised and living the majority of her life in central Illinois, Lynn moved to a suburban community just south of Nashville to discover a creative fate. Carrying her Journalism degree from Southern Illinois University, a laptop and vivid imagination in the nap sack of wonderment, she began writing for audiences. Stepping beyond normal life situations, her characters are interestingly flawed in stories written to encourage readers toward interpreting the unexpected or unconventional. Always including an underlying theme of hope, her faith in God is the seasoning that binds. You will find more of her stories at **Lynnsstories.com**.

**Ric Minch** started early in his contracting career, word-smithing proposals to make the subject more appealing, selling points to entice thought for additional recognition. Later as a speaker for the Oregon Food Bank, speech writing was required for maximum impact. Since then, articles have been written for church and volunteer information. Currently retired to the Washington coastal community of Surfside on the Long Beach Peninsula, his second career has begun to flourish in the field of fictional writing. Currently, completion of his first novel is in progress.

**Ginger L. Moore** is a Christian wife, mother, entrepreneur, homeschooler and writer with a "modern southern belle" personality. Born and raised in the beautiful hills of southeast Tennessee, she still lives there with her husband of over twenty years and their only child, a son born to them later in life, and their rescue dog, Miss Dottie. Ginger has been involved in Christian ministry for most of her adult life. She and her husband have held positions of leadership within the church in various ministries. Most recently, they both have been involved in personal counseling, Biblical teaching and encouraging others how to be over-comers and discover their identity in Christ.

With a lifelong interest in natural and alternative health and beauty, Ginger has devoted much of her time to learn more in this area and eventually launched her premium handcrafted cosmetics company, Neos Skin Care™ in 2009. The mission of Neos Skin Care™ is to bring women trustworthy skin care products made with fine ingredients, excellence and decadence while embracing southern inspiration and charm. Her website is **Neoscreations.wordpress.com.**

In 2012, Ginger started At Home Woman™, a community and blog for women with at home roles, ministries, and businesses. At Home Woman's mission and ministry is to give women the opportunity to be real, encourage, share, support, have fun with friends and learn from one another in a safe environment, with a Christian faith-based foundation. From this arena, Ginger also plans to write books that she hopes will minister to and help moms, women and other home educators.

**Ellen Peacock** is a wife, mother, and sister. She enjoys art, making soap, painting silk, drawing, cooking, and just about anything creative. She owns a small online business Ellen's Essentials, **Ellensessentials.com** and created a line of colorants especially for handcrafted soap makers Peacock Dyes **Peacockdyes.com**. Being a former legal assistant, she loves research. If there's something she wants to do, but doesn't know how she's willing to go the extra mile and dig until she figures it out.

**Cheri Perry** lives in Battle Ground, Wash., with her husband of nearly twenty-five years, Dean Perry, and their teenage son, Tyler Perry. Dean and Cheri are the co-owners/founders of **Total Merchant Concepts**, a national credit-card processing company that provides a variety of business services to merchants and credit unions. The success of the Perry family business and Cheri's love of public speaking have yielded many opportunities for her to present on topics ranging from *Small Business Success* to *Passionate Partnerships*. Her personal passion for excellence in service, business development, heartfelt leadership, and relationships is something she lives and loves to share. The Perry's experience with deep personal loss and a rejuvenated marriage have inspired Cheri to share their story to offer hope and healing to others.

**Deborah Petersen**, a single mom of one, Annie Grace. She loves the Lord with all her heart. She works with bringing healing to children whose parents are recovering addicts. She is a world class coffee maker and an aspiring speaker and author. Deborah's blog is **Anniemom2912.blogspot.com**.

**Karyn Pugh** is a business consultant and writer. She lives in the South with her husband and two children, and does most of her writing in the wee hours of the morning, fueled by copious amounts of caffeine and chocolate. Her hobbies include hiking, running, tae kwon do, traveling, reading and baking.

**Lane Reed** is a dancer, inspirational speaker, lover of stories, music, cooking (and eating), shopping and traveling.

**Linda Reinhardt -** Raised in beautiful Washington State, since age eight, Linda J. Reinhardt has contributed to church newsletters, a puppet ministry curriculum, and wrote/directed a Christmas play and Women's Bible Study play, and has written for Girlfriend 2 Girlfriend online magazine. Linda wrote a song performed at her wedding, which has now become a lullaby to her daughter before bed. She is now a speaker for StoneCroft Ministries and has also lead writers' workshops.

She is the author of the Sister Blue Thread series, and has co-authored, with Sharon Bernash Smith and Rosanne Croft, the historical novel *Like a Bird Wanders,* Book One in The McLeod Family Saga, as well as the Christmas classics, *Once Upon a Christmas* and *Always Home for Christmas,* and co-authored with Sharon Bernash Smith another Christmas classic, *Starry, Starry, Christmas Night.*

Linda is a stay-at-home mom. Her favorite activity is spending time with her best friend and husband and her miracle daughter. She also enjoys sitting over a cup of coffee with her sister or a friend, sharing the details of her heart. Passionate about ministering to post-abortive women, Linda is active in leading small group Bible studies: HEART (Healing and Encouragement for Abortion Related Trauma), Time to Heal, and Life Groups. As an avid believer in the power of prayer, she has met for the last nine years with a prayer group dedicated to supporting family and friends. See her on Facebook, Twitter, LinkedIn and at **Lindajreinhardt.blogspot.com** and **Sisterbluethread.blogspot.com**.

**Mandalyn Rey** is a freelance poet, musician, and inspirational speaker who is passionately in love with Jesus. Her greatest joy comes from mentoring younger women who struggle with identity wounds, depression, or finding their place in the body of Christ.

**Debbie Richards** is a professional soapmaker and business owner. Her professional career has spanned more than two decades and includes positions as a software trainer, help desk manager, technical writer/editor, research and development lab technician and quality assurance manufacturing manager. Debbie's eclectic interests include cooking from scratch, mentoring others on healthy lifestyle living, organic gardening, and playing guitar. She currently lives and works in Sugar Grove, Illinois with her husband and two backyard hens. Her website **BigFatSoap.com**.

**Loral Robben** served as a marketing manager, creative director and managing editor in the higher education and financial services sectors for fourteen years in Chicago. In 2013, Loral exchanged architecture for natural beauty and relocated to Franklin, Tennessee. She is currently a freelance writer, editor, marketer and project manager. Loral earned a Master of Journalism from the University of Kansas. In her free time, she enjoys dancing, hiking, reading, cooking, paddle boarding, kayaking and traveling. Loral's website is **www.loralrobben.com**.

**Lisa Rodgers** spent eleven years in the cosmetic industry as a manufacturer of natural spa, bath, and body products. In 2009, her passion for creating bath and body goodness took a turn for the unexpected. Lisa plays as hard as she works, and at the end of the summer in 2009, she damaged several fingers on her left hand playing volleyball. Long story short, after much soul searching, Lisa made the gut wrenching decision to close the manufacturing side of Cactus & Ivy.

Shoot Y'all Photography was born out of a love for photography, cabin fever due to a snow storm, and the need to carve out a new journey. It's a strange combination, and one that flowed together like the words to a poem. Lisa is a natural light photographer, she lives in the south, and she uses the word y'all . . . a lot! Lisa loves candid; not posed. Flowing; not stiff. She shoots pictures based on the life that surrounds her clients. In addition to people, she shoots animals, landscape, architect, products and more. In a nutshell . . . she captures life.

Lisa is working on photography book, "_____ {*blank*} *Doesn't Define Them*" which will show beautiful, passionate people fighting a diagnosis with grace, faith, determination and strength. This photography project will cover people living with Breast Cancer, PTSD, Autism, Downs Syndrome, Brain Cancer, Prostate Cancer and the list goes on. I have an overwhelming urge to photograph individuals dealing with a diagnosis or disease, and show there is beauty that lies within them, that what they are going through does not define who they are.

Spending time with family and friends is what Lisa loves the most. In her spare time, you will likely find her on their volleyball court or simply relaxing in the country surrounded by twenty-four fuzzy paper weights {aka cats}, Lucy the dog, and the love of her life, her husband Prevo. Her website is **Shootyallphotography.com**.

**Prevo Rodgers, Jr.** joined the military fresh out of high school. When Prevo put pen to paper and fingers to chords for Veteran's Hand, he was serving a tour in Iraq. It wasn't until he returned home that he finished the song. By the time Prevo retires, he will have spent thirty years serving his country. Veteran's Hand is thought provoking and serves as a reminder what soldiers have sacrificed and continue to sacrifice for the United States of America and its citizens. Freedom is not free. Prevo resides in South Carolina with his wife, Lisa, a dog and twenty-four cats, aka, Fuzzy Paper Weights.

**Sara Shay** is a mama to three precious gifts and wife to a man who lovingly calls her "his nutter." She started pushing her family into real food a few months after she started blogging. They will forever be on the road to real food and natural health. Balancing art and logic in her daily life and work, God's balance of creation and healing is quite clear to her. She loves creating, experimenting, and learning. Whether it be food, health or crafting. She is navigating her family through healthy frugality – trying to THRIVE, not merely survive this life. She shares this journey at Your Thriving Family which can be found at **Sarabethshay.com**.

**Tammy Lovell Stone** is a pastor's wife, writer and homeschool mom. She started writing poetry at the age of ten as a way to express her negative emotions and fell in love with how words written on a page can transform us. She is currently working on her first book, *Rediscover the Apron* that is expected to be finished in April 2014. She has been married for the past twenty-seven years to her high school sweetheart, Kenny Stone. They have three children Ashton, Charley, and Gabe; two grandchildren Britt and Boone. They live in Minnie Pearls hometown of Centerville, Tennessee. Tammy enjoys homesteading, playing the piano and gardening. She is a prayer warrior and active in music, women's and children's ministry. Tammy is available on Facebook. She may also be reached on her webpage, **tammylovellstone.com**.

**Debra Sturdevant** lives in the country hills of upstate NY with her husband Bob and several feline fans. She has two grown sons and an inherited dog from her mother named Timmy who thinks he is a real boy. She loves gardening, music and living the simple, country life. She has reopened her handcrafted, herbal soap and sundry shop after caring for her mother for several years. Educated in fine art and business she now runs her little eclectic piece of heaven and enjoys life and living while savoring every day to its fullest.

**Michelle Titus** is a writer/storyteller who lives with her two children in Franklin, Tennessee. She is a National Novel Writing Month participant and 2013 winner. Her novel Cut of the Cloth is available as of June 2014. Michelle can be found on Facebook.

**Melodie Tunney** is a marvelous vocalist, award-winning songwriter and top-notch arranger, and a gifted worship leader as well. Mel's journey as a vocalist began at the age of eighteen with the Christian group, TRUTH where she met future husband, Dick, the group's keyboard player. Mel had a successful career as a studio singer in Nashville, TN working on background vocal sessions, choral projects as well as regional and national jingles. The "studio season" brought new relationships with fellow singers Bonnie Keen and Marty McCall. Together they founded the group First Call in 1983. They held a featured slot on tour with Sandi Patti, a record contract with WORD records, live performances on the Grammy Awards telecast and the Tonight Show with Johnny Carson. As well as opportunities to tour with Christian artists Amy Grant and Bebe and Cece Winans. Mel (along with Dick Tunney) continued to write songs that found their way to recording projects by Larnelle Harris, Steve Green, Sandi Patti, First Call, Glad and others. The couple was also lauded with one Grammy Award and ten Dove Awards for writing, singing and recording.

Mel and Dick spent four years as Worship Leaders/Artists in Residence at First Baptist Church of Columbia, TN and now spend several weeks each year leading worship at parachurch events for organizations like *The Jesus Film Project, Cook Communications International, The Fellowship of Christian Athletes* and the *Christian Management Association*. She is also now the Minister of Music and Worship at the Haywood Hills Baptist Church. As well, Mel has found a new passion in teaching women on subjects such as *How to Study God's Word* and *Learning to Hear God's Voice*. This season of ministry for Mel Tunney is described in one of her favorite scriptures, Eph. 3:20: *"God is able to do immeasurably more than anything we could ever ask or imagine, according to His power at work within us."* Read more at **Tunneymusic.com**.

**Rachel Turner** is the owner of Music City Suds in Nashville, TN. Her work has appeared in The Sun, Metropolis, Japanzine, and a variety of online publications. She currently lives behind a white picket fence with her husband and a pack of very short dogs. Rachel's website is **Musiccitysuds.com**.

**Dorothy Wagner** is a full time wife and mother. She is forever a Twinless Twin after the unexpected death of her twin sister Tracy. She discovered the organization Twinless Twins Support Group International in 2009 as she sought ways to connect after the loss of her twin. She discovered that she is not alone in her grief, nor will she ever be alone.

Dorothy also found the athlete inside of herself when she joined Team in Training with The Leukemia and Lymphoma Society. She has since walked two full marathons and one half marathon to raise money to find a cure for the disease that took her twin sister Tracy.

**Wayne Watson's** voice and songs helped define an entire genre of Christian music throughout the '80's and '90's. As a songwriter he is known for his remarkable depth and relevancy has just brushed past the milestone marker of half a century—most of it shared intimately on the trail with God and his music. Much of the journey has been chronicled within the library of songs contained on more than two dozen album projects since his memorable breakthrough album *Working In The Final Hour* caught the imagination of an entire generation of Christian music listeners and radio with its release in 1980. To say his vocal styling and lyrics of open, honest communication of God's presence in everyday life circumstances helped lay the foundation on which today's contemporary Christian music is built would in no way be an overstatement.

Wayne Watson's connection with his audience has to date produced twenty-three number one singles on Christian radio—including *Friend Of A Wounded Heart, When God's People Pray, Almighty, Be In Her Eyes, Watercolour Ponies, More Of You, Another Time, Another Place,* and *Home Free* (which became the most played song on Christian radio in 1991).

Wayne's litany of career credits includes a half dozen Dove Awards wins. He has twice been nominated for the Grammy Award—both for his performance of Watercolour Ponies (1987), and for Best Pop Gospel Album in 1992 with his stunning A Beautiful Place project. Wayne's books include: *Watercolour Ponies, For Such a Time as This, Wayne Watson Home Free* (Piano Songbook), and *When God's People Pray* and *The Way Home* (Artists Devotional). His website is **Waynewatson.com**.

**Marc Whitmore** was born in Springfield, Missouri and attended Missouri State University. Moving to Los Angeles after college, he became an agent and later a personal manager of recording artists, actors, writers and directors in Hollywood. He is a strange mixture of Midwest values and West Coast living. While he enjoys writing, he's an avid reader and lover of literature (having read well over two thousand books) and has represented a number of best-selling authors. He resides in a quiet, mostly literate, neighborhood in Los Angeles.

**Lisa LaCross Wethey** is a celebrated flutist from the concert stages of the world, including Carnegie Hall and La Scala Opera House. She and her husband Bruce left highly successful careers in the mainstream classical music world to pursue full-time instrumental music ministry. The ministry of BRUCE & LISA has taken them from church concerts to conferences nationwide. They have led worship for special prayer services at the Pentagon, and have appeared with the ministries of both Chuck Swindoll and David Jeremiah. They have recorded for many artists and have been guests on numerous television and radio programs, including Washington D.C.'s *Janet Parshall's America* radio broadcast.

Lisa's amazing experience as the survivor of multiple brain tumor surgeries, radiation five days per week for six weeks over the past several years and a major stroke just a short time ago, has given birth to a strong, new side to their ministry. Lisa has become a sought-after women's ministry speaker bearing witness to the power of prayer and God's healing.

Bruce & Lisa use their gifts in music ministry trusting God to provide for their needs every step of the way. They spend their lives serving as the Lord calls, wherever He calls them including churches, rehab programs, convalescent homes, women's ministry and serving people from all walks of life. During their Christian concerts they take their direction from the throne of God as they share music, amazing testimony, unique stories and scripture. You can follow Bruce & Lisa on Facebook and their website is **Bruceandlisa.com**.

**Carol Wilson** is a writer and part-time drug abatement tester for a national airline. She has enjoyed facilitating Bible study support groups for post-abortion healing since 1991 and speaks occasionally about the sanctity of human life and the devastation caused by abortion. She is currently writing a book designed to help women heal from post-abortion pain. Carol and her husband, Kevin, live in the glorious Pacific Northwest. They enjoy traveling and she always has several books to read anywhere she goes. She can be contacted at **cwilson7145@gmail.com**.

**Jessica Mills Winstead** is a lifelong resident of Morristown, Tennessee. Upon completing her B.S. in education at East Tennessee State University in 2000, she married and began raising her children in Morristown. She also began working at First Baptist Church Morristown as the coordinator of pre-school ministries, which she has continued for fourteen years. She completed her master's degree in education at Carson-Newman University and her ED.S. in Education at ETSU and taught classes at Walters State Community College in Morristown.

After losing her ten year old son, Noah Dean, in July 2012, Jessica became an advocate to raise awareness for Electric Shock Drowning, which claimed Noah's life at a marina at Cherokee Lake near Morristown. She is on the board of the Electric Shock Drowning Prevention Association and she is currently working toward the passage of a state law in Tennessee to safeguard the public from the risk of electrical shock injury and death at marinas and boat docks. Jessica has also turned to blogging as one of the ways to work through her grief and allow it to become part of the healing process. In addition to carrying on her son's memory, Jessica is mom to thirteen-year-old Haleigh Raye, who gives her reason to live every day and strive to make the most of each day.

To read more from Jessica at **Bendintheroadblog.blogspot.com**.

Find out how to become a **360 Degrees** contributing author at
**360DegreesBooks.com**

# ACKNOWLEDGMENTS

While I was still raw from the grief of losing my mother, God nudged me with the idea to publish the book you are now reading. As I often do, I questioned God. *How can I manage what you are calling me to do?* Just as I asked, my mind was divinely filled with a "to do" list of the steps from A to Z.

On the long road to publication I found the authors, editors, graphic designer, and encouragers who made this book a reality. When I ran out of steam to push forward a word of encouragement would be spoken seemingly out of the blue. I am grateful to all the people who obeyed the nudge God gave them to walk with me.

I am thankful to each author who poured raw emotion out onto the page. They wrote with transparent hearts in hopes of being a beacon of hope to the reader. I am humbled by the trust put in me to care for their words, stories and gifts.

Thank you to the editing team who spent countless hours reading submission after submission, voting and pouring over every line to prepare *360 Degrees of Grief* for publication. I am forever grateful for Carol Wilson, Debbie Richards, Mary Humphrey, Robin Schmidt, Shila Laing, Kim Jones, Darcy Hickey, Ginger Moore, E.F. McAdams, Carol Hattaway-Richey, Rose Cunfer, and Caiden Fioravanti. Thank you Lynn McLeod for offering a fresh set of eyes at exactly the moment I prayed for help. You have been a great blessing. Special thanks to Carol Wilson for staying with me from the very first word of this book to the very last one. Thank you Selah Fioravanti for drawing the 360 Degrees Books logo.

Thank you Dennis, Selah, and Caiden for putting up with me on the days I sat at the computer from sunrise to sunset editing in my jammies with my geriatric cat Star on my lap. Her imminent death seemed to be postponed from sitting together as I worked.

Dawn Fitch took only a wisp of direction from me to create a beautiful cover beyond my imagination. Lisa Rodgers is the very definition of awesomesauceness. Really! It is a real word. I submitted it to the Urban Dictionary to legitimize my use of it. Without Kim McCrea Wilton, Sue and Steve Nadel this book would still be on my computer in a Word document. Many thanks to Lannie Cates for handling all the legal details. I am grateful to Graywolf Press for granting me permission to reprint the poem *Circle of Breath* by my favorite poet William Stafford.

Volume I of *360 Degrees of Grief* is only possible because God nudged me, David Sanford educated me, my parents nurtured me, my husband empowered me, the authors shared with me, and the editors directed me. Thank you all for playing your role in turning a nudge into a reality.

I owe praises to my Lord Jesus for the gift of writing and above all for the certainty of His saving grace. "Whatever you do, work at it with all your heart, as

working for the Lord, not for human masters, since you know that you will receive an inheritance from the Lord as a reward. It is the Lord Christ you are serving."
Colossians 3:23

# REFERENCES

English Standard Version Bible. New York: Oxford University Press, 2009. Print.

Milne, A.A. *The Many Adventures of Winnie the Pooh*. Disney Book Group, 2010. Print.

Milne, A.A. *Pooh's Grand Adventure, The Search for Christopher Robin*. Grolier Books. 1997. Print.

*New International Version*. Bible Gateway. Web. 29 Jul. 2013.

*New King James Version*. Nashville: Thomas Nelson, 1982. Bible Gateway. Web. 7 Feb. 2010.

Peterson, Eugene H. *The Message: The Bible in Contemporary Language*. Colorado Springs: NavPress, 2002. Print.

The Free Dictionary © 2012 by Farlex, Inc

*The Holy Bible, King James Version. New York:* American Bible Society: 1999; Bartleby.com, 2000.

*The Holy Bible: New International Version*. Grand Rapids, MI: Zondervan, 1984. Print.

William Stafford, "Circle of Breath" from *Ask Me: 100 Essential Poems*. Copyright © 1960, 2014 by William Stafford and the Estate of William Stafford. Reprinted with the permission of The Permissions Company, Inc. on behalf of Graywolf Press, Minneapolis, Minnesota, www.graywolfpress.org.

# INDEX BY AUTHOR

Made in the USA
Charleston, SC
14 April 2014